THE
SPANISH WATER DOG

Di Williamson and Wanda Sooby

Published by First Stone Publishing
An imprint of
Corpus Publishing Ltd
PO Box 8, Lydney, Gloucestershire GL15 6YD
on behalf of
Stellareach Publications Ltd,

First Published 2007
© 2007 Stellareach Publications, Di Williamson, Wanda Sooby.

ISBN 1 904439 63 2

Printed and bound in Singapore

10 9 8 7 6 5 4 3 2 1

CONTENTS

FOREWORD

by
Angi Hodges
Owner of Spanish Water Dogs and member of CanTech Lowland Search Team

There have been hundreds of books written about the care and training of hundreds of dog breeds. Now… finally… here is The Spanish Water Dog.

Whatever it was that attracted you to this breed in the beginning, you will no doubt have had some surprises over the time you have been living with it – some welcome, others possibly not. And, if you are still just at the attraction stage, and haven't yet embarked on life with your "curly treasure(s)"… well, you've got it all to come!

These little animals force us to re-think pretty well everything we thought we knew about living with dogs. This book about their nature, history, care and training is a reflection of the knowledge, enthusiasm and commitment of the two authors, both of whom have a wealth of experience not only in this breed but also in others, going back over many years.

The Spanish Water Dog is an ancient breed with a fascinating history, and it is a constant source of wonder to observe how that history informs the behaviour of our own dogs. Hardy, intelligent, resourceful and independent, they have for centuries offered their skills to human beings to assist in a whole variety of different occupations. Proud and sensitive as they are, the passage of time has in no way diminished this work ethic, and they deserve every assistance to take advantage of all the opportunities that exist in our own society for them to contribute to the daily lives of their owners. A Spanish Water Dog will do pretty well anything you ask it to – except nothing.

This book is an absorbing read for anyone with an interest in dogs, whether you are a long-standing, experienced owner or waiting for your first Spanish puppy, researching the breed for suitability or just someone with an interest in dog breeds who would like to expand their knowledge base. There is something here for everyone. Enjoy.

Angi with her fully operational search dogs, Luz and Marron

A NOTE FROM THE AUTHORS

If, as you peruse the book, you become aware of the repetition of certain themes or ideas, be reassured that this is intentional on our part. We consider it of such importance for certain aspects of the nature of the Spanish Water Dog to be fully understand that they need mentioning more than once. The breed is so complex we feel that it should be portrayed as it really is, warts and all.

If you are totally undaunted by the length of the book and the material it contains, you may want to read it from cover to cover. On the other hand you may have bought the book to use as a source of information, to dip into as you feel necessary. If the latter is the case, vital points made in earlier chapters could be missed; thus the reiteration of such points is needed throughout the book. We have tried to be as succinct as possible; the relevance of any repetition becoming clearer the more you read.

Please be aware that the views expressed in this book are those of the Authors and no criticism of any individual or third party is intended.

Throughout most of this book we refer to the puppy as 'he' for ease of writing since the constant use of 'he or she' will become boring for you, the reader, as well as us!

Miguel and Squiffy

Without them, this book would not have been written

INTRODUCTION

At different times and in completely different circumstances we each acquired our first Spanish Water Dog, each a white one with brown markings. We knew little of these dogs as a breed, only that these curly coated, workman-like creatures had caught our attention and subsequently, captured our hearts.

In our naivety we expected our dogs to be just like other dogs that have been part of our lives, to live and grow with us, to join in our activities and fit into the scheme of things without any more than the usual problems that go with taking on a puppy. How wrong we were. Almost immediately it became apparent that these dogs were different and, at the time, we did not fully understand why. Not satisfied with accepting this, each of us in our own way, set about finding out what made these dogs so different, why we were faced with difficulties and also why they had found their way into our hearts so quickly and so effectively.

Separately, we endeavoured to read about, research and learn where the breed came from, what they were originally bred for and how this influenced their behaviour in the environment in which they were now being asked to live. We have pondered, discussed and theorised at great length until finally we decided to join forces and put together our knowledge and research in this book.

This book is written for anyone interested in Spanish Water Dogs; owners, prospective owners, breeders and exhibitors alike. Within its pages we hope you will find useful information to help you understand your own dog and to give you an insight into how this breed thinks and works. We have included the history of the breed from early writings of curly coated dogs on the Iberian Peninsular to modern times when Spanish Water Dogs can now be found in numerous countries worldwide. We have considered various aspects of the breed: how to live with these dogs, train them and understand where they are coming from. We hope this book will be a useful handbook that you can dip into at leisure or refer to when things are not going to plan with your dog.

We both hope that not only will you perhaps learn from these pages but also enjoy them and consequently see your own Spanish Water Dog in a new light.

Happy Reading
Di Williamson and Wanda Sooby

This book is dedicated to our respective first Spanish Water Dogs, Miguel and Squiffy, who opened our eyes and changed our lives

1 ORIGINS AND HISTORY OF THE SPANISH WATER DOG

HISTORY

The Spanish Water Dog (Perro de Agua Espanol) is considered to be an ancient breed, its curly coated ancestors having been recorded in writings and documents as far back as the Eighth Century, Tenth Century, the early Twelfth Century and again in the Middle Ages. Yet this breed, having worked alongside shepherds and farmers as a herding dog and guardian of flocks for hundreds of years, has lived in anonymity until the early 1980s. Documentation exists which strongly suggests that Spanish Water Dogs, also known as Turkish Andalucian Dogs, originated from the Near East and, by studying ancient maps and references, it is possible to follow the movements of this type of dog westwards. Along with written texts are also engravings that show the essential characteristics of the breed set in rustic environment, displaying its function. In the book 'Varia Conmensurancia' by Juan de Arphe (1587) a reference to a water dog with typical characteristics indicates that they were already recognised as a type, if not a breed.

Several theories have been put forward about the origin of this breed and how it arrived on the Iberian Peninsular but these remain theories and none have been proved beyond doubt. It is commonly accepted that the development of the breed was within a pastoral setting, closely linked with that of Merino sheep and these active, quick thinking little dogs were used for herding. Merino sheep are descended from early breeds of sheep originally domesticated in Asia. Through careful breeding the quality of the animal and its wool was improved and with well established trade routes this breed found its way across Europe and into North Africa, particularly during Roman times when trading was at its height. Merino sheep arrived in Southern Spain from North Africa and were regarded as a rich source of income for many centuries, suffering a decline in the 'Dark Ages', followed by a revival in the Middle Ages. It has been suggested that a curly-coated water dog with a strong constitution was introduced from North Africa along with the Merino sheep by the Moors and arrived in Southern Spain, particularly in the region of Andalucia, in the year 711 around the time of the Muslim invasion.

There are records of dogs in North Africa, which resemble Spanish Water Dogs, being used for hunting in water, although none are found there today. Certainly, throughout the Middle Ages as the Merino sheep thrived, so also did the curly-coated, medium-sized, robust dog that was being used for herding as well as a variety of other tasks.

Many would argue that Spanish Water Dogs, which lived and flourished in the salt marshes of Southern Andalucia, are the forefathers of the breed and this is where the breed originated from before its spread throughout the Iberian

Spanish Water Dogs have been used in Spain for herding sheep for hundreds of years

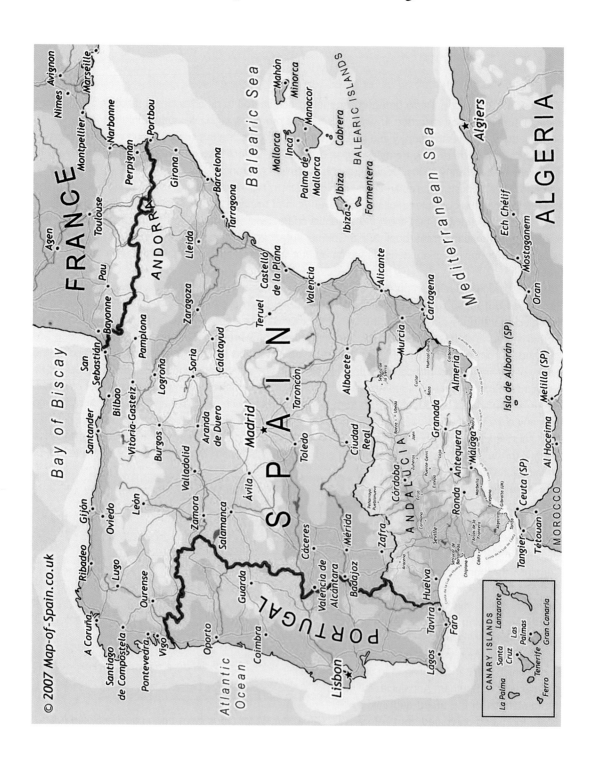

© 2007 Map-of-Spain.co.uk

Peninsular. Certainly, there have been sheep in this area for many centuries and it is possible that the breed evolved alongside the development of better quality sheep.

Another theory suggests that the Spanish Water Dog's ancestry can be traced back to Eastern Europe where other curly-coated breeds including the Puli and Komondor were developed. It has been suggested that they were introduced by the Barbarians in their various raids on Spain or more likely during the Eighteenth and Nineteenth Centuries when ships from Turkey were involved in the establishment of the trade in livestock, in particular Merino sheep, from Spain to Australia. In order to move the sheep onto the awaiting vessels, a sizeable dog with a strong character was needed to persuade what is essentially a stubborn species to move into 'unknown territory', the dog also having the agility to move out of the way of or over the backs of the sheep. In its study of the Turkish Andalucian Dog, the University of Cordoba cites 'reliable testimony' that a dog very similar to this breed exists on the coast of Turkey. It is assumed that the Turks brought with them their own dogs, a curly-coated type, which was introduced into Southern Spain and became known as 'El Turco Andaluz' or Andalucian Turk. Whether this is so, again, is debatable but the name has remained through the centuries along with several other names including Perro de Agua, Laneto, Perro de Lanas, Perro Patero, Perro Rizardo, Churro, Barbeta and, as it is now known, Perro de Agua Espanol.

During the Eighteenth Century movement of livestock took place across the Iberian Peninsular. This movement from north to south and back again in search of better grazing mirrored an activity that was taking place right across the more mountainous regions of Europe and this pattern still exists today in more remote areas. Known as 'Transhumance' (Transhumancia) the efficient movement of livestock in this way required the assistance of Spanish Water Dogs. This led to the breed becoming scattered across the country so, when the Napoleonic Wars resulted in plots of land, livestock and dogs being given to farmers, this brought an end to transhumance. The breed became isolated in rural communities, particularly in Andalucia.

As the impact of the Industrial Revolution was being felt in Northern and Central Spain other breeds of herding dogs from Germany and Belgium became more popular. Southern Spain remained much as it had been, continuing to use these useful curly-coated water dogs for a variety of tasks. At the same time, Spanish Water Dogs continued to be used by the fishermen in the Northern ports to assist with the nets along with other maritime tasks.

Further north of the Iberian Peninsular in other European countries there are a number of other curly-coated breeds and there is a suggestion that these all have a common ancestry. Through dispersal around Western Europe they became established as separate breeds, which included Poodles, Barbets, Portuguese Water Dogs, Irish Water Spaniels, the Old English Water Spaniel (now extinct) as well as Spanish Water Dogs. This breed, having become established in coastal regions of Cantabria, worked alongside the fishermen and, although now separated by some distance from the Spanish Water Dogs already established in the south, the northern dogs still retained the outstanding character and physical attributes of those in the south.

Along with the movement of dogs through transhumance regular trading had been taking place between the ports of the north and the Low Countries along with the ports in the south of Spain. Trade with the southern ports was centred around those near Seville where the presence of water dogs has long been recorded. Cattle trading took place between the north of Spain and Flanders, the cattle being accompanied by dogs. Certainly the dogs in the north, having adapted readily to the climate, were taken on by local fishermen who were eager to take advantage of the many talents that these dogs displayed

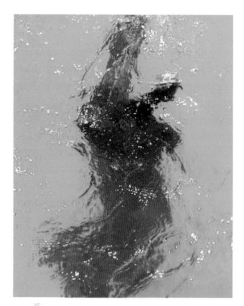

Spanish Water Dogs are excellent divers and can dive to a depth of several metres

when working in water. Even if these water dogs had originally been brought from the south by sea or overland they displayed some of the type and attributes of other breeds of water dog already established in other parts of Europe, so a genetic link is certainly possible.

References in the past to the presence of Spanish Water Dogs in the north of Spain can be found in the book 'Laredo en mi Espejo' (Laredo in my Mirror) by Maximo Busoa, published in 1932. In it he mentions on two occasions that a 'dog of wool' was to be found in the ports of Catalonia (Santander, Laredo and Santona). On the first occasion he writes that a shipwreck took place when, on returning to Laredo for the fiesta of The Virgin of the Port of Santona, the ship foundered in a sudden storm. 'The dog, almost drowning, was carried along by the woolly coat that covered its body. Swimming shorewards it reached a pillar and then the beach where it was found all wet, nervous and barking pitifully. It was then that the size of the catastrophe was realised.'

The next mention was about an incident that took place in the time of Ferdinand VII. 'A woolly dog lived at night in the house of the Tagle family. When it was time to light the streetlamp the dog would scratch at the glass in the door. The owner would give a lighted taper to the dog which it carried in its mouth and, with help from the owner, would light the streetlamps. Once the street was illuminated the dog would follow its owner home.'

It was only thirty years ago that the modernisation of the fleet of the Cantabrian ports took place. Prior to this, in these ports, water dogs or 'woolly dogs' of Cantabria and of The Basque region had an important part to play in the lives of local fishermen. These men of the sea lived in conditions of hardship and dogs were not kept as pets or on a whim but were employed in the process of ensuring that food was on the table. A dog possessing these exceptional abilities, capable of numerous functions, became an essential part of the work of the fishermen. Their dogs were resilient, had a predisposition for learning quickly and a natural desire to work. It is because of these attributes that the water dogs became needy companions of the fishermen and quickly gained the trust and respect of their owners, remaining with them in their employment.

They were capable of retrieving objects from the water, gathering fish that had escaped from the nets as the catch was landed, carrying the end of the mooring rope from the boat to the jetty, alerting the crew of the presence of fish or if a sailor fell overboard into the water and, finally, guarding the catch once it was landed. So important was the contribution of these dogs that they became a necessity.

These useful little dogs were also used for hunting in the wetlands, catching marine birds and partaking in other activities associated with fishing. The water dog, being an excellent retriever, readily carried objects back to its owner.

Spanish Water Dogs lived wherever the owner's possessions were kept, be it on the boat, in the storeroom or at the house. They frequently wandered freely around the port when not on board. The character of these dogs and their faithfulness guaranteed that they did not wander far away but remained within a distance where they could guard and protect 'their own'.

Known as 'woolly dogs' because of their appearance they became effective guards but still retained a friendly demeanour. There are numerous anecdotes of these dogs being reliable messengers having the capacity of remembering and carrying out simple errands. There are people who can recall a dog on its own, carrying a dish containing breakfast from the store to the boat. Crew members have related how, at only the slightest mention of a fishing trip, the dogs were eager to go.

The fishermen of Northern Spain appeared to have a preference for lighter coloured dogs; white, cream, bi-coloured and beige, most probably because it was easier to see them in the water. Conversely, the shepherds and goatherds of the south seemed to prefer darker coloured dogs that could easily be distinguished within the flocks and herds.

Historically, the Spanish Water Dog has lived in a poor environment where there was little food to spare for the dogs and because of this, the breed can live frugally while still retaining its strength for the different tasks required of it and the capability of coping with what life throws at it.

THE BREED IN MORE RECENT TIMES AND TODAY

In more recent times the breed has become scattered around Spain in rural settings, particularly in and around Malaga and Cadiz, where the primary role has been one of work. Although the majority of them could be found in Southern Spain, others were to be found in Northern Spain along the coast and in the ports. Separated by geography in isolated pockets of rural and mountainous areas it appears that minor variations in type emerged. These types differed slightly in height, structure and the purpose for which they were used, varying according to the needs of the owners.

A Spanish Water Dog could be used to move several hundred goats

Regardless of the differences in geographical location this breed has been developed purely as a working dog. The tasks it was required to do depended on the environment in which it was raised and the occupation of its owners. If the main occupation was fishing then the dog was used to assist in and on the water. If the rearing of sheep or goats was their livelihood then these dogs were used for herding.

Very often owners were involved in more than one activity and the dogs would be utilised accordingly, which could include hunting, water work, herding, guarding and as companion animals for the family. As a result, the Spanish Water Dog of today is multi-talented, very responsive to training, an independent thinker and can be taught to work in almost any sphere. Today, this has certainly been proved to be the case and in these pages you will find a variety of disciplines that Spanish Water Dogs are currently involved with in the UK.

In Spain today, this tough little dog can adapt to and operate in almost any environment. It is sure-footed, agile and has the capacity to think on its feet and problem solve. It appears to have a strong resistance to infections and parasites, making it an ideal dog for the countryside, salt marshes and the coast.

As a herding dog it is not unusual to see this breed working up to five hundred sheep or goats, which they learn to control often with only the minimum of training from the herdsmen. This would suggest that the skills are possibly acquired by observation of more experienced dogs or even that they are inborn. The dogs will follow vocal commands or signals given by the herdsmen or, through constant scrutiny of the flock, will work on their own initiative to ensure that the animals are kept together and are following the correct route.

The 'working' clip, showing trimming round the eyes and feet

As far as the coat is concerned, very little maintenance takes place apart from an annual clip in the Spring when the sheep are shorn. Some shepherds choose to cut hair away from the eyes and around the feet between yearly clips to allow the dog to see clearly and prevent tangling of hair between the toes.

In Southern Spain the breed is not used in the ports today but has been in the past on the River Guadalaquivir in Seville where it was given the task of retrieving mooring cables that were thrown in the water so that the dog could swim to the shore with the cable in its mouth.

Because of its ability to penetrate thickets and remain on a scent without barking, this breed is still used by some for hunting rabbits and occasionally ducks on lakes and rivers.

The natural wariness of strangers that still exists in the breed makes the Spanish Water Dog a useful guard of property and gives warning to the owner that someone is approaching.

As the world around us has become subject to changes, so the role of the Spanish Water Dog has evolved accordingly. Because of its superior scenting ability, agility and tenacity this breed has proved to be an excellent rescue dog in areas of natural disasters. They have been used to search out bodies in areas subjected to earthquakes in several countries around the world. Spanish Water Dogs have been trained to search out drugs and firearms, proving to be a useful asset to the police and the army.

Apart from its usefulness as outlined above, what, perhaps most of all, makes these dogs so special is its function as a companion. Anyone who has owned a Spanish Water Dog will understand how different this breed is to so many others. It may be the attractive looks that first catch the eye but when you really get to know your curly friend you will find a dog that has a sense of fun, often at your expense, a mischievous streak and the capacity for learning tricks to show off in front of an audience. However, beneath those irresistible curls is a deep thinking, complex dog that can confuse and baffle you and one that you will struggle to understand.

For a long time, while other foreign breeds of dog have been admired and kept by enthusiasts, this breed has been inadvertently overlooked. At last, this great Spanish breed has gained the recognition it deserves and a significant increase in the breeding of these dogs has led to a boom in numbers. Although this may be considered to be advantageous, it is important that today's breeders work together to conserve those aspects of the Spanish Water Dog that have been nurtured for generations and to retain them for the future.

REVIVAL OF THE BREED
Prior to the 1980s this breed was to be found almost exclusively in isolated rural locations, particularly in the mountainous areas of Malaga and Cadiz, being used for its original purpose in a working capacity but it still remained unrecognised as an accepted breed by the Kennel Club of Spain. Because of the isolation of these dogs from other breeds they tended to remain true to type without too much obvious out-crossing, if any.

Around 1980 a Mrs Mesdag brought a Spanish Water Dog to a dog show in Malaga where two people, Santiago Montesinos Rubio and Antonio Garcia Perez, recalled having seen numerous examples of these dogs throughout their lives but could not understand why they were not recognised as a breed in Spain. Santiago Montesinos also recalled his father mentioning repeatedly the existence of these dogs in the Province of Seville twenty-five years previously.

Having realised the untapped potential and the importance of this breed in ecological terms, these two enthusiasts united forces in order to revive the breed and make its presence known in its native country. With the help of others who knew the region intimately, they began a campaign of travelling around the villages and rural communities, buying, borrowing and acquiring from shepherds and goatherds those dogs they considered to be the best specimens. Their travels covered the mountainous regions of Malaga, Cadiz and beyond. The chosen dogs displayed the typical features and peculiar characteristics of the breed, some of which had come from families that could trace ownership back three centuries. Having established the basis of a gene pool they then began a breeding programme in earnest. In 1980 The Asociacion Espanola del Perro de Agua Espanol (The Spanish Association of the Spanish Water Dog) was formed and the first president, as well as founder member, was Santiago Montesinos. Because of the determination and generosity of this gentleman, along with his invaluable knowledge of dogs, the search for typical specimens was able to continue. The breed was studied, photographed and recorded but up until 1983 numerous letters to the Kennel Club of Spain and requests to take part in shows failed to get a response.

Meanwhile, through careful breeding by selecting only the best dogs and bitches, the Spanish Water Dog as we know it today became established. This was consequently followed by exposure of the breed at various dog shows in Spain in a non-competitive role. In late 1983, having been seen by the President of the Spanish Kennel Club at the Madrid World Show a breed standard was drawn up by Antonio Garcia Perez and in 1985 the breed was provisionally accepted by the Spanish Kennel Club and FCI, being put in Group VIII (flushing dogs).

Antonio Garcia Perez, ecologist and grandson of shepherds, is President of the official Breed Club in Spain (La Asociacion Espanola del Perro de Agua Espano) and is considered as 'the father of the breed'. His 'de Ubrique' affix is world famous amongst Spanish Water Dog owners and enthusiasts and 95% of dogs with a pedigree can be traced back to this kennel. Antonio was brought up with these dogs and is passionate about the breed that he has nurtured and developed over the last few years. His priorities are to keep the rustic appearance, working ability and sound temperament of this breed first and foremost.

Antonio's life is dedicated to his dogs and all his spare time is taken up with working, training, playing and just being with them. All his dogs love and respect him and you only have to see him working his dogs to appreciate the rapport he has built up with them. His knowledge and understanding of the breed, their pedigrees and bloodlines is boundless and he remains the foremost authority on Spanish Water Dogs.

Antonio Garcia Perez, 'Father of the breed' with Fin. Sp. & WW Ch. Zula de Ubrique, in Finland

Antonio has proved to be a great supporter of people who wish to become associated with the breed for the right reasons but will give his honest opinion about anyone who chooses to become involved in the breed for personal gain or to change the appearance or natural character of these dogs. He continues to take an active interest in the breed worldwide and will happily travel to wherever the correct advice on various aspects of the breed is required.

INTRODUCTION INTO THE UK

A group of four people from this country, Audrey Murray, Chris McQueeney, Faye Allen and Diane Phillipson, joined together to make the trip to visit The World Show in Valencia in June 1992. Their only reason for going was simply to enjoy the show, having no idea what they were letting themselves in for.

As two of them were watching the dogs in the show ring they were fascinated by a medium sized, woolly-coated breed. Almost simultaneously, the other two were observing a demonstration of similar dogs doing agility, Spanish style. It was only after some discussion, a visit to the breed stand and an introduction to the breed by Antonio Garcia Perez did the four realise that not only were the two groups of dogs the same breed but they were still in the early stages of full recognition. On further investigation of the breed and with the aid of Antonio's video, showing what these talented dogs were capable of, they were hooked. Having caught the imagination of the four travellers, on return to the UK a partnership was formed in order to work together to introduce Spanish Water Dogs into this country.

The 'Partnership'
Audrey Murray, Chris McQueeney, Faye Allen and Diane Philipson

This was followed by the careful selection and acquisition of two dogs and two bitches purchased from the foundation kennel 'Ubrique' owned by Antonio Garcia Perez, whose help was invaluable.

The first four imported Spanish Water Dogs

Sp. Ch. Cila de Ubrique   White bitch
six years old

Relampago de Ubrique   White and
black dog three years old

Topo de Ubrique   Cream dog
twelve months old

Dilita de Ubrique   Black and white
bitch eighteen months old

Cila and Relampago arrived into quarantine kennels in November 1992 followed by Dilita and Topo in January 1993 and on release from quarantine a breeding programme began in this country under the joint affix of 'Canagua'.

The initial development of the breed was carefully planned and guided by the partnership. From the birth of the first Spanish Water Dog in the UK, a single pup born in quarantine kennels in 1992, up until August 1st 2001 when The Kennel Club accepted the Spanish Water Dog onto the Imported Breeds Register, there were 16 litters registered with a total of 70 dogs.

The members of the Partnership met regularly to set down a series of guidelines in order to protect and advance the interests of the breed. They were only too aware that this delightful breed could prove to be very popular and sought after, but not necessarily for the right reasons. Prior to being accepted onto the Imported Breeds Register it was not possible to show these dogs in this country but members of the Partnership became actively involved in other pursuits with their dogs including field sports, agility, flyball and working trials.

Perhaps the final words here ought to be from the members of the Partnership themselves....

" What made us decide to embark on such a venture and nearly bankrupt ourselves in the process? Everyone asks the same question. Well, it is not always easy to say why anyone becomes attracted to a particular breed without liking everything about them or at least most things. None of us have regretted becoming involved with this enchanting breed and we look forward to seeing them worked to their full potential. We do not want them to become a fashion dog bred for their coats or colour. Judging by the behaviour of all the youngsters we have seen, they need something to do, their brains need working and are perhaps not a novice owner's dog. As you will know, bright dogs are also quick to learn bad habits as well as good."

"The Partnership consider themselves as guardians of Spanish Water Dogs in Great Britain. It is up to us to protect the breed and keep it true to its native country."
Audrey Murray, Chris McQueeney, Faye Allen, Diane Philipson, 1993.

Sp. Ch. Moro

2 THE SPANISH WATER DOG CLUB

The establishment of the breed in the UK began with four owners with a vision and four dogs imported from Spain. For the next nine years the partnership and a small number of new owners began a carefully planned programme of breeding. As numbers increased and new imports were introduced, there came a point in the history of this breed where it was essential to have common aims, common ideals and a solid foundation for owners and interested parties to work from. This role could only be filled by the introduction of a breed club with rules and regulations and a code of ethics to work from.

On September 14th 2002 an inaugural meeting was held at Markfield, Leicester with the late Mr Harry Baxter chairing the meeting and thus The Spanish Water Dog Club was formed. Harry Baxter had a wealth of knowledge about the less well-known breeds in Europe and followed the progress of the Spanish Water Dog from when it was first introduced into the UK. He wrote several articles on the breed in his regular column in 'Our Dogs' newspaper and remained an enthusiast until his death only months later.

The purpose of the Club was, and continues to be, a forum for bringing together a group of like minded people, owners and others interested in the breed, and to offer them an opportunity to learn about their dogs and to work, play with and compete with them through educational, competitive and enjoyable activities organised by the Club.

Within the Club there is very much an awareness that dogs of this particular breed appear to be conveniently sized, easily maintained, non-shedding and pretty, in fact, the perfect pet. Accordingly, they will appeal to many potential dog owners on appearance alone. However, it needs to be understood that the breed is much more complex than that and was bred specifically to fill a working role in its native country. Its character, temperament and rustic appearance very much reflect that. This is not a cuddly, 'teddy-bear' dog that will be satisfied to sit by the hearth in a haze of inactivity. It is a quick thinking, sensitive creature, a puzzle-solver and enthusiastic worker and very much requires a stimulating environment to bring out the best in it. It can often work independently and, most importantly, has a strong guarding instinct. Because of its sensitive nature coupled with a natural aptitude to guard this dog does not adapt easily to harsh or forceful handling and in the wrong hands it would be easy for this type of dog to become unpredictable, defensive or apprehensive.

Those actively involved in the Club feel it is vitally important that they are able to educate current and potential owners and give guidance and advice throughout all stages of the dog's development. Within the membership there is a diversity of experience in numerous aspects of canine activities including obedience, agility, flyball, search work, water work, showing and canine behavioural counselling. There is a great enthusiasm amongst the members and a willingness to share, educate, help and support all members wherever required.

The Club is also responsible for monitoring, collating, and recording any ongoing health issues within the breed and subsequently educating its membership accordingly. It sets standards and gives guidelines in the area of breeding so that future stock is produced as free from inherited diseases as is possible within the constraints of our current knowledge and understanding. The opportunity to increase our knowledge and understanding of a variety of canine issues is made available through annual breed seminars where the expertise of canine, genetic and health specialists may be called upon. Already the Club is aware of two specific health problems that have occurred in the breed and has taken steps to encourage testing, monitor progress and record results in the breed archives. These are discussed later in the book.

Since their debut onto the Imported Breeds Register in 2001 Spanish Water Dogs were frequently campaigned at championship and open shows around the country. Certainly, the unusual corded coat in a variety of colours and overall athletic and attractive appearance has caught the attention of many people, handlers and judges alike. As a result, a number of experienced show people have become owners with a view to showing their dogs. The Club is very much aware of the desire from Spanish quarters to maintain the natural and rustic appearance of the breed in this country and this includes the show ring. It also tries to ensure that anyone coming into the breed is aware of this so that the appearance of the dog is not changed or enhanced in any way by shaping or brushing the coat specifically for showing. One major way that this can be achieved is through education within the framework of the Club.

January 2008 marked another milestone in the history of the Club when the breed was transferred onto the Kennel Club Breed Register and, whereas previously, the Club could only hold Breed Matches it can now hold Breed Shows under Kennel Club rules.

Apart from its role of support and education The Club provides a number of activities throughout the year for members to participate in with their dogs. These involve learning new skills, finding out what their dogs are capable of and most importantly, having a great deal of fun.

"Somebody said 'Sit down'..............you're confused?!"

Almost nine years prior to the formation of the Club, in his column in 'Our Dogs' (April 1993) Harry Baxter wrote a piece about the introduction of Spanish Water Dogs into the UK. In it he included his thoughts about the future of the breed with regard to being shown and recalls his 'famous last words'......
"It is after all a beauty show". He then asked, 'whether a Spanish Water Dog breed club could properly fill its conservation role if, for its promotion of the breed, it relied on a programme of shows and show-related activities'. Well, Harry, you can rest in peace in the knowledge that the main aim of the Club is to maintain the true characteristics and working ability of the breed. This, hopefully, will continue to remain the focal point for the Club and all that it stands for in the years to come.

THE SPANISH WATER DOG CLUB MATCH

The First Three Years

Two talented brothers: Miguel (left) winner of the Club Match 2005 and Pablo (right) winner of the Club Match 2004

*2004
Joan Hubbard
with Pablo*

*2005
Di Williamson
with Miguel*

*2006
Lynn Napier-
Wong with Bibi*

They look cute but 'cute' has another meaning!

The three 'wise' monkeys!

3 DESCRIPTION OF THE BREED

The Spanish Water Dog is a medium-sized, curly coated, active dog, renowned for its all-round working ability, especially in water. In its native Spain it has, for several hundreds of years, been used for herding, guarding, hunting and fishing and has an incredible capacity for learning and remembering. It is faithful and hard working, gaining pleasure from being given tasks that stretch its abilities. It enjoys the company of its owner and very much wishes to be part of the family, preferring to be close to humans rather than living apart. It is brave and bold, especially when working, but can be reserved, particularly with strangers, preferring to meet and assess people in its own time and on its own terms. It is watchful, learning by observation, and readily adapts to most situations and environments. Its senses of sight, hearing and scent are well developed, complimenting its working ability.

Moby displaying the typical corded coat

The breed should be robust for its size, athletic in appearance and well muscled. It should be slightly longer in the body than height measured from the withers to the ground (9:8) with a level top-line rising slightly towards the rump due to well-muscled hindquarters. Further details of height and weight can be found in the breed standards of the Kennel Club and FCI.

The head should be well defined and strong with a flat skull, which is very much a feature of the breed. There is a small occipital crest and the planes of the skull and muzzle should be parallel to each other with a slightly marked stop between. The nostrils should be well defined and the lips should be well fitting, not slack. The jaw is strong and dentition should display a scissor bite with the upper teeth overlapping the lower and all the teeth being present at maturity.

Eyes are oval-shaped and very expressive, the colour varying according to pigmentation, the darker the pigmentation the darker the eye. Ears are v-shaped and dropped with a slightly rounded tip, being set slightly above the level of the eye.

The neck should be short and well set into the shoulders with no dewlap, the forequarters should be

An example of a flat skull

strong, displaying good angulation of shoulder and forearm, elbows set close to the body and front legs straight and parallel.

The chest should be deep with a good spring of rib, indicating an active dog with plenty of heart and lung room. Hindquarters should be moderately angulated and well muscled with hocks well let down. Altogether, the body should give the appearance of robustness without the impression of being heavy in the bone. There should be no excess weight, the muscles being well defined and solid to the touch. Feet should be tight with strong pads and webbed for efficient use in water.

The breed was customarily docked, the dock being medium set and, when attentive, decidedly raised. The undocked tail should taper towards the end and be carried like a scimitar but not curled. It is not unusual for Spanish Water Dogs to be born with a 'natural bob' or shortened tail.

Docked tail

Full tail

Half tail

Born tailless

THE COAT

The coat is curled and of a woolly texture and should have a natural, rustic appearance which is never groomed out or shaped. The curls form cords when long and, as they grow, should be separated using fingers only. The dogs are clipped at least once a year, as was the custom in Spain, when dogs were clipped along with the sheep in the Spring. The clip should be even all over with no shaping or sculpting that alters the outline of the dog. Much emphasis has been placed on correct presentation for the show ring from Spanish experts in the breed and it is the aim of a number of owners, especially those who were responsible for introducing the breed into the UK, to uphold that tradition in this country.

Full coat

Spanish Water Dogs can be shown with a short, medium or long coat although it is generally accepted that they are not shown newly clipped or with over-long coats. Correct lengths of coat for showing can be found in the FCI Breed Standard. Coat care will be covered in more detail later in this book.

The texture of the coat can vary slightly from one dog to another, sometimes being harsher or wiry, sometimes softer. The texture can even vary on a dog that has two distinctive colours, the white often being softer than the solid colour.

Medium coat

Clipped

Coat colours in Spanish Water Dogs vary and any solid colour is considered acceptable. These colours include black, various shades of brown, orange, cream through to white. All of these colours are also acceptable with white markings or the coat can be predominantly white with coloured markings. Tri-colour, black and tan and brown and tan are considered undesirable. It is understood that albinos are considered undesirable also and flecking is not to be encouraged.

Skin pigmentation, eye colour and nose leather can vary but should match the colour of the coat; generally speaking, the darker the dog, the darker the eye colour and also the pigmentation, but some light coat colours may be complimented by darker pigmentation.

Pigmentation can vary from black through to pink and eye colour from very dark brown to a yellowish colour. Nail colour generally also matches the coat colour and a dark coloured dog will have black nails, a dog with white feet will have pink nails but occasionally both colours may be present.

One inherited factor frequently seen and which affects coat colour in this breed is the fading or greying gene. A dark puppy pales with age, the fading beginning soon after birth in some cases or after a period of a few weeks and this continues until maturity when the pale colour establishes itself permanently. For a period of anything up to two years of age, each time the dog is clipped, it seems to be a shade lighter. Fading is first evident when the coat is parted on a young puppy, the lighter shade showing at the roots.

Taffle at three weeks

Taffle at ten weeks

Taffle at three years

The effect that fading has on the original colour is that black can become blue or grey, brown can become fawn or beige and red can become roan. If, when you choose your puppy at the age of seven or eight weeks of age, you have a particular colour in mind do not be surprised if this is not the colour the dog ends up. Perhaps it is better to consider other factors when making your choice rather than the colour!

One interesting observation that can be made where the fading gene is present is that of injuries to the skin. If the skin is damaged in any way, either as a consequence of a clipper burn, abrasion or infection

you will find that when it has healed the hair grows back the same colour as the puppy was at birth. As an example, a dog that was brown at birth but fawn at maturity will have a brown patch of hair where the skin was damaged. With time, this patch will gradually fade to the colour of the rest of the coat. It's open to speculation but one possible reason for this is that the fading gene is controlled by temperature. Where the skin is warmer, the coat is subject to fading but where the skin is cooler, the original colour is evident. Damaged skin will have fewer blood vessels near the surface; therefore the temperature will be slightly lower. As the skin repairs itself, the blood vessels are reformed and the temperature consequently rises.

Brio showing the bleached hair on his face

Brio with the hair on his face wet showing his true colour

Another feature of this breed is the tendency for the tips of the curls to bleach in the sun. This is not an extra colour but the effect that the sun has on the colour that is present. A black coat will have tips of brown, even orange in the summer. To prove that the coat has bleached, rather than the dog having black and tan colouring, one has only to wet the coat. This bleaching of the coat is an accepted occurrence and adds to the overall attraction of the breed.

STRUCTURE AND MOVEMENT

The overall appearance of the typical Spanish Water Dog is one of athleticism and alertness, a very natural looking dog that, although attractive and eye-catching, can be appreciated equally for its working ability, giving the impression that it can do a full day's work with the minimum of effort. When newly clipped the true outline of this breed can easily be appreciated. An active and fit specimen will carry no excess fat, appearing lithe and lean. However, when hands are placed on the dog, a firm and well-muscled body can be felt. A well-sprung rib cage gives plenty of room for heart

Coco showing overall balance

and lungs to facilitate breathing and strong hindquarters give power and drive to movement.

An old fashioned way of knowing whether your dog is the correct weight or not can be utilised after your dog has just been clipped. The tried and tested method amongst some gundog folk is to run your hands over the dog and you should be able to clearly feel three vertebrae and the rib cage. Then take three steps back and you should not be able to see them.

On the move the dog should cover the ground effectively and efficiently, giving the appearance of effortlessness and drive. There is little need for a Spanish Water Dog to waste time and energy in lifting its legs high in a prancing action when moving, as can be seen in some other breeds.

This natural, easy movement should be particularly evident in the show ring in order for the judge to appreciate the workmanlike aspects of the breed. However, presenting a Spanish Water Dog on a tight lead, causing the dog to high-step in order to take some pressure off the neck, can so easily spoil the whole picture! This may be considered by some as attractive and does, to some extent, look flashy but it is unnatural and incorrect for this breed. A dog that is allowed to move freely on a loose lead will be correctly balanced and able to demonstrate parallel movement to better effect, the fore and hind legs remaining in the same plane.

4 CARE OF YOUR SPANISH WATER DOG

THE COAT AND CLIPPING

The Spanish Water Dog's coat is very distinctive and it sets this breed apart from so many others. It is naturally curly and, when long, forms into cords. In its native country the coat was never brushed or combed but the accepted look was achieved through parting the cords with fingers, which is then further enhanced by regular swimming.

Detail of the corded coat

The coat is described as having a natural, rustic appearance and it is important that all those who have Spanish Water Dogs or acquire them in the future are aware of this and endeavour to preserve it. This is how the breed has been kept for centuries and it would be a travesty if it were ever changed. A groomed out or sculptured look that is evident in some other breeds, like Poodles for example, would suggest a lack of understanding of the history of this breed and the purpose for which it was bred.

Traditionally, Spanish Water Dogs were clipped out in the Spring at the same time as the sheep were sheared. This presumably was the easiest way of maintaining the coat when it was getting too heavy and cumbersome for the dog to work with and allowed the dog the freedom and comfort of a short coat through the summer months. As a result it has been accepted that the coat should never have more than one year's growth.

Once the coat has reached a year's growth or 12 cms in length it should be clipped. If you choose to take your dog to a professional groomer you will need to have a photograph with you of a newly clipped dog to demonstrate that you want your dog clipped out completely, the same length all over and with no sculpting. The groomer may try to persuade you otherwise but you will need to stand firm. It would be a good idea to warn the groomer that your dog will look very strange, once clipped, and that you are prepared for this! Many Spanish Water Dog owners have invested in clippers and have learnt to do it themselves. Although this appears to be a daunting prospect at first, it soon becomes easy to do and will save a fortune in professional groomers' bills. Choosing the correct clippers and blades is another time consuming task but sound advice can be obtained from other owners who have acquired their own. Different owners have preferences for different makes so you will need to do some research. Advice about the clipping procedure should also be sought before you tackle your first clip. Very often other owners are willing to lend a hand to start you off or you may have seen a demonstration of clipping at a Spanish Water Dog Club event. The first time is always the hardest but after you have clipped your own dog a few times you will become quite expert.

Just remember, unlike some other breeds that have curly coats that are shaped or have longer hair left on certain parts of the body, the correct way to clip a Spanish Water Dog is to take off all of the hair **uniformly** all over the body. There should be no shaping, sculpting or topiary! After as much coat as possible has been removed then it is necessary to tidy up and finish off with scissors. Professional grooming scissors are what is required for this job and it is worth investing in two or three pairs of differing sizes. Although expensive to buy, they give a better cut and will last.

Before Clipping (Can't see!)

Half Way (Tea break!)

Finished (That's better)

Your newly clipped dog may appear somewhat strange at first but the curls will soon begin to grow back within a week or two. Any mistakes you may have made when clipping will have 'disappeared' after three weeks. Don't worry if the weather turns cool and you are concerned about your dog feeling cold. There are some very attractive dog coats that can be purchased for cold weather and your dog will soon adjust to wearing one.

Once clipped, the curls soon come back and, as the coat grows, the curls separate into single strands which form cords as the coat gets longer and thicker. These cords need some encouragement from the owner to stay separated and by taking hold of the cords with the fingers they can be gently prised apart, so preventing large mattes from forming.

Points to remember are that a brush or comb should never be used on a Spanish Water Dog and that hand grooming only is the correct method.

Maintaining the Coat

There are no hard and fast rules about how long or short you should keep your dog's coat if it is not being shown. As a member of your family your dog needs to fit in with what suits you. It may be that you do not wish for the coat to grow into cords nor to have to work at separating them. A well-kept long coat looks spectacular but it is also very good at harbouring all sorts of vegetation and debris picked up on walks.

If you feel that you prefer a more easily maintained, shorter coat then there is no reason why it cannot be clipped two or three times a year. If your dog is regularly in water or is frequently exercised in areas with long vegetation then a shorter coat will be much easier to keep and will dry more quickly. You may prefer the look of the full coat and enjoy the hand grooming, which can be a very relaxing hobby if done in the evening in front of the TV for instance.

Whatever your preference, whether it be short or long, the important point to remember is that the coat still maintains the natural and rustic appearance so typical of this breed.

Swimming is the most natural way of keeping the coat in good condition but without access to regular dips the dog may need bathing from time to time, although this is not ideal and does not always give the desired finish to the coat. Removal of the natural oils through frequent bathing can lead to the coat turning fluffy.

Occasionally, however, your Spanish Water Dog **will** need a bath, especially if it has begun to smell, rolled in something unsavoury or has just been clipped. You should use warm, not hot, water on the coat, along with a mild shampoo. It is as well to have a large plastic jug handy so you can dilute the shampoo in ten parts of water to one part shampoo. 'Neat' shampoo should not be applied to the coat or skin. Tea Tree Oil or Aloe Vera shampoos are ideal; another product worth considering, especially where there is an occurrence of coat or skin problems is 'Malaseb', which is available from your Vet or via the Internet but advice from your Vet is desirable. Spread the shampoo all over the coat and massage well in. Rinse thoroughly with cool water to remove all traces of shampoo and finish off by patting with a towel but do not rub vigorously as this will encourage the coat to go fluffy. Let the coat dry off naturally in a warm room to allow the curls to form correctly and avoid using a dryer. Do not brush or comb the coat.

A well-maintained, fully corded coat readily repels water and encourages drainage down the cords away from the skin when working in water.

The Puppy Coat

When a Spanish Water Dog puppy is born it has a very short coat, which is usually wavy once the pup has dried out. The coat begins to grow immediately so that within a short space of time the waves have become the beginnings of curls. By the time the pup goes to its new home at seven or eight weeks of age the curls are quite long and well defined.

The coat soon after birth

The puppy coat

However, the texture of the coat at this stage is very different from the adult coat. It is still very soft and fluffy compared to the crisp curls of the mature dog.

At about the age of five or six months the beginnings of the adult coat can often be seen coming through at the base of the puppy coat and already the texture has started to change. This is the time that the first clip should take place. Removal of the soft puppy coat will allow the adult coat to come through unhindered. Different breeders have varying views on exactly when the first clip should take place but the most important aspect of this is that your pup has been well prepared for the procedure.

If you are a new Spanish Water Dog puppy owner your breeder should have explained when to clip and how to train your puppy to cope with the experience well beforehand. It is as well to let an experienced groomer or your breeder do this for the first time, although eventually you may wish to acquire all the necessary equipment and learn how to clip yourself. Preparing the puppy starts very early on, soon after you have settled it in to its new home. On a regular basis lift your puppy onto a table, having made sure that it is standing on a non-slip surface. Be very careful not to allow your pup to jump or fall off and when you have finished always lift it down. Run your fingers through every part of the coat and over all parts of the body. Handle its ears, around the head and lift each foot up, holding them for a very short while. Use a gentle voice and praise your pup each time it allows you to touch or hold a specific part of its body. Avoid gripping it tightly or forcing it to be held as this will only frighten it or teach it to resent being handled. Clicker training is very useful here if you have experience of it.

At a later stage introduce an object that makes a noise similar to clippers, an electric toothbrush for example or an electric razor. Hold the object away from the puppy to begin with until you are certain that it will not react adversely. If the puppy happily accepts the noise move the object closer and ultimately run it up and down the coat. Remember to spend time allowing the puppy to get used to the feeling of vibration around its head and legs, as when the clippers are used on bony areas the sensation can be very frightening. Praise your puppy at every opportunity. Keep these sessions very short to begin with, making them slightly longer as the weeks go by. If your puppy has quite happily accepted these simple exercises it should have no major problems the first time it is clipped.

If you have chosen to take your puppy to a professional groomer for the first clip it is advisable that you insist on being present so that you can make the groomer aware of the potential problems that may arise. Spanish Water Dogs are different from so many other breeds and need correct handling at times of stress. Even though you have prepared your pup well in advance it does not ensure a problem free experience of the first clip. Your puppy's reaction may be one of uncertainty and fear, which could be the cause of major problems in the future. Ensure that the groomer is aware of your concerns and is prepared to handle the puppy gently, reinforcing correct behaviour but not reacting to anything adverse. Also, you need to remain calm and to avoid the temptation of making a big fuss of the pup when things are not going well. Expect the first clip to take a long time and don't strive for perfection in the quality of the clip. The puppy's well-being is more important at this stage.

EARS

Because the ears of a Spanish Water Dog are quite long and pendulous it is not easy for air to circulate and this may create an environment that bacteria can flourish in. It is vitally important that ears are inspected on a regular basis to ensure that the hair is not growing inside the ear canal and that there is no infection. To encourage the hair to grow outwards all you need to do is gently rub the hair away from the ear canal using nothing smaller or more pointed than your thumb. Avoid using cotton buds or poking any other instrument down the ear as this could cause damage to the delicate membranes or push dirt and foreign bodies further down.

If the hair grows very thickly inside the canal it may be wise to gently pluck out the hair that you can reach easily or use a product such as 'Ear Clear' (Thornit). This breaks down the wax and aids the removal of loose hair that may have built up.

You will notice that your dog's ears have a mild 'yeasty' smell but, provided they are not inflamed or causing a problem, you should consider this as normal. If the dog is constantly shaking its head or scratching its ears causing them to become reddened and painful or if the smell is more powerful than normal this is a sign that there is a problem and it needs treating immediately. On inspection you may find the inside is more moist than usual or the wax is a lot darker. The cause of the problem may be a foreign body lodged inside such as a grass seed, there may be an infection or it could be the result of ear mites. In a case such as this we would recommend you seek the advice of your veterinarian who can use an instrument to see deep down into the ear canal and find the cause of the problem. It is imperative that you follow the course of treatment prescribed carefully and you continue to check your dog's ears on a regular basis.

TEETH

Altogether a dog has forty-two teeth and, provided you assist with the care of these, they should be strong and healthy well into old age. Care of the teeth requires correct diet and allowing your dog to chew on a suitable toy or object. When constantly fed moist or sloppy food the teeth will become covered in tartar and ultimately infection will set in. Dried food as part of the regular diet encourages your dog to use its teeth and this will help to keep them clean. There are dog toys and products specifically designed for chewing on like 'Nylabone' toys or dental rasks and these should be made available. Raw bones are ideal if you can get them but make sure they are big enough not to be broken into fragments when chewed. Roast bones very often crack and break up into sharp pieces that can be dangerous. Cooked chicken and lamb bones should be avoided for the same reason but are safe if fed raw.

There are toothbrushes or finger gloves and toothpaste specially designed for dogs so you can brush your dog's teeth daily. In order to clean the dog's teeth you must hold its head by passing your hand behind the neck, and introduce a brush from the side (never frontally because the dog will bite the brush). Don't put too much toothpaste on. Regular brushing will slow down the build up of tartar. Avoid using products designed for humans, especially toothpaste.

Inspect the teeth regularly and if you see signs of infection or damage it is best to seek the advice of your veterinarian.

NAILS

Before your puppy came to you the breeder may already have trimmed its nails several times. Puppies' nails are very sharp but quite easy to trim back, in fact a small pair of nail scissors may be all you will need.

If your dog is very active or runs around on hard ground you may find that clipping is not necessary or only needs doing infrequently. It is as well to train it to sit quietly and have its feet handled in preparation for the times when clipping is required. This requires short sessions of picking up the feet, each in turn with lots of praise for desired behaviour. A quick inspection of the nails will indicate whether or not they need attending to. It is much easier to see how much needs trimming back on nails that are light in colour but black nails are much more difficult to assess. In light coloured nails the quick, which is pink, can be clearly seen and only the white part of the nail should be cut. When clipping black nails it is a good idea to take a little bit off first then decide if you can take off some more. Don't forget the dewclaws on the inside of the front legs. These do not wear down and can become quite long, sharp and curved. If overlong they catch on fabrics and soft furnishings when your dog jumps up and they are easily torn off causing a lot of pain and bleeding.

It is as well to invest in clippers designed specifically for trimming nails and these come in two distinct forms; guillotine and scissor shaped trimmers. Ensure that they are always sharp and have non-slip handles.

INTERNAL PARASITES

It is usual practice for the bitch to be wormed prior to mating and for the puppies to be wormed two or three times before going to their new homes. Very often neither the bitch nor the puppies have shown evidence of having a worm problem but they may still be present, so treatment is just a matter of course.

The two main worms that can be found in dogs are Roundworms and Tapeworms. There are others but they are difficult to see evidence of and can easily be removed as part of a systematic worming programme.

Roundworms can lie dormant in the bitch in the form of larvae and the hormones associated with pregnancy will activate the larvae of the worm causing them to be passed to the puppies via the mother's milk. Part of the cycle includes eggs being passed into the environment via faeces and being picked up and ingested by another dog; thus the cycle continues.

Tapeworms are transmitted to dogs by ingesting fleas that are carrying the eggs or by the dog eating a small animal that is infested with them. Tapeworms are made up of segments that are attached to each other in a long 'chain'. The segments then break off, being passed via faeces, where they can then become attached to the hair around the anus. This is an indication that the dog has an infestation.

It is worth bearing in mind that worms found in dogs can be passed on to people so a regular worming regime is important, especially if there are children in the family. If there are other dogs and also cats in the household then your worming programme should include all of these at the same time. There are various worming preparations which can be bought from pet shops but these may not be as effective as products acquired from your veterinarian, where you will also receive sound advice about how frequently to worm and which product to use.

When considering the possible infection of children it is as well to note that it may not only be dogs that are the potential source of contamination. Urban foxes and hedgehogs visiting your garden can easily cause infestation, so the solution here is a sensible routine of washing hands before eating.

EXTERNAL PARASITES

From time to time the majority of dogs will play host to something unpleasant in their coats. The three main parasites to be found on dogs are fleas, ticks and mites but these can either be prevented or dealt with quite easily. Fleas are more likely to be picked up when the conditions are warm and moist and when your dog is in close contact with another carrying them or from a cat. Once the fleas have made themselves at home on your pet they can multiply at an alarming rate.

The first sign that your dog has 'visitors' will be when it persistently scratches itself. You will need to investigate the dog's coat by parting the hair right down to the skin, particularly round the neck and the base of the tail. If you do not actually see a flea you may see tiny specks of what looks like dirt. Remove some of these and drop them on a damp paper handkerchief or into a bowl of water. If the specks dissolve and turn a red brown colour then it is a sign the dog has got fleas. These are flea droppings of dried blood. As fleas lay large numbers of eggs which drop off into the bedding or carpets, both dog and house will need treating. Flea treatments can be acquired from your veterinarian and come in two main types. There are drops that you can put on the back of the dog's neck, which is a preventative method, or you can use a spray. Advice on using these can be obtained from your vet or the receptionist if a consultation is not necessary. Remember to vacuum your house thoroughly and wash the dog's bedding as well.

Ticks are picked up by your dog from bushes and undergrowth. They lie in wait and when a suitable host passes they jump onto it in preparation for a feed. You may not notice that there is a tick on your dog until it has had a large blood meal, after which it will have a distended, grey coloured abdomen. The tick itself will have buried into the dog's skin and the head and legs will be out of sight, gripping tightly under the surface.

Ticks need to be removed carefully because pulling them out roughly may leave the head and legs under the skin, which, if left, will cause an area of infection. The trick is to firmly take hold of the tick as close to the skin as possible with a pair of tweezers and gently twist in an anticlockwise direction until it comes loose. Check it to see that it is intact, then dispose of it in any way that you think is appropriate. It's worth investing in a small plastic implement called a tick remover. This has a v-shaped indentation, which you slip round the tick then twist to remove it as above.

Sarcoptic mange mites (scabies) are highly contagious and are easily passed on if your dog has close contact with an infected dog. The mite itself is very small and burrows under the skin, causing intense itching. Signs include hair loss, a skin rash, and crusting. Skin infections may develop secondary to the intense irritation. In order to treat this problem it is necessary to consult your veterinarian who will prescribe a course of treatment, which involves medication and shampoos. People who come in close contact with an affected dog may develop a rash and should seek treatment from their doctor.

Demodectic mange is dealt with elsewhere in this book.

Any signs of persistent scratching, hair loss or inflamed skin should be investigated and treated immediately before the problem really takes hold.

ANAL SACS

Dogs have two anal sacs, one either side of the anus. Provided the dog is fit, healthy, active and is fed a diet that includes dried food or roughage, the chances are that these will not present a problem, in fact you may never have even noticed them. There's a saying, "If it ain't bust, don't fix it"! This is a philosophy close to my heart and I have never had need to consider problems with anal sacs in all the time I have owned dogs.

However, there may just be the occasional problem cropping up with your dog and the sign to look for is your dog 'scooting' its rear along the ground. Most dogs will do this very occasionally but if your dog is scooting frequently it may be because the anal sacs are impacted and need emptying. This is not a pleasant job as the fluid has a strong, unpleasant smell. If you feel the need to have this investigated it is as well to consult your veterinarian who will do the emptying for you if required.

Some people will tell you that the scooting is a result of worms. It is certainly possible but it is more likely to be associated with the anal sacs. If in doubt, seek advice from a professional.

5 LIVING WITH A SPANISH WATER DOG

We cannot, however, promise this level of service

Spanish Water Dogs are incredibly intelligent and quick to learn. They have phenomenal memories and can learn anything it is physically possible for a dog to do that you are capable of teaching, and quite a lot that you may not have to teach at all! They are inquisitive to the point of nosiness and believe they have the right to know what is occurring at all times. Spanish, unlike most other breeds, are capable of learning simply by watching and may learn to do something because they saw you training another dog. They are rustic, unspoiled working dogs but they are still learning how to live in a modern world. For hundreds of years they have lived on their wits, done all that was expected of them and been left to make decisions on their own. They are still eminently capable of doing this. However, the life they live here in the UK is very different from the one they live in Spain. There are no privileges for working dogs in Spain. They are fed and housed and expected to work in return; end of story! In our modern, pet loving society dogs with working brains become very confused when they are treated as lap dogs. If there are no boundaries they believe they still have to work on their own initiative and this can cause problems. Understanding what makes a Spanish Water Dog tick and teaching him from day one that he has a leader, and there are rules, will ensure he grows into a happy, sociable family companion of which you can be proud.

Clever dogs are apt to learn the wrong things as quickly as they do the right ones! They are also adept at training their owners and this can prove problematic, as they are so inherently 'bossy', and inclined to take matters into their own hands if they believe themselves to be 'in charge'! Spanish Water Dogs are often perceived as 'cute'. They are cute – very – but not only to look at! With their curly coats and sparkling eyes they look adorable but in reality they are German Shepherds in sheepskin coats! They can do anything we wish to train them to do but they are **very** sensitive, they **do** guard and they **do** like to be in control. If you are thinking of taking on a Spanish as a cuddly toy, a couch potato or a bed warmer stop reading now, throw this book away and go find yourself a Poodle or a Bichon Frisé.

Lola flying – hair and all

Like all puppies Spanish Water Dogs have a 'fear imprint' stage (a period when, if a pup is frightened by something, that fear could remain 'imprinted' in its mind for the rest of its life) that occurs between four and seven months of age. How you deal with this will have a permanent impact on the puppy, for better or worse. If you reassure your puppy when he or she is afraid all you will achieve is a puppy that believes that you are afraid too, and that showing fear is rewarded. Behaviour that is rewarded will be repeated and eventually your dog will be fearful of more and more situations until you end up with a truly nervous dog. If, on the other hand, you act in a happy and confident manner and ignore your puppy **entirely** you will be setting a positive example for the pup to follow and he or she will grow into a confident dog that can cope with the stresses of everyday life. Give the puppy time to recover from the initial fear of the unknown situation or object then, **when** he is happy again, reward him for being positive.

Whilst other breeds do have a second 'fear imprint' stage most of them do not present too much of a problem but with the Spanish Water Dog it can be a very difficult time. It starts at around nine or ten months and lasts until between twelve and fifteen months as a rule. At this time, however, the pup is entering puberty, hormones are beginning to play their part and it is now that problems with aggression or fear can sometimes occur, especially if the pup believes he or she is 'cock of the roost' – in other words 'Leader of the Pack'. Learning, from the start, how to be the 'Leader' yourself, as far as your puppy is concerned, is the best way to be certain that you can control the difficulties with which you may be faced during this adolescent period. If you, or any of your friends, have older teenagers I am sure you can remember being horrified when they turned from polite, loving children into argumentative Neanderthals! With firm, loving parenting they eventually revert to human beings! If your pup believes that you are important enough to deal with situations that are fearful, he or she is more likely to look to you for advice on how to behave. On the other hand, a pup that believes he or she is in control may be more likely to 'take the law into it's own hands' so to speak. This fear period is not going to present a problem in every dog and there are no hard and fast rules as to how it manifests itself with regard to the sex of the dog. However, when it occurs in males it can result in a period of apparently aggressive or unsociable behaviour. A female, particularly during the month prior to her first season, may suddenly become inexplicably nervous of people when previously she was outgoing and friendly.

As previously mentioned, Spanish Water Dogs are a sensitive breed and part of that sensitivity can be connected to their ability to cope with stress. Stress is a normal part of life, for dogs as well as humans. In normal circumstances reasonable levels of stress are actually beneficial. If stress levels are too high or too constant the animal's well being will begin to suffer and its behaviour will deteriorate. Puppies should be exposed to stressful situations from the very beginning, starting with very low levels, ignoring any negative response and only gradually increasing the pressure. Were a puppy to be protected from all such stimuli until it was older, the effect then would be catastrophic as it would never have learned to develop coping mechanisms. A dog that has slowly built up levels of tolerance will not be phased by some new and potentially shocking experience when it reaches maturity.

It is vital that a Spanish Water Dog is trained by modern, motivational methods, and never subjected to any form of abuse, either physical or mental. Harsh training methods, choke chains, physical punishment and 'firm' voice control will result in a dog that doesn't trust you or other people and which will therefore become unreliable. A dog that is trained in a positive, meaningful way will respond with alacrity!

The Spanish Water Dog has a very well developed sense of humour. No matter how well you have done your training there will be times, especially in front of an audience, when your normally beautifully

Anton showing exactly what he thinks of the photographer!

behaved little darling will go through his own repertoire offering every behaviour he has ever learned except the one you have asked for! In a situation where it doesn't matter accept this for what it is – a bit of Latin temperament and the dog's way of having fun at your expense. When the chips are down and disobedience could be unacceptable or dangerous you will occasionally need to take control again. If you have trained correctly without resorting to aggression or punishment you will be able to assert yourself and let him know you're less than pleased. Your Spanish will jump to attention, look up at you angelically and say, "Oh, you want me to do **that?** Why didn't you **say** so?" He will then give you the behaviour you asked for as if the thought of arguing would never have entered his head. Your Spanish does not need to be turned into a robot. They are fun loving dogs with a great zest for life and it would be a shame to try to stamp out the very characteristics that probably drew you to the breed in the first place.

Breeders are often asked the question "What are they like with children and other dogs?" I could be flippant and answer, "How long is a piece of string?" but the sensible response would be that they are only as good as you have prepared them to be. Let us consider children first. A puppy needs to be socialised with children as early as possible, ideally while still with the breeder. The children should also learn to respect the puppy, not treat it like a toy, not interrupt it while sleeping, not poke pencils down its ears but also learn how to have fun both in play and by joining in with training. With regard to other dogs it has to be said that while the Spanish is a very dog-sociable breed with extremely well developed canine communication skills, it is also a very assertive breed. Please do not confuse assertiveness with aggression. Low levels of what we see as aggressive behaviour are part of normal canine conversation and should not

Pip and Katie know each other well enough to exchange a kiss

be inhibited or interfered with. However, the Spanish Water Dog does not generally take kindly to being at the bottom of a pack so, although they are quite capable of getting along happily with dogs of all breeds and both sexes, they are inclined to "strut their stuff" and boss other dogs around! A problem will only ensue should they meet other dogs of equal status and similar feelings of self-importance. At times like this your training should enable you to put a stop to any **fistipaws!**

Whilst on the subject of 'assertiveness' it is timely to mention the Spanish Water Dog's ability to assess the emotional and physical condition of the people he comes into contact with. If a person is in a vulnerable condition, either through illness or injury, a dog of this breed is perfectly capable of recognising that this is a weakness and taking advantage of the situation. This may manifest itself in

Behaviour this 'rude' can be quite intimidating

excessive barking, jumping up and possibly even the grabbing of clothing. Although there may be **no** aggressive intent it can still feel quite intimidating.

As a herding breed the Spanish Water Dog may show an inclination to round things up, possibly children as well as sheep, deer, ducks etc. Bicycles could also provoke a chasing response. Another 'endearing' trait that may be observed in dogs of this breed is an inclination to 'head butt' in order to control or manipulate situations to their advantage. This can be applied to humans as well as other dogs! Many a Spanish will produce a toy in an attempt to elicit play and, if ignored, will thrust it forcefully at the object of their attention. This ploy, if unsuccessful, may well be followed by some

serious head butting, or punching with the front feet! Respond at your peril! If you don't want a dog that controls everyone who enters the house this behaviour should be ignored. Good training and learning how to harness natural tendencies will prevent these traits from ever becoming a problem.

Spanish Water Dogs are somewhat "vocal" and love the sound of their own voice. Their bark is quite intense and fairly high on the Richter Scale when it comes to noise-level. When a Spanish hears a noise he will wake up, leap to his feet and

Max saying "Pay me some attention – Now

bark all in the same split second, which can be very startling for the owner. I have 'worn' more than one cup of coffee I would have preferred to have drunk when my dogs have 'alerted' me to something they perceived to be threatening! At it's best the bark of a Spanish sounds like that of a much larger dog but, if he feels the situation demands action and he is not sure what that action should be, the bark can become almost hysterical and is usually accompanied by much leaping, spinning and possibly the frantic grabbing of a toy. Then again, when he is playing, a Spanish can sound like a silly puppy! The range is extensive and very expressive of the dog's emotions but if allowed to get out of control may well reach nuisance levels. Controlling excessive barking is dealt with elsewhere in this book.

As a working dog and being classified as a gundog breed, it may be thought by some traditionalists that the Spanish Water Dog will be happy living in a kennel. Nothing could be further from the truth. They are sociable dogs with a highly developed sense of 'family', both canine and human, and as such make poor kennel dogs. A Spanish would be miserable living in a kennel full time, would probably become very bored and could easily raise noise levels to a degree that might up-skittle friendly relations with your neighbours! The old argument in the gundog fraternity that a working dog living within the family will be 'ruined' by the wife and children is not a good enough reason to put a Spanish in prison. My advice would be to train the wife and children, a Spanish is quite clever enough to know the difference between work and play!

Another frequently asked question is "Are they one-man-dogs?" The answer is emphatically "No!" A properly socialised Spanish, whose family have all taken part in his training, will react equally well to each of them. In fact, most Spanish who have been well trained will work for whoever has hold of the lead, even complete strangers.

Whilst on the subject of 'work' it is timely to point out that the Spanish Water Dog is a 'Jack of all trades' but definitely not 'Master of none'! Most Spanish will do well in more than one discipline so if one member of the family wishes to do agility and another fly-ball and yet another working trials that family will not need to come to blows or buy another dog. They will be able to share the dog and have equal pleasure from their chosen activities. The dog will be the winner and will have a fascinating and rewarding life.

The desire to 'retrieve' is very pronounced in the Spanish; puppies will probably be carrying toys long before they leave their mother. If a puppy is given lots of toys, especially of the soft, furry variety, he will be much less likely to damage your home in pursuit of something to do with his teeth. Carrying a toy is this breed's answer to boredom or stress – when in doubt pick up a toy! It is an endearing trait and if it helps a dog to cope when people are 'invading the home' it has a positive benefit for the dog and the owner. Controlling his insistence on giving visitors a toy and telling them what to do with it is another matter entirely, which will be discussed elsewhere!

A Spanish demonstrating the 'dirt collecting' qualities of his coat!

Many people become interested in Spanish Water Dogs because they, or a member of their family, may suffer from allergies. The non-shedding nature of these dogs makes them an ideal choice. However, it would be advisable to spend some time in the company of one or two dogs in case the allergy is to something other than hair. Whilst the lack of dog hairs on the carpets and furniture is a very attractive proposition it needs to be borne in mind that when a Spanish has a reasonable length of coat it will, if allowed to behave naturally, bring all manner of filth and debris into the house!

It has been observed that some Spanish react in quite an intriguing way to the length of their coat. If the coat is allowed to grow long enough for the hair to cover the eyes the effect of clipping can be quite interesting. Some dogs seem to jump for joy and become quite skittish, behaving like young lambs on a glorious spring day. Other, perhaps less confident, dogs that have been 'hiding' behind their coats, may become quite withdrawn and wary of contact with people for a few days. This passes quite quickly and should give no cause for concern, but should not be reacted to. Conversely, there are dogs that perhaps feel insecure when carrying a long

Perdi demonstrating how easily she can learn to climb ladders – this was her first attempt

coat because they don't have a clear view of the world and are suddenly much more outgoing and confident once they have been clipped and are no longer peering at the world through a curtain of hair.

When considering a working breed one must think about the effect upon the owner's life of a dog that wants to be busy doing things a great deal of the time. Collies and English Springers generally put their owners under a lot of pressure because their desire to work is so hard-wired that they can't relax. Whilst the Spanish has a strong work ethic and will do whatever you ask, whenever you ask it and for as long as you like, he does have an effective 'off-switch'. As his Latin temperament suggests, he will work hard, play hard and then happily flop down for his siesta, relaxing to a degree that could almost persuade you to forget you have a dog in the room. However, it is possible to break even the most efficient 'off-switch' by allowing the dog to manipulate you into playing on demand, so beware!

Baxter's 'off-switch' is clearly in good working order!

In a nutshell, living with a Spanish Water Dog is interesting, rewarding, sometimes frustrating, amusing, mind expanding and, on the whole, great fun. However, there are responsibilities that come with the package and these need to be addressed so that you get the very best out of your little Spaniard.

6 CHOOSING AND BUYING A PUPPY

Once you have carried out your research into the Spanish Water Dog and have ensured that each and every member of your family agrees that this is, indeed, the Breed for you, it is time to begin your search campaign for the ideal puppy. This may not be as easy as it sounds. It is true to say that, at the time of writing, numbers are increasing steadily but it is still a numerically small breed in the UK. If you have preferences as to gender and colour this will prolong your search considerably and you may need to wait patiently for the right puppy to come along. It will be worth the wait!

Your first consideration should be the Breeder. There are many questions you need to ask and you, in turn, will be expected to answer some yourself. A Breeder who does not delve deeply into your motives for wanting a puppy and is not forthcoming with answers to all your queries is not the kind of person from whom you should be buying a puppy. Purchasing a puppy is not like buying a washing machine, (although you might need one of those as well when you see the mud the coat can carry into the house!) even though both are covered by the Sale of Goods Act. If a new washing machine is defective it goes back, is replaced and the problem is solved. Should a puppy develop serious health or temperament issues that impinge on its well being and your happiness the Law states that the same rules may apply. However, you do not fall in love with a washing machine. Assuming the Breeder is prepared to accept the responsibility of taking the puppy back, this is an option that few new owners are prepared to consider. The solution then is to assure yourself that you are buying a puppy that is sound in mind and body, thus reducing the risks of complications as it grows and becomes a valued member of the family.

The temperament of the parents should be your first consideration. If Mum and Dad have nice friendly, outgoing attitudes and are not nervous or aggressive their pups will probably follow suit. You will always be able to meet the mother and assess her nature. If not there is something desperately wrong and you should leave at once. Only in extreme cases where the bitch has died should you even consider a puppy if the dam is not available for viewing. Meeting and assessing the father is often more difficult as the Breeder will probably have travelled some considerable distance to mate the bitch. However, in a breed like the Spanish Water Dog there is a close community spirit between Breeders, so you should be able to discuss the attributes of the stud with a number of people besides the Breeder if you are unable to visit him.

Health issues should be your next concern. Ask the Breeder to discuss with you the known health problems within the breed and to explain what steps have been taken to prevent them occurring. At the time of writing the two known major health problems that need to be addressed are Hip Dysplasia (H.D.) and Glaucoma but there have also been incidences of Demodex. Great effort is being made in the UK, by the Spanish Water Dog Club and its members, to reduce the incidences of all genetically inherited conditions. The conditions themselves are explained in much greater detail in Chapter 15, BREEDING. For the purposes of this chapter it is necessary only to describe how to ensure that your puppy has been bred from animals that have been screened and are as free as possible from predisposition to these debilitating problems.

Ask to see all the relevant health certificates pertaining to both parents. A responsible Breeder will gladly show you the BVA hip score certificates, or copies thereof, and should your request to have sight of them be met with a refusal, or a statement that the hips were "X-rayed but not sent away for scoring", extreme caution is advised. With regard to the 'gonioscopy' test to determine predisposition to Glaucoma, there is, at present, no certificated scheme. However, there should be some sort of records of the opinion of the eye testing specialist(s) who examined the dogs and these should be explained to you and copies made available. Ask your Breeder if there is any evidence of Demodex in the bloodlines of the parents and hope that you receive an honest reply. Demodex is mentioned in more detail in Chapter 15, BREEDING.

Having ascertained that all the health screening is in place and temperaments are sound the next step is to assess the way the Breeder will be rearing the puppies. As mentioned elsewhere in this book socialisation is of paramount importance in the Spanish Water Dog. The puppies should be reared within the home in a social setting, with the family, hearing, seeing and experiencing all the sights and sounds of normal everyday life. Do not even consider buying a puppy that is going to be brought up in a shed outside. A beautiful clean, well-equipped whelping room is fine for the first three weeks but if the pups were to remain there until they left for their new homes with no other life experience they would be ill-equipped for what is to come. Stay away from the kind of Breeder who allows the bitch to whelp inside the house, keeps her there with her puppies until they "become too much trouble" at around three to four weeks and then throws them outside where they will not cause so much work! A utility room is often chosen for rearing puppies because it is so easy to clean. This is fine for putting them somewhere safe at night or if the Breeder goes out but should not be a permanent residence. Having a television in the room with the puppies is a great idea for getting them used to all sorts of loud noises and other sounds but only **in addition to,** not instead of normal socialisation.

Make sure that the puppies have enough access to their mother. It is **her** job to teach them canine communication skills and basic good manners. If she is not allowed to do this your puppy will have all sorts of problems later on, especially in adolescence, and especially with other dogs. Of course the puppies will need to be weaned onto solid food and the time their mother wishes to spend with them will naturally decrease as time goes by but she **must** be allowed to spend some part of every day with them until they are seven weeks old. The bitch must also be **allowed** to discipline them as she sees fit and should not be punished for telling them off. Much more on this subject can be seen in Chapter 15 BREEDING. It will help you and your puppy enormously if the Breeder has taken the litter out in the car a few times before they leave so that the trip home will not be traumatic.

Look for signs of mental stimulation. The

*Mum being **allowed** to do her job.*

A perfect, safe environment – a variety of toys, suitable beds and toilet areas

puppy pen should resemble a children's nursery with toys of various types and textures available, including those that make all sorts of different noises. Puppies need to stretch their minds as well as their legs and this variety of toys teaches them to amuse themselves while learning to solve problems.

Sometimes people are tempted to buy two puppies from the same litter, usually because they believe it is good for them to have each other for company or because two members of the family have fallen in love with two different puppies. It is a grave mistake because firstly the pups will relate more to each other than they will to the owner and will prove very difficult to train, and secondly you will have to deal with 'sibling syndrome'. The puppies will become a single unit with a dominant leader and a follower. One of them will almost certainly be very nervous and unable to cope without the other. Ironically, it tends to be the dominant one that falls into this category.

Single and orphaned puppies need consideration here, as they may crop up from time to time. Orphaned puppies will receive no maternal education so it will help enormously if they have had access to another mature bitch who may have helped to show them the way. Be wary of a litter that has been completely hand reared with no canine influences at all. Singletons, even when reared by the mother, can present all sorts of problems, especially in communication with other dogs and with regard to hierarchy. Single puppies have never had to compete and when placed in a family environment can occasionally be very forceful, finding it difficult to understand that they have to earn privileges and their place in the scheme of things.

Eventually, if all goes well and your chosen Breeder has a puppy for you there is the question of the age at which you should collect your puppy. In my opinion seven or eight weeks is the optimum age to ensure that the puppy has plenty of time to learn about his new life. Be very wary of buying an older puppy unless you are certain the Breeder has socialised it extremely well because every week lost is a week less in which you can prepare your puppy for a normal life. In Chapter 8 SOCIALISATION you can read all about the developmental stages that a puppy goes through and understand the importance of early association with new situations and experiences.

I'm ready! Where's my new home

Finally, there is the paperwork and the trip home to consider. When the great day arrives you should be prepared by having either a crate or a cardboard box for the puppy to travel in safety. Line it with some veterinary bedding or a blanket and give him something to chew. Holding him on your lap is not a good idea as it would set the seal for future journeys and, if the puppy were worried, there would be a huge risk that you could be reassuring him! Reassuring a frightened puppy is the best way to guarantee that he will continue to be afraid of new situations in the future! Relax and ignore any apprehension on the part of the puppy and he will soon learn that there is nothing to worry about. You will need water and a bowl and, if it is a long journey, some food for the puppy. He may well refuse to eat it but it would wise to have some to offer, just in case. You should also take some kitchen roll, wipes and plastic bags in case of any accidents or toilet needs. Remember that the puppy will have no protection against disease at this stage and cannot be put down at the side of the road. As soon as you arrive home your basic training of the puppy should begin so please turn immediately to Chapter 7, EARLY DAYS and Chapter 12, TRAINING to ensure you start as you need to go on.

You should be given the Kennel Club registration document, signed by the Breeder, so that you can transfer ownership of the puppy into your name with the Kennel Club. This will allow you to take up the Kennel Club's offer of six weeks free insurance, which is valid from the date of transfer. Some Breeders will arrange some insurance cover themselves but this can be discussed beforehand. Most Breeders will have 'endorsed' the puppy's Kennel Club papers and should explain to you what this means and why it has been done. There are two types of endorsement, 'progeny not eligible for registration' and 'not eligible for an export pedigree'. The former is to protect the puppy from indiscriminate breeding and, in the case of the Spanish Water Dog, to comply with the Club's Code of Ethics. Some Breeders will explain that they are willing to 'lift' the endorsement once the puppy has passed all its health checks if it has been agreed that you may breed at a later date. The second endorsement does **not** mean that you can never take your puppy abroad on holiday! It is to prevent an export pedigree being obtained so that the puppy cannot be **sold** to someone in another country. **Only** the Breeder may lift the endorsements.

The Breeder should also supply you with a signed pedigree, a copy of the parent's hip and eye test results, a record of worming and a feeding chart. It is vital that you know what food has been given to your puppy so that you can continue to feed the same, at least for the time being. Most Breeders will give you enough food to tide you over for a few days. The move to a new home is quite traumatic enough without the added stress of a sudden change of diet. Your puppy may have been micro-chipped and, if this is the case, you need the certificate so that you can have your own details put on record. Responsible Breeders will also give you a pack of useful information on rearing and training your puppy. Alternatively they might suggest the most suitable books, DVDs or videos to help you on your way. There is a list of useful titles at the back of this book.

Vaccinations are unlikely to have been carried out if your puppy is only seven to eight weeks old since most Vets agree that at such a young age there is still sufficient immunity from the mother. If, however, your puppy is slightly older the first vaccination should have been administered and you will be given the certificate to take along to your own Vet so that the second vaccination can be given two weeks later.

You will be asked to sign a Contract between yourself and the Breeder. Contracts vary considerably but they are generally used to protect the puppy in the event of a change in the new owner's circumstances, resulting in him needing to be rehomed or returned. Provided you have been given the opportunity to read and agree to the terms and conditions and, if necessary, have certain aspects explained to you there should be no difficulty. It would be advisable to discuss the contract on an earlier visit to see your puppy rather than the day you collect him, thus avoiding any misunderstandings at the last moment. Most caring Breeders are acutely aware of their responsibility towards the puppies they have produced and want to do all they can to make their future secure.

Your chosen Breeder will wish to keep in contact with you when you have taken the puppy home. This can be a great help if you ever experience any problems, as you will be able to discuss things more easily with someone you know and feel comfortable with.

Don't be fooled by the 'victim look'.
This puppy didn't fool the breeder but did a good job on her owner
until he wised up to what a manipulative little madam she really was!

7 EARLY DAYS

Finally, you have arrived home with your gorgeous little ball of fluff and together you are ready to step out on life's great journey. You will, by now, be aware from all that has been said previously regarding this wonderful breed, that you have to think carefully about how you live with your puppy so that he grows into a dog of which you can be proud. This chapter is devoted to getting things off to a good start in ways that the puppy understands, keeping the signals clear in dog terms and laying down ground rules that mean something to the puppy. Your puppy does not understand the way the human mind works (who does?) and he cannot interpret our language or emotions yet. The information that follows will help you to understand your puppy and rear him in such a way that he becomes a healthy, happy member of your family, a credit to his breed and a loyal friend for many years to come. There are some references to 'clicker training' in this chapter. For more details please refer to Chapter 12, TRAINING, Clicker Training.

FEEDING GUIDE

This is a guide to feeding an eight-week-old puppy. Your Breeder should have given you a comprehensive diet sheet and, if that is the case, it would be advisable to follow it, at least for a while. The quantities will depend on the requirements of the individual pup and will need to be increased as he grows. It is also necessary to know that puppies go through different growth rates from time to time. Consequently, if he is on four meals and consistently refuses to eat one of them, he is probably going through a rest period and needs less food. On the other hand, when a period of rapid growth starts, he may require more food than the chart tells you, so please adjust accordingly!

James Wellbeloved is possibly the best commercial dry food, (and Nature Diet the best wet food), you can possibly give your puppy, producing the best results, but I do realise that you may wish to use a different diet for reasons of your own. If you do choose to feed James Wellbeloved start him off on Puppy, then progress to Junior at around 4 or 5 months. The instructions on the bag will suggest later changeover times but experience has shown that keeping pups at a higher protein level can be counter-productive. The change to Adult food should be made at around 8 months of age. Since the Spanish Water Dog is still somewhat 'primitive' it is possible that some high quality foods may not be ideal once he has finished growing. A suitable alternative is Skinners Field & Trial, Duck and Rice or Salmon and Rice, Hypoallergenic, which has ingredients of equal quality but in different proportions with a lower level of protein. Too much protein is shown to reduce the production of seratonin in the brain, which may result in problems with the dog's 'feel good' factor. An alternative to using commercial food is to feed your dog on a completely natural diet. This an excellent method, generally known as 'BARF' (Bones And Raw Food) but needs to be fully understood so that the dog receives the correct balance of nutrients. It is not possible to go into the subject fully in a book such as this so, if you are interested, please consult the bibliography for a suitable book that will help you decide whether or not to go down that route.

At 8 weeks he should be having four meals per day. He should be weighed and his whole daily ration weighed out according to the guide on the bag. This should then be split into four meals, which should be given throughout the day after he has seen you eat, even if you only eat a biscuit. The food should be left down for 15 minutes only and any he leaves can be added to that which is weighed out for his next meal. **Absolutely nothing** should be added to these high quality complete diets. Plenty of clean, fresh water should always be available to drink. Any tit-bits needed for training purposes can be taken from the daily ration, except where higher value rewards are required when you could use 'Puffed Jerky' (dried lambs' lung) or 'James Wellbeloved Crackerjacks' or 'Minijacks'. Should you wish to give the puppy some milk it is advisable to use only goat's milk, or **good quality** evaporated milk mixed with equal amounts of water. Do not be fooled into believing that he doesn't like the food if he refuses to eat - just remove it and offer nothing in it's place!

At 12 weeks the meals should be reduced to three, but everything else remains the same except that from now on milk should not be given at all. Puppies over 12 weeks of age cannot digest milk properly and feeding milk may cause skin or temperament problems.

At 6 months you can reduce the meals to two per day, which should continue for the rest of his life.

Additives

Do not use any additives if your puppy is fed on James Wellbeloved or any other **good quality** complete diet. If feeding a different diet, such as BARF, take further advice, but do be very careful not to feed extra calcium if there is sufficient in the food. Too much calcium may cause excessive bone growth, which could lead to problems later in life.

WORMING

Your pup should have been wormed regularly and the Breeder ought to have given you a worming certificate. He will need dosing again so speak to your Vet, making sure that he knows what has already been given, and he will advise on future treatment. I would recommend that you only buy worming treatments from your Vet. Regular worming is essential to keep the dog in good condition and to prevent the risk of infection in children. This should be carried out three to four times a year for the rest of the dog's life. Remember that, if you have other dogs or cats, it is essential to carry out worming for all of them at the same time otherwise they will simply re-infect each other. You will also need to administer flea treatment occasionally although adding garlic capsules to the food will help to keep the fleas at bay.

VACCINATIONS & MICRO-CHIPPING

Be sure to visit the Vet for a 'social call' before taking the puppy for his vaccinations so that he doesn't associate the Vet's surgery with an unpleasant experience. This trip will also help to show the puppy that not **all** car journeys are traumatic. It will give your Vet the chance to confirm that he is in good health with no obvious problems and it is an ideal opportunity to discuss worming and perhaps to ask for details of micro-chipping at a later date. Take a little bit of his food with you for the Vet to give him while he is being examined.

Have your pup vaccinated as soon after that as your Vet will do it, the sooner the better. Ideally the first vaccination should be administered at eight weeks but certainly no later than nine. Puppies have a very short time in which to absorb new and possibly frightening situations and the younger he can be socialised and accustomed to the outside world, the more confident and reliable he will be. If he is worried when receiving his first vaccination please **do not reassure him.** Simply ignore any fear but keep rewarding, with food if possible, his acceptance of the situation.

EXERCISE

Your pup does **not** need loads of exercise! To begin with, to enable you to lead train him, short sessions in the garden will be plenty; just enough to learn good manners! He will get all the exercise he needs from playing around the house and garden. Make sure you socialise him, though, by taking him in the car to places of interest. This is discussed in much greater detail in SOCIALISATION, Chapter 8. As he grows you can increase the amount of time spent walking on the lead very gradually so that by the time he is twelve months old he is strong

Some early lead training in the garden may help to prevent your puppy knitting a jumper with the lead

enough, and sufficiently well developed to cope with all the exercise you feel up to giving him. Keep an eye on his weight while he is growing; a fat puppy is likely to grow into a fat adult with associated health problems in later life.

INSURANCE

Ideally, your breeder should have insured your puppy for the first six weeks with one of the many Insurance Companies that offer cover for dogs. If so, they will contact you to give you the option of continuing to insure him with them. It is advisable to do this as veterinary fees are increasing all the time! More importantly, you will be insured against Third Party liability so that if your dog ever causes an accident you will be fully covered for any claims made against you.

TRAVELLING WITH YOUR DOG

Puppies that are accustomed to car travel from a very early age, especially by the breeder, will become good travellers. Once you get him home take your puppy on short, pleasant journeys as often as you can, not just to the Vet's surgery! Don't cuddle him and certainly don't reassure him if he is worried.

Give him a safe, secure, comfortable place in which to travel, ideally a car cage, and leave him in peace. Not only does a car cage offer the puppy a feeling of security it will actually protect him and your family in the event of an accident. In a car crash a puppy that is not contained will become a missile that could seriously injure someone in the car as well as being badly hurt himself.

If you are planning to travel abroad with your dog you will need to make preparations for 'passporting' well ahead of time. The process takes a little over six months so it is wise to discuss things with your Vet as soon as possible. He will explain the vaccination and worming requirements and talk you through the process. If you are left in any doubt at all you should contact DEFRA.

CHILDREN & DOGS

It is wonderful for children and dogs to grow up together, but common sense must prevail at all times! Whilst it is essential for your dog to learn how to behave with children, it is also necessary for children to learn how to behave towards the dog! The responsibility cannot lie with just one or the other! Make sure children are not allowed to torment or abuse the dog and teach them to leave him in peace to eat and sleep. If you have no children around please try to 'borrow' some. You can always give them back! See Chapter 8, SOCIALISATION.

A DOG IS A DOG!

A dog is a dog! I am sure you are now saying to yourself "What a stupid thing to say - we all know that!" The problem is that an awful lot of us forget that simple fact and treat our dogs as if they were human. How often do you hear someone say, "My dog understands every word I say" or "He's almost human" or "He knows when he's done wrong"? The thing we need to realise before we can ever truly understand our dogs is that he **doesn't** understand every word we say; he is **not** human and, most importantly, he **doesn't know when he has done wrong!** By treating our dogs as if they are human we are being quite unkind to them because we expect them to behave in ways they just don't understand and then we get cross when they fail. A dog is **not** a human being in a fur coat! No matter how intelligent he may be his instincts are those of a dog and his actions and reactions are governed by his **being** a dog. Once we understand that, we must then realise that the moment we acquire a dog the whole family becomes a pack, at least as far as the dog is concerned. His behaviour for the rest of his life will be decided by his position in that pack and his understanding of how we treat him in the home.

A pack must have a leader, and the pack leader has certain rights and privileges. He has first choice of all available food; he goes wherever he likes; he has the best, and probably the highest, place to sleep; when he's asleep no-one disturbs him; he enters and leaves the den (house) first and all the other pack members obey him, or else!

At this point it should be made clear that **dominance** (i.e. pack leadership) and **aggression** are **not** the same thing. Do not assume that because a dog is, by nature, bossy, pushy or wanting his own way, he will necessarily become aggressive. An aggressive dog, one that bites, is very often this way because he is frightened rather than naturally dominant. He may be protective of **himself**, but his incorrect upbringing has forced him into a position of unwanted authority. Leadership involves responsibility and that responsibility can cause stress if the dog is not a natural leader. It is **your** job to be the leader so that your dog can relax and enjoy life further down the pack where he has nothing to worry about!

So, you bring home your Spanish Water Dog puppy, and make him comfortable. You give him a nice, soft bed and as soon as he cries you feed him before you eat yourselves. When you think he needs to

Don't panic, I'm on guard duty

Oh, and by the way, we can climb trees too!

My 'off-switch' is in good working order, as you can see

relieve himself you rush to the door and push him through it, and everyone joins in the excitement. When he falls asleep on your best chair you leave him in peace because "he's only a baby". When he cries in the night, you come running down to see if he's alright and may even relent and take him back to bed with you, "just until he settles down". When he jumps up you say "Oh, isn't he cute?" Are you beginning to get the picture? This may be an extreme example, but it does show how, in a very short time you have **taught** the dog that he is much more important than you are. As he grows this idea settles in his mind and eventually you may end up with a hooligan who calls the shots with the whole family. The dog is not bad - you have simply trained him to be the Boss! And when a Spanish reaches that second 'crisis' point mentioned in Chapter 8, SOCIALISATION, he may be driven to control the people he meets because he 'thinks it's his job' when, actually, he can't cope with the responsibility!

OK, let us begin again. No, we **don't** have to be hard on the dog, or unkind to him. We certainly must not resort to force! We just have to behave in a way that he understands, and which shows him that we are at the top of the pecking order and he is at the bottom - where he should be! Here are a few simple rules for you to follow, the 'Ten Commandments', if you like, to help your puppy learn his place in the pack. It is **vital** not to **confront** him if, as he gets older, problems do start to occur. If this should happen you **must** seek advice from an expert on behavioural problems. Don't take chances! Once your dog has accepted his position he will be a pleasure to live with and easy to train. He will also be happy and relaxed because he will know where he stands!

1. Do not allow the dog to go wherever he likes - make some parts of the house out of bounds to him, especially the bedroom. Ideally, a dog should never go upstairs at all, and pups under twelve months of age can sustain damage to their joints if they do. If an older dog does have to go upstairs for some reason, then make sure that you go up first, allowing him to follow you. **Never** allow him to go up first so that he can stand at the top looking down at you.

2. Do **not** feed the dog before the family eats. Feed him after he has seen you eating. If you are not having a meal try to eat a biscuit or sandwich in full view of the dog, and also pretend to eat from his bowl, before putting his food down for him. Having done this, allow him to eat in peace! Allow 15 minutes for him to eat the food then remove the bowl whether he has finished or not. Do not offer any alternative food and do not feed again until the next meal is due. If there are already other dogs in the family put their food down in order of hierarchy, with the puppy last! Cage the puppy at mealtimes, if necessary, to teach him that he cannot help himself to the food of another dog.

3. Always go through all doorways, gateways and entrances of any kind before the dog and allow him through afterwards. Do not speak to him or use the lead to do this. Use your legs or body to bar his way until he stands back and accepts that he cannot barge past. In this way you are using body language, rather than commands, to make him understand he **does not** have the **right** to go first.

4. If the dog is lying across a doorway, or anywhere else that you want to go, do not step over him or go round him - ask him to move out of the way by **pushing** him with the **side** of your foot. Do **not** kick him! If, as you do this, you say "Excuse me" or something similar he will learn that the words mean that he should move because it is **your** doorway, gateway etc. and he **does not** have the right to block your way nor to try to guard it. He will probably move as you approach but it will be out of respect, not fear.

5. Play with the puppy when **you** want to, **not** when he tells you to! Spanish **love** toys and will instigate play at the drop of a hat. They love to carry toys around, especially when they are excited and when visitors arrive. **Do not** play with the pup with the toys that belong to him (i.e. toys he has all the time). Most certainly you should play with your dog as often as you can, but **you** decide when; **you** decide for how long and **you keep the toys** that you play with together and put them away when you have finished. See 'Playing with your puppy' later on in this chapter. **Never** let anyone play-fight on the floor with the puppy, especially children, nor allow him to be physically above people.

6. Your puppy needs to 'Learn to earn' everything, including your attention and attention from visitors. Learn to read your dog's body language! When you are sitting in a chair and he comes and plonks his paw on your knee he is **not** saying "I love you!", he is saying "I'm in charge. Fuss me **now**!" When he leans on your visitors or gently takes their arms in his mouth he is saying "Watch it, baby, this is my pack, don't try anything." Learn to **ignore** your dog when he does these things, and teach your visitors how to ignore him, too! **Fold your arms; turn your head away; don't look at him; don't speak to him; don't touch him!** Once he is sitting politely or has come when called you can reward him with fuss, a tit-bit or play. If a dog has to **earn** your attention he will be much easier to train and will be well-behaved and polite around people.

7. Do not allow your puppy to get on the furniture. If he gets on of his own accord **don't shout at him or try to drag him off**. Go and sit next to him and **shove** him off with your elbow (not your hand) and **immediately** fold your arms and turn your head away to show him that it is **your** furniture and **you** are in charge of it. Children should not be allowed to try this with an older dog. If he gets on your lap **sweep** him off quickly (don't push or he will just push back) and then ignore him in the same way; immediately folding your arms and turning your head away again. When he has gone away and settled down you can call him to you and praise him. If, when the puppy is older, you want him on the furniture; teach him he can come up when he is **invited!**

8. Do not allow any puppy or older dog to hold your hand or arm in his mouth, even in play, and don't allow him to lead you or your visitors anywhere in this manner. Fold your arms, turn your head away and completely ignore him.

9. If another dog is present in the household the puppy should be introduced carefully so as not to upset the pack structure. By making a great deal of fuss of the newcomer you will be raising his status in the eyes of the established dog, thus forcing him to show the pup his authority. If the resident dog feels the need to 'tell the pup off' please don't interfere. Don't elevate the puppy by carrying him around in front of the older dog, or sitting with him on your knee. Always put the older dog's food down a split second before the newcomer's. Later on, if the newcomer is destined to be top dog this may change, but that bridge can be crossed at a later date when the pup's true character has developed. See Chapter 13, PROBLEM SOLVING.

10. Grooming is a privilege of pack leadership and **would** reinforce your superiority as pack leader. However, normal grooming is not suitable for a Spanish Water Dog because of the type of coat, so you should 'hand groom' instead. Start this with your puppy straight away by separating the coat with your fingers, checking behind the ears for early signs of matting and pulling the hair apart to prevent the mattes forming. Your Breeder should have given advice on grooming and it is covered in Chapter 4, CARE OF YOUR SPANISH WATER DOG. Don't shout at the puppy or get rough if he doesn't like it. Do a little at a time and reward him with a tit-bit when he is good.

All of these things will lower the rank of your dog without causing any distress. By using body language and the giving and withholding of privileges you are talking to the dog in language he understands instinctively, so his response is immediate and you don't have to teach him. You have learned to communicate in 'dog' rather than expecting the poor dog to try to understand 'human'! You will eventually have a happy, relaxed, well-adjusted dog that respects you, but also loves you because you have not used physical force or punishment to control him. He will be your friend and loyal companion because you have **allowed** him to be a dog!

CRIME AND PUNISHMENT

Before punishing a puppy for committing a 'crime' there are two things you need to ask yourself. Firstly, does he know what he is being punished for? Secondly, is the punishment likely to prevent him committing the same 'crime' again? Dogs do not reason in the same way as us, so if we hit him or shout at him after he has done something that is perfectly natural to him, but unacceptable to us, what is he likely to learn from the experience? Not a lot actually, except that humans are strange things that can hurt you if you get too close to them!

Ask yourself these questions: Is he actually 'committing a crime' or simply doing something perfectly natural to him, but unacceptable to you? Has he **learnt** whatever you are trying to teach him? In other words, are you teaching him what you want him to do or punishing him for not doing it? Will punishing him teach him what you want him to learn? Will the punishment stop him from doing it again?

For example, it is perfectly natural for a pup to chew but it is unacceptable to you if he chews your best shoes! Smacking him, or shouting at him, will not teach him not to chew, because he **needs** to chew, but it will teach him to be afraid of you when you enter the room or raise your voice! If he has already discovered that lying on the sofa is great fun, yelling at him won't stop him doing it again, it will teach him not to do it when you are watching! Also, at this point, you should think about what you actually say to your puppy. If you have taught him that "Down" means lie flat on the floor how can you expect him to understand that he is in the wrong when he is lying flat on the sofa? He's lying down, isn't he? He's going to be quite confused if you say "Down".

It is natural for a dog to relieve himself anywhere except his own bed, but it is unacceptable to us when he does it on the carpet. How is he supposed to know this? Will hitting him, shouting at him or (Heaven forbid) rubbing his nose in it teach him? All he will learn is that it is safer to head for the hills whenever a human enters the room. He will also learn that it is safer to hide when he relieves himself. If there is a puddle when you come down in the morning and the first thing you do is shout and point your finger or punish him, you will actually be punishing him for coming to greet you, not for making the puddle. If you punish a dog for something he has done while you were absent he will gradually start to worry, as soon as you leave him, about what will happen when you return. The stress this causes can result in more chewing and loss of bladder or bowel control, so the problems just get worse.

Please don't make the mistake of thinking that because the dog cringes when you come into the room and find he has done something wrong it means he 'knows he has done wrong' or 'feels guilty'. He cannot feel guilt or remorse, he simply feels fear because he senses your anger and has learnt from past experience that something unpleasant is about to happen. He is actually using body language that is designed to stop an attack so, when you punish him, you will confuse him even more. Generally speaking, you will teach a pup far more quickly and effectively if you follow the golden rule - **reward the behaviour you do want and ignore the behaviour you don't!** Show him what you want and praise him for doing it. When he's running round with the video remote control in his mouth tell him to "Leave", take it from him and replace it with his chew-toy. He'll soon get the message!

Squiffy demonstrating the so-called 'guilty' look

The exception to all this is 'play-biting' which is a perfectly natural thing for puppies to do but which must not be tolerated or encouraged under any circumstances. Neither should it be punished. See Chapter 8, SOCIALISATION.

One of the commonest mistakes we make is when a dog is more interested in other dogs, interesting smells, etc. and refuses to come when called. This quickly turns into a game for the dog when the owner chases after him in an attempt to catch him. Very often tempers get a bit frayed which results in the dog being grabbed with varying degrees of roughness, shouted at or even smacked when he is finally caught. If this happens when the dog has finally returned of his own accord the damage done is tremendous - he will certainly be less likely to return next time you call him! **Returning to the owner must be a pleasure to the dog.** This way he will always want to come back. See 'Recall', Chapter 12, TRAINING.

CHEWING

All pups need to chew - it is perfectly normal behaviour! The puppy is not being 'naughty'. He is not doing it just to upset you! The fact that it is unacceptable to us when he has chewed our best shoes is totally irrelevant to him! Scolding or punishing him will not make the act of chewing any less pleasurable. It will only make him afraid of you being there and will probably ensure that next time he chews he will make sure you are not around to see! In fact, if he begins to worry about your reaction every time you enter the room he is quite likely to chew (and possibly urinate) even more because he is stressed. If you find the pup chewing something inappropriate take the item from him and replace it with something he **may** chew, such as a 'Rope Ragger' or a 'Nylabone Plaque Attacker', that you can get from any reputable Pet Shop, and which he will love! Learning to tidy up while you have a young puppy would be a great idea! If it's on the 'dog shelf' who can blame the puppy for thinking it belongs to him? Preventing a puppy chewing dangerous and immovable items, such as electric cables and

*"It felt **so** good – how was I supposed to know it was for the dustbin men?"*

furniture, can be achieved by the liberal use of "Bitter Apple Spray".

Puppies have **two** teething stages - the first, which everyone knows about, is up to six months of age, while the baby teeth are being shed. The second, and less well known, even by some Vets, is from around seven to eleven months, while the permanent teeth are settling in the jaw. During this time the pup has a pathological need to chew, and if nothing suitable (or unsuitable!) is available he may well chew some part of himself, usually his legs or feet. Prevention (by making sure he cannot reach the things he shouldn't) and substitution (by giving him safe, appropriate objects he **can** chew when he is left alone) will be much more successful, and humane, than constant nagging and punishment. Train your pup to enjoy using an indoor kennel (crate) as his bed so accidents can't happen and remember that he is a puppy; he needs to chew; and you are an intelligent human – **Put things you do not want him to chew where he cannot reach them!!!**

PLAY BITING

Biting is what puppies do! It is how they learn 'dog language' and communication skills. All puppies will play-bite until they learn that we do not like it. Whilst you may be able to ignore it, or laugh at it, your family and friends may not! This sort of behaviour can be quite frightening to children and elderly people, and very off-putting to visitors who may not be terribly fond of dogs. There **are** people who don't like dogs, and their feelings must be respected, too!

Telling a pup off, or smacking him, for biting will confuse him, tell him that people are unpredictable and aggressive, and will only serve to make matters worse. It will **not** teach him how to behave.

The best way to teach a puppy that biting your hands, feet, clothing etc. is unacceptable is to react as another puppy would – shriek as if you are in pain, stop playing and **ignore** him! A puppy will almost always stop biting once he realises he is hurting you. Resume playing after a few moments.

Puppies need to learn something called 'bite inhibition'. See Chapter 8, SOCIALISATION.

JUMPING UP

The reason a puppy jumps up is that we are big and he is small. It is as simple as that! He jumps up to get closer to our faces and receive attention. If you do not want your puppy to jump up when he is older do not allow or encourage it while he is young. Remember that puppies repeat behaviour that works. The hard thing for us to understand is what 'works' for the puppy! When a puppy jumps up and we push him off, yell at him and stare him in the face we are, believe it or not, giving him three reasons to do it again! Touching him is a reward; yelling at him is a response and looking at him is an invitation! As the 'intelligent species' it is up to us to figure out a better way of getting the message across to the puppy. In the dog world a superior dog would deny the puppy attention by turning it's head and refusing to interact. We can copy that behaviour in the following way: **Fold your arms, turn your head away and wait for the jumping up to stop. Don't** speak to him, **don't** touch him and **don't** look at him.

Fold your arms and turn your head away

Wait for polite behaviour

Quietly reward the behaviour you want

If he changes sides to look into your face turn your head the other way. Keep your body facing the puppy—only turn your head. If you twist your upper body you will be inviting him to play, which will confuse him completely.

   Don't tell the puppy to "Get down", and don't push him down with your hands, as this would be giving him the attention he is demanding, although you may think otherwise! Don't look at him, as this will invite him to jump up again! If you are sitting down and he persists in scrabbling on your knee flick him off sharply with your elbow (not your hand) and then immediately fold your arms and turn your head away. Do not give him any attention until he sits on the floor or goes away. If he sits, 'click&treat' so that he understands that sitting is acceptable behaviour and jumping up is not. The acceptable behaviour

Turning your body away invites the dog to play and may result in him jumping on your back. Not what you had in mind

gets a reward, the jumping up does not! If he goes away call him back to you, 'click&treat' or fuss and praise him for coming. When you decide the interaction is over send him away again by folding your arms and turning your head **before** he chooses to go himself. This will ensure that your pup is never a nuisance and will also help to make him understand that although you are the Leader, and more important than him, you will always reward him for positive, polite behaviour and ignore him if he is 'rude'. This strategy will have great benefits later on when you teach your puppy to 'Recall'. It will also make him the sort of dog your friends are happy to meet when they visit!

HOUSE TRAINING

A young pup will always need to relieve himself upon waking, after feeding and when he has been playing. If you always take him outside at these times, ignore him until he starts to 'go', give a cue such as "Be clean!" **while he is performing**, praise well as soon as he finishes (click and **throw** the treat to him if you are using a clicker) and then allow a little playtime before returning indoors, you will find the process a lot easier. This way he will learn to 'go' on command. Never call the pup into the house to reward him or he will come in for the treat without bothering to go to the loo first! At other times watch out for the pup walking round in circles, sniffing, with his tail slightly raised - all sure

You are supposed to praise him, silly!

signs he wants to 'go'! When the pup does have an accident **do not scold or punish him** - he doesn't know that your carpet is not the place to do it! If you catch him in the act - remove him outside at once, giving the cue when you get there and remembering to praise when he has completed the job. If you arrive after the event, even if it is only a few moments, there is nothing you can do! **Ignore it**, but try to be quicker next time! **Never even** raise your voice if you enter the room after the event. Scolding a puppy for performing a perfectly natural bodily function, even though it is in the wrong place, will only teach him to fear you - **it will not teach him where he should have done it.** Praise the good results, ignore the bad, and you will soon have a pup who goes confidently to the door to be let out, and who also knows that it is safe to approach you when you enter the room! Please understand that a dog **does not 'know he has done wrong'** - he has simply learnt, the hard way, that when your voice sounds angry something bad is about to happen, so he cringes, or heads for the hills and we wrongly assume that he is feeling guilty! Guilt is a human concept and is totally unknown to the dog. Don't forget to give him time to gain control of his bladder before expecting him to hold on all night.

Toilet Training Out of Doors

This information is intended to support the advice on house training which outlines the principles of how the puppy understands the way we teach him to go to toilet in the right place. Provided that has been followed carefully, so that he is not confused about where to go, you can move on to teach a specific area outside that you want him to use as his toilet.

• When you are out for a walk, every time the dog urinates or passes a motion, you must say the word that you have been using at home as a cue to toilet. You must always say it at the time he is performing in a very nice, but quiet, voice and immediately follow it with praise. If using a clicker – click as soon as he finishes then throw the treat to him.
• Once you have been able to use this new cue word several times on a walk you can start introducing it at home by taking him to the place of your choice, on the lead, at a time you know he needs to 'go'. Don't start saying the word over and over again and expect him to understand - **wait** until he starts to go then say it and praise exactly as you did on the walk. Reward with a tit-bit if your dog is interested in food or a short play session if not.
• After a few days he should be getting the message so you can start to say the word to actually tell him you want him to 'go'.
• Once you are sure he has got the idea you can take him out off the lead and tell him to 'go' in the chosen place. Remember to reward him every time.
• If he slips off and chooses his own place don't tell him off - simply take hold of him by the collar in mid-wee, escort him back to your chosen place and quietly start again.

CRATE TRAINING

If your pup must be left (for reasonable lengths of time) it is a good idea to invest in (or make, if you have a handy-man handy!) an indoor kennel. This is simply a fully enclosed, rectangular crate, made of mesh, with an integral floor and a door at one end. It should be of such a size that, when the dog is full-grown, he can stand up, turn round and lie comfortably in it, but no larger. There should be some sort of covering in the base to protect the dog from lying on the mesh, and it should have suitable bedding (such as veterinary bedding) to make him feel at home. Do not think of it as a prison! Once a puppy gets used to his crate he will regard it as a safe haven - a place of refuge where he can have peace and quiet. As a result, when you come home, only nice things happen to him because he has not had the opportunity to do anything that might upset you!

Make the crate a nice place to be

For a crate to be successful the pup must be introduced to it carefully. Initially, it should be left in the room with the door open so that he gets used to the sight of it. From time to time lure him inside by holding a tit-bit in your hand, in front of his nose, and leading him into the cage with the tit-bit, saying the cue word "Bed!" in a nice voice as he steps inside. As soon as he is in the crate give him the tit-bit and lots of praise - "What a good boy!" The puppy should be fed inside the crate, but with the door still open, until he will go and lie happily in it whenever he wants to go to sleep. At this point the door may be closed, but

only for a few moments. Reward the puppy with praise and a bit of food while he is inside then, as you open the door and let him come out, **completely ignore him.** If you are using a clicker, click once the puppy is inside and give the treat. Over a period of time start leaving the room momentarily and going to the crate when you return to 'click&treat'. Make sure you randomise what you do when the puppy is in the crate: sometimes leave the room; sometimes stay in the room; sometimes leave the house; sometimes reward him when you re-enter the room; sometimes ignore him when you return; let

Generally speaking it is the dog that should be in the crate

him out at different times and occasionally put him straight back in again. The common factor through all these variations is that he is rewarded for being in the crate and coming out is boring!

In the early stages do not leave him so long that he starts to cry. If he is let out while he is crying he will learn that he can demand to be let out whenever he likes! Gradually increase the time the door is closed until he will happily stay inside long enough for you to leave him when you have to go out. Remember to supply some water if you are leaving him for any length of time, and a chew toy, such as a 'Plaque Attacker' or a hollow chew toy smeared on the inside with cream cheese, paste or **smooth** peanut butter. Don't forget that he will need to go to the toilet - he will not be able to hang on for hours and hours!

Once the puppy is happy in the cage it can also be used in the car, when visiting or when going on holiday, and will prevent many of the problems usually associated with rearing young puppies. However, don't expect the puppy to spend his whole life in it just for your convenience! He must have adequate playtime and mental stimulation if he is to become a valuable member of your family! The general rule is that a puppy that is crated overnight should be in the crate for no more than four hours during the day. However, these four hours can be split up to suit your personal circumstances.

TEACHING YOUR PUPPY TO COPE ALONE

Separation anxiety (fear of being alone) occurs when dogs become too dependent upon the people (or other dogs) that they live with, either because they have never been left alone or because they have been spoiled and given too much attention. Even if your dog can cope while you are out at work he may still become distressed, and possibly destructive, if left alone while you are in the house simply because he **expects** to be with you whenever you are at home. A dog who believes he is 'pack leader' will become worried if separated from you because, as far as he is concerned, it's his 'job' to look after you; you are his responsibility instead of him being yours!

The easy way to avoid this situation occurring is by teaching the puppy that his world does not fall apart when he is not with you. Do not spend every waking moment with your puppy. Right from the start get him used to being left alone, initially for short periods, especially when you are actually in the house!

Follow 'A Dog is a Dog' very carefully so that your dog realises -that you are the leader and consequently he has no responsibility. Be sure to read, understand and follow the advice offered in 'Crime & Punishment' so that you do not exacerbate the problem by punishing your puppy when you return for something he has done, possibly through stress, while you were out.

Reduce the puppy's dependence on you by leaving him alone in another room when you are in the house. Do this for **very** short periods to begin with – maybe just leaving the room, closing the door and immediately returning. Upon return **completely ignore the puppy.** You must make the initial separations brief otherwise he will either scratch the door or make a fuss and if you return under these circumstances the puppy will believe he has controlled you and made you return. If you leave him too long he will become stressed and the problem will continue, rather than be cured. Gradually increase the time you can leave the puppy alone without him becoming upset. Always ignore him for at least half an hour before you leave and again for five to fifteen minutes when you return. **Never** go to him and tell him not to worry, or that you will be back soon etc. as this will make your leaving him too important and stressful – this sort of behaviour works with humans but has entirely the wrong effect on dogs. Making a fuss when you return teaches the puppy that your return will be exciting so that he looks forward to it too much. This may result in him worrying as soon as you leave and being unable to cope with you being away.

Remember that making a fuss, cuddling and re-assuring your dog if he is worried about something will only make things worse – you will be rewarding the very behaviour you wish to cure!

Squiffy being 'rewarded' for looking worried!

If at any time you begin to feel frustrated or irritated by the amount of time this exercise is taking **Stop!** Go away for a while, have a drink or a ciggie, phone a friend, watch a bit of television or go for a walk on your own – whatever it takes to relax you before starting again! Nothing will ever be achieved if the dog senses you are cross with him.

PLAYING WITH YOUR PUPPY

Spanish Water Dogs love to play. Playing with your puppy should be fun for both of you and forms an important part of the learning process when it comes to manners, as well as being fun! Dogs play 'status' games to help them establish their position in the pack. To maintain **your** position as Pack Leader and prevent your puppy learning that he has the ability to train **you** it is essential for you to be in control of playtime.

Your puppy needs toys of his own. He needs toys of different types and, especially, different textures. He needs toys he can throw, some he can carry, some he can get his teeth into and maybe one or two to curl up and sleep next to. You should **not** play with him with any of those toys!

You must have toys that belong to **you** and are kept out of reach of the puppy. These are the toys you use to play with your puppy. This may sound a little over the top but, believe me, Spanish Water Dogs are experts at manipulating people into playing on their terms and if allowed to do so their 'off switch' may become faulty!

Play with **your** toys when **you** choose to and stop when **you** say so. As well as being a great source of fun for you both a toy can play a large part in training your puppy, by getting his attention and being used as a reward. Spanish are very 'toy focused' so making certain toys 'valuable' will be very useful later on.

The puppy must **want** the toy

In the unlikely event that your puppy is not interested in **your** toy you need to know how to awake his interest. Get family or friends together and play 'piggy-in-the-middle' without letting the puppy get the toy. Stroke the toy and talk to it as if you really love it! Alright, you'll feel stupid but you'll get over it! Once the puppy wants to join in with enthusiasm put the toy away. Repeat several times. Now you can play constructively as follows but **first** you must teach the puppy to Take & Leave, Chapter 12, TRAINING.

Learning to earn playtime

Bring out the toy and ask the puppy to 'sit', 'stand' or 'down' and as soon as he does what you have asked for say your 'release word' (the word you use to tell your dog he can do as he pleases. See Training, CHAPTER 12) and then say, "Play!" in an excited voice. If you are sure the dog will not refuse to come back with the toy you can throw it for him, let him play for a moment or two then call him back. When the dog is close to you hold out your hand to take the toy and say, "Leave!" in a nice, but fairly firm voice. If he runs off do **not** chase him. Run away in the opposite direction again so that he follows you then try again. Take the toy from him and throw it again, run away and take it from him as before, remembering to say, "Leave!" Repeat the whole process one more time. If you know he will clear off with the toy attach some string to it or play a 'tug' game instead without letting go of the toy. After a moment or two ask him to "Leave". If he refuses, take hold of his collar **underneath his neck** with your free hand and **stop pulling the toy**. Let the dog pull against his collar and, without pulling the toy at all, simply wait for him to open his mouth. As soon as he does say "Leave, good boy!" and take the toy. Reward him by immediately playing again. Repeat several times.

Ending the game

By now the puppy should be really excited. **Now** is the time to stop! Don't wait until the puppy gets tired or fed up and goes off for a sleep. **You** are the leader. **You** end the game. Take the toy, say "Stop!", "Finished!", "Game over!" or whatever word you choose, as long as you stick to the same word, and put the toy away where the puppy cannot get it. Ignore any attempts made by your puppy to persuade you to continue playing. Remember, ignoring means no speaking, looking or touching. It does **not** mean having a conversation with the puppy about the fact that you no longer wish to play with him!

Playing in this way will make you valuable as the 'leader' and the source of all the good things in life, whilst allowing the puppy to realise that nothing comes for free. Play as often as you can throughout the day for very short periods. Once these words and practices are established you will be able to use play as a powerful reward during control training exercises and as a distraction in difficult situations. As your puppy grows up the desire to play will remain strong and you can continue using toys for fun and reward but his 'off switch' will be in good working order!

CONCLUSION

The first few days that a puppy spends in his new home are probably the most important of his life. Understanding how his baby mind works will help you to forge a secure future. Chapter 5, LIVING WITH A SPANISH WATER DOG should have given you an insight into the complexities of this wonderful new addition to your family. **However, there is much more to learn and to teach him so, please, whilst continuing with the advice in this chapter until adulthood, move on to** Chapter 10, TRAINING.

Keep a happy balance between sleeping, playing and quiet relaxation. Puppies need to sleep, they need to play and they need time on their own. Too little sleep and too much play or too much time in isolation would be detrimental to the well being of your puppy.

8 SOCIALISATION
(preparing a puppy for life in the real world)

The word 'socialisation' will crop up in this book so many times that you may become heartily sick of reading it! The very good reason for so much repetition is that it is probably the most important part of bringing up your puppy. An untrained dog can be trained at any age, even an unruly hooligan can be put back on the straight and narrow with correct handling. An **unsocialised** dog is damaged for life and will never reach the potential he was born with. Improvements may be made through huge amounts of sheer determination and endless patience but there will be gaps in that dog's confidence that can never be filled. The Spanish Water Dog is still, as yet, fairly un-domesticated, semi-feral if you like, and as such has a more highly developed 'flight or fight' response to threatening situations than breeds that have been selected to live closely within the family for generations. Socialisation is important in any breed to enable puppies to cope in our hectic modern world but the Spanish needs more positive stimulation than most, especially as, added to its primitive nature, it is also a breed with strong guarding tendencies.

Socialisation does not begin when the puppy leaves the Breeder; neither does it begin once the puppy has been vaccinated and can safely venture out into the world. There is a critical period in which the commencement of socialisation needs to take place and this is before the puppy becomes alert or wary to strange sounds and movements. The optimum time is before the eyes are open; therefore it begins in the nest. This chapter, consequently, is relevant to the Breeder as well as the New Owner.

BIRTH TO SEVEN WEEKS
(THE BREEDER)

Full tummies and a clean bed, what more could you ask for?

Puppies go through various stages of psychological development during which they are more capable of learning things than at other times. During the critical period of three to seven weeks of age a puppy is programmed to learn the basics of canine communication and good manners from its mother. At that time, if it were a wild dog, it would also learn to fear anything its mother perceived as dangerous or threatening. To prepare a puppy for today's world, therefore, we need to make sure that what it learns in the nest is positive rather than negative. It is also necessary to ensure that the mother is setting a good example so her temperament is of the utmost importance. A sensitive, nervous mother may have become that way through life experiences rather than genetic influence but she will, if allowed, still teach her puppies to copy her behaviour.

From birth to three weeks all a puppy is expected to do is eat, sleep, crawl about a bit and then eat some more. If hungry, it will cry and it will be fed. If cold, it will seek warmth and if too hot, it will try to avoid the source of the heat. Mother will see to the necessities of toileting and digestion by stimulating the puppy with her tongue and cleaning up the results. All the Breeder needs to do during these few short weeks is provide adequate safe accommodation, suitable furnishings, food of the highest quality for the mother and some moral support. The mother will feel protective during this time and may not welcome any intrusion. Give her some space and let her decide. If she wants your company and support she will let you know! The first three weeks are her responsibility and she knows best.

However, even at this age, the puppies should be handled. It is helpful to hold them as the bitch would by grasping them gently with your first finger and thumb around the neck and your remaining fingers around the shoulder area. This causes the pup to 'dangle' in your hand, which might look awful to you! However, holding the puppies in this way encourages them to produce endorphins, which is nature's way of helping them to relax. When you pick a puppy up you should raise it slowly. A puppy that is lifted from the box to human height quickly suffers an effect similar to that of a human ascending in an express lift and it can become quite distressed by it. Handle the puppies as often as the bitch will allow but do not scold her if she is unhappy about it. There is evidence to suggest that if puppies are subjected to low levels of stress during the first three weeks of life they will be better equipped to deal with stress as adults and may be easier to train and quicker to learn. There is a handling regime called 'The High Achievers Programme' details of which can be found in the bibliography at the back of this book. It is an interesting concept that has been performed on only a very small

number of Spanish Water Dog litters, as far as I am aware. One litter was too young, at the time of writing, to establish the value of this programme and this litter hardly constitutes a scientific survey! Nevertheless it may be something you wish to consider. I feel compelled to say that should you attempt to carry out this form of early training the programme **must be followed to the letter** with no deviations or exaggerations.

Scientific studies have shown that at approximately three weeks of age puppies go through a dramatic period of development where, having opened their eyes and gained their hearing, they are capable of responding to sound. Sharp or loud noises produce a 'startle response'. It is during this critical period in the life of the puppy that contact with humans can form bonds that will last a lifetime. Social relationships such as this will never be formed as easily later in life, if at all.

At the age of three weeks canine learning begins in earnest. Mother will begin to assert herself and educate the little ones as to how to behave. She may be quite forceful in her attempts to discipline and it is now that the Breeder should take a deep breath, step back a little and trust her to know how much force she can use. So often I have heard people say that they had to remove the puppies early from a bitch because she didn't like them any more, or they felt the need to punish her for being 'aggressive' towards them. The bitch has a series of signals that the puppies need to learn, starting with her turning her head and holding it very still. This means, "stop whatever you are doing!" If this does not produce the desired response from the puppy she will then lift her lips and give a silent 'smile'. This, if ignored, will be followed by a low growl and some strong eye contact. Should the puppy be foolish enough to believe she doesn't mean it she will then follow it up with a quick snap using the side of her mouth so that she doesn't actually harm him. He may well scream his head off at this point, roll on his back or run away yelping for all he is worth! What he is learning from this experience is that it doesn't pay to ignore the first signals. The body language the bitch uses gives him the chance to learn how to behave and avoid the punishment in future. Unfortunately humans sometimes don't

Puppy 'lip licking' to appease Mum, who is refusing to play.

notice or understand the body signals that were warning the puppy and only see and react to what they perceive as 'aggression' thus misunderstanding what she was endeavouring to a achieve. Interfering in order to 'protect' the puppy is likely to undermine the bitch so that she stops trying to do her job and this will give the puppy a licence to be a thug. Preventing the bitch from doing her job is a recipe for disaster when the pup goes to its new home. Unfortunately, Spanish Water Dog mothers sometimes fail to discipline their puppies in this way. Should this be the case, access to another bitch or, in some cases, a sensible male will help to ensure the pups learn some manners.

"Yeah I'll play, pup, but only on my terms!"

As the pups grow the mother will play, but only on her terms, and insist on carrying out necessary grooming and cleaning, using as much force as she feels is necessary. She will gradually reduce the time she spends feeding the pups and will begin to ignore their vocal demands for her attention unless she perceives a genuine problem or threat. She will spend more time away from them, returning when **she** feels like it! This is not a signal to the breeder to take the pups away from her; she still has work to do. Make sure she can get away from them to a space of her own but do not prevent her returning when she wants to. The mother is the Breeder's greatest ally in producing puppies that are ready for what life holds in store. All in all she is teaching the puppies how to be dogs and if she is prevented from doing this their communication skills will be at best under developed and at worst non-existent. Puppies who leave the nest with no boundaries or canine etiquette make very difficult pets, are harder to train and have the potential to become dog aggressive later on.

If a decision has been made to breed from a bitch that has some nervous tendencies, because it is certain that they are learned rather than inherited, some consideration must be given to how to manage the situation. It is essential that the puppies do not, in turn, learn from her that people are to be mistrusted. If the bitch is likely to bark hysterically or show fear when strangers enter the room I would advise that she is removed before people are allowed to see or interact with the puppies. Whilst it is always stated, quite rightly, that prospective puppy buyers should see the puppies **with** the mother, it is perfectly reasonable to explain why they are meeting her separately, as long as you stress that she still has regular access to them. Under these circumstances it would be wise to explain the reasons for her apprehension and offer some sort of reassurance that it is not a problem within that bloodline and as such will not be inherited by the puppies.

SEVEN TO TWENTY WEEKS (THE NEW OWNER)

Splendid isolation does not make a splendid dog!

There are three deadlines facing you as you introduce your puppy to his new life. In order to reach your socialisation targets by these deadlines you must arrange for your pup to be vaccinated as soon as possible. Most Vets will now give the first vaccination at eight weeks but this does depend, to a degree, upon the choice of vaccine. If the first one can be given at eight weeks and the second at ten weeks the pup will be ready to hit the road by eleven weeks. However, there is much you must do before that time comes. What you cannot do is sit at home with your puppy in isolation until that time, then begin socialisation when he is almost three months old. **It will be too late!**

SEVEN TO TWELVE WEEKS—**Socialisation with people:**
From the moment your puppy arrives in your home you must begin to socialise him with people: lots of people; all sorts of different people; men and strangers in particular; children especially, and boys in particular; people of different races; men with beards or wearing hats; babies crying and toddlers running around or in pushchairs. The list is endless and is spelt out for you, with tick boxes so you can keep track, at the end of this chapter. Your puppy needs to meet several new people every day and should have met at least a hundred by twelve weeks of age. A new puppy is the best excuse I can think of for giving your social life an enormous boost! It is also an excuse to go to the pub. Even pubs that do not generally allow dogs will consider letting you sit there

with a puppy that has to stay off the floor. So, invite all your friends and family round. Invite the local Mother and Toddler Group for a coffee morning. Have a Tupperware Party (oh, alright, not a Tupperware Party, but you get the gist?). In short, do anything and everything you can to get hold of as many people as possible before it's too late. But the puppy can't go out until vaccinations are complete I hear you say. Of course he can. He just can't walk around where other dogs have been, that's all. Puppies become infected through direct contact with infected material such as faeces, urine, vomit or, in the case of kennel cough, droplets or mucus from the infected dog. As long you do not allow your puppy to sniff or touch any of these or have direct contact with a dog, and provided you wash your hands if you have touched any risky substance or another dog, the risk is minimal. The risk to the future of the dog through lack of socialisation is far greater and can, in extreme cases, be terminal. You can carry the pup to the park, the railway station, the trolley bay at the supermarket, the bus station and the town centre. You could even take him for a ride on the bus or train. A

This is a novel way to take your pup into the outside world before vaccinations are complete.

trip to the school gates, still in your arms or snuggled up in a puppy travelling carrier (it looks like a soft padded beach bag with a hole at one end for the head to poke out!) is an ideal way of getting started with children. Take a pocket full of treats and your clicker and reward any positive, confident behaviour by clicking and passing a treat to everyone you meet to give to the puppy. The golden rule when going to all these places is to act in a happy and unconcerned manner, even if the puppy is afraid initially, and to ignore him completely until he is happy and relaxed. If your pup shows fear of any unfamiliar sight or situation you **must** ignore him. This may seem cruel to you, but if you fuss your pup to reassure him when he is afraid you are actually teaching him that fear is the correct response - you are praising him for it and it will make him worse, not better. By the same token, you should not try to bully him out of his fear. Just leave him alone to come to terms with it so he can get used to the thing he is afraid of. Carry on talking (to yourself, if necessary!) in a normal, happy voice or even sing if the people around you can stand it! Once he knows you are not afraid he will see that actually there is nothing to fear. It is perfectly normal, and acceptable, for an inexperienced puppy to 'startle' in an unfamiliar situation. It does not mean he is nervous; simply that he is a bit surprised and apprehensive. He will recover, normally within seconds, if left alone. If the fearful behaviour is 'rewarded' it will continue and worsen. Puppies repeat behaviour that gets a response from you. Behaviour that is ignored will die out.

Socialisation

Puppies need to learn to accept all sorts of strange things that people do to them or around them. Being hugged or held tight is completely unnatural to a dog so gradually teach the puppy to put up with it and welcome it. Ask people, initially close family and people the pup knows well, to hold his collar, touch his feet, handle his tail area, look in his mouth, put their faces close to his and generally invade his personal space. Make sure it is done very gently at first and always reward his quiet acceptance with a click and a treat. As he becomes accustomed to these invasions of his privacy ask strangers to do the same thing. Be careful not to reward the wrong response and never force him to cope with more than he is ready for. All this handling experience will stand him in good stead when children want to play with him or he needs to visit the Vet's surgery. The Spanish Water Dog needs to be clipped on a regular basis, starting at around five months, so prepare your puppy for this, too.

Many dog owners, especially men and boys, think it is fun to play rough, fighting games with their puppy, winding him up until he is completely over-excited. They do not realise that if the games are out of control, they are teaching the pup that it is perfectly acceptable to challenge humans to a fight and that most of the time he can win. This gives him the idea that, as he reaches adolescence, and hormones come into play, humans are fair game and battles are worth fighting. It is great fun to play with your dog, there is nothing wrong with a bit of rough and tumble but there are two golden rules: even the gentlest of biting should result in an abrupt end to the game with the pup believing he has 'hurt' his playmate (even if he has not) and the human should be able to stop the game and calm the pup at any point. All that is necessary to achieve this is the use of body language in conjunction with a word or phrase that the pup will learn the meaning of. As soon as you decide you want to stop, fold your arms, turn your head away and say "Game over", "Stop", "Enough" or some other word of your choice. Be consistent, always use the same word and make sure that other family members know what it is too! After very few repetitions the word itself will be enough to end the game. Ask for a 'sit' or a 'down', quietly and gently reward the pup for complying and then rest for a while. A good way of rewarding the pup for stopping and calming down is to play again! What you are teaching your youngster is that playing is great, roughhouse is fine but, at the end of the day, you are the 'Leader' and when you say "Stop" it is easy to calm down and be rewarded for doing something on cue. What you are **really** doing is making sure the 'off switch' is in good working order!

SEVEN TO EIGHTEEN WEEKS— **Bite inhibition:**
Puppies bite! It is a perfectly normal thing for a puppy to do. So that your puppy grows into a safe, reliable dog with no inclination to bite people (or, for that matter, other dogs) it is essential that he learn to 'inhibit' his bite. That is to say, he learns to control the pressure he exerts with his teeth even if he is angry or afraid. Bite inhibition is an incredibly important part of canine etiquette. You could teach your puppy not to bite at all, you could punish him when he bites you so that he learns it is a bad idea but one day in the future, when someone accidentally

hurts him, he may bite to defend himself. It will be a bad bite. His teeth will sink in. The resulting problems will be difficult to deal with. If you have taught your puppy to inhibit his bite when that day comes he will still snap, out of shock or fright, but he will not bite. He will not break the skin. He will probably not even cause a bruise because he will have learnt not to bite hard, even when things go wrong and he bites because he is in pain or afraid. **Smacking will prevent a puppy from learning this vital skill.**

In order to teach your puppy not to bite you should behave in the same way as another puppy. When puppies play they bite each other but if a puppy bites too hard the bitten puppy will yell and refuse to play for a few moments. The biter then realises that his roughness has ended the game. He learns, by trial and error, how to bite more gently so that his playmate does not go off in a huff. You can adopt the same method to teach your puppy to inhibit the power of his bite. As soon as your puppy bites any part of **your body or your clothing** let out a shrill, high pitched "Ouch!" and immediately walk away, or even leave the room, for about twenty to thirty seconds. Return, call the pup to you, ask him to do something for you such as 'sit' and then reward him by resuming the game you were playing before. When the biting starts again do the same as before, let out your yell of pain and leave. Over a period of time the puppy will realise that your skin is so weak and feeble that even the lightest touch of his teeth hurts you and he will stop using them. It will dawn on him, too, that your clothes are part of your body and that biting them stops the game abruptly. The more often you do this, and allow other people and especially children to do it, too, the safer your adult dog will be. He will have learnt how to control the power of his bite which will make him as safe as it is possible for a dog to be.

The cream puppy is invading the gold puppy's space and, because he is restricted by the lead, the gold one feels the need to use apparently 'aggressive' behaviour to keep him at bay. If he was off-lead he would be able to escape.

SEVEN TO TWENTY WEEKS— Socialisation with other dogs and the outside world:
By twenty weeks your puppy must have learnt all he needs to know about how to be a nice, reliable, confident dog. After twenty weeks anything you have missed out of his education will be lost forever. So don't wait until the last minute. **Long before twenty weeks,** ideally as soon as vaccination is complete, you should have enrolled your puppy on a good, motivational puppy-training course. You should have been along to your local training classes without the pup and watched for hints as to the type of training on

offer. Spanish Water Dogs do not respond well to the old fashioned 'stamp and pull' type of training methods. Generally speaking, trainers who use clicker training have studied the best way to motivate and train puppies of all breeds. They will usually have an open mind and, even if they have never seen a Spanish Water Dog, they will be sufficiently intuitive to understand the idiosyncrasies of different breeds and types of dogs. If you see dogs wearing choke chains, owners being told to use a 'firm voice' and leads being jerked to correct the dog's position walk out at once and find another class. There is no excuse these days for old-fashioned bullyboy tactics. Since the dog training revolution began with John Fisher in the 1980s there is now a wide choice of good, sound training available if you know where to look. If clicker training is not for you, so be it, but at least try to find a class where the trainer will have the knowledge and understanding to help you train your puppy without force or punishment.

Socialisation is the most important aspect bringing up any puppy, but in a primitive breed such as the Spanish Water Dog it is vital that it is approached and carried out sympathetically, thoroughly and **at the right time.**

The following chart has been reproduced from the 'Fast Track Puppy Survival Kit' with the kind permission of the Authors Lyn Fleet and Helen Roberts. When you have found perfection produced by someone else, why try to improve on it?

Details of their book can be found in the bibliography.

Tick each item off as your puppy experiences it.

I HAVE SOCIALISED MY PUPPY WITH.....

Your puppy needs to have had **good** experiences of everything listed below while he is under twenty weeks old. Be sensible. Be calm. Be inventive.

Never force your dog into a situation he isn't comfortable with. If he's unsure, then casually let him make up his own mind from a distance and then praise him when he shows interest. Don't reassure, as he might think he's being praised for his fear. Simply let him take his own sweet time about it.

PEOPLE

- ❑ Adult men and women of various ethnic groups
- ❑ Children aged 0 - 6 months
- ❑ Toddlers
- ❑ Children aged 6 years
- ❑ Children aged 12 years
- ❑ Children in pushchairs
- ❑ Person with walking stick
- ❑ Man with beard
- ❑ Person wearing a hat
- ❑ Person wearing sunglasses
- ❑ Person wearing a uniform
- ❑ Person who delivers the post/milk/newspapers
- ❑ Strangers outside the house

- ❏ Strangers coming into the house
- ❏ People on bicycles/roller skates/skate boards

DOGS

- ❏ Other puppies at the Vets
- ❏ Other puppies at socialisation class
- ❏ Black dogs
- ❏ Dogs with short muzzles (e.g. Bulldog, Boxer)
- ❏ Dogs with heavy coats (e.g. Old English Sheepdog)
- ❏ Small dogs (e.g. Jack Russell Terrier, Shih Tzu)
- ❏ Big dogs
- ❏ Dogs held in someone's arms

ENVIRONMENTS

- ❏ Busy town centre
- ❏ Walking past school playground at playtime
- ❏ Railway stations
- ❏ The Pub
- ❏ Vet's waiting room
- ❏ The countryside
- ❏ The car
- ❏ Other people's cars
- ❏ Other people's homes
- ❏ Other people's gardens
- ❏ Grooming parlour
- ❏ City farm or real farm
- ❏ Parks
- ❏ Seaside
- ❏ Sand dunes

OBJECTS

- ❏ Bin bags caught on railings/in tree
- ❏ Balloons
- ❏ Aeroplanes
- ❏ Helicopters
- ❏ Shopping trolleys
- ❏ Christmas trees
- ❏ Halloween masks
- ❏ Motorised children's toys
- ❏ Other animals (e.g. cats, rabbits, guinea pigs etc.)
- ❏ Livestock (e.g. sheep, cattle, pigs, horses etc.)

This list is by no means exhaustive so use your imagination. Introduce your puppy to the rich pageant of human life.

They'll never spot me here!

Say "queso"!

9 THE PROBLEMS OF ADOLESCENCE

Teenagers the world over cause their parents anguish. It's their job! Your puppy will probably be no different. As stated previously, Spanish Water Dogs can become quite difficult when they are going through their second 'fear imprint' stage of development. As this time clashes with the onset of puberty the resulting emotional and hormonal mix can be quite problematic, and even a really confident, well-socialised puppy may suddenly 'go off the rails'.

Bitches may suddenly become nervous during the months prior to their first season. They may start 'herding' people and/or other dogs. Previously sound 'recall' could become seriously shaky! They may become very vocal and slightly 'guardy'. If these behaviours are dealt with correctly most bitches will return to their former sweet, biddable selves once the season is over.

Dogs occasionally become **very** 'guardy'. They may start to drive people away and sometimes will herd at the same time, even running in behind and threatening the backs of legs! Their 'recall', like the bitches', might become so unreliable that you cannot believe you ever trained it in the first place! If you own a bitch your young male might take it upon himself to 'protect' her from what **he** perceives as threatening situations or other dogs. Nervousness, again, could suddenly manifest itself, even though there was no sign of it before.

Both dogs and bitches can occasionally begin to back off from people they do not know well. They may even start to growl as they retreat, especially when on the lead. Going to the Vet's or into boarding kennels can become traumatic.

The natural human response to all these situations is very often the wrong one! Throughout this book you will find advice on preventing and curing the type of problems that may arise. The following table is a 'quick find' for the solutions:

Problem	Solution
• Suddenly starts barking at people or dogs	• Teach 'Leave' and follow with **rewarded** 'Recall'. See Chapter 13
• Backs away from people or growls	• Teach 'Say Hello'
• Shows signs of nervousness of people or unfamiliar situations	• Completely ignore the behaviour and show that you are not worried
• Shaky 'recall'	• Re-train in safe, secure area and increase value of reward
• Guarding inappropriately at home	• Teach 'Goody Jar' as visitors arrive
• Herding or chasing (livestock, people or dogs)	• Practice 'Recall'. **Teach** 'So you want to chase? Chase this!', Chapter 13
• Fear of Vet	• Visit Vet often for purely social call. Teach 'Sit to Greet' or 'Say Hello' in reception/surgery with Nurses and Vet
• Boarding kennels	• Prepare dog for first visit well in advance, ideally before puberty. See Boarding Kennels, Chapter 10
• Excessive or unacceptable barking	• Ignore barking, don't shout. Reward **quiet** behaviour. See Chapter 13

10 THE AGGRESSION MYTH

There are four times in the life of a Spanish Water Dog when people who do not understand this breed will make the assumption, wrongly, that the dog is aggressive. Spanish Water Dogs are primitive and sensitive. Sometimes, when they are truly afraid, they growl and show signs of what we humans think of as aggression.

VETERINARY SURGEONS

These are usually the first professionals with whom our dogs come into contact. Correctly socialised puppies do not normally have a problem when they attend for vaccinations but, during the onset of puberty and the second fear-imprint period, many dogs are taken to the Vet's surgery for castration or spaying. They are left alone, possibly for the first time in their lives, with people they do not know and who do not understand the psyche of a breed like this. Some of these dogs react, through fear and apprehension, in the only way they know how. 'Aggressively', or so the Veterinary Surgeon and his staff will believe. The dog may be returned to the owner on two leads, held at a safe distance, with the report that he is "The most aggressive dog we have ever seen". The owners, who know and understand the dog, cannot believe their ears. If only the dog had been prepared for the situation. If only he had been shown that being away from his home and all he knows is normal. If only he had visited the surgery for a social call and realised it was a perfectly normal place to be. If only professional animal carers had more knowledge of how the mind of a primitive dog works. So many 'if onlys'!

It would have been so easy to make sure the poor, misunderstood dog had been properly prepared for this new and frightening experience. A few social visits to the Vet's with treats from the staff; a night or two away from home with friends or family; plenty of opportunities to go off for a few moments with 'strangers' when out and about on the lead; being acclimatised to a kennel or cage environment beforehand. The list of opportunities to make the dog feel safe in uncertain situations and environments is endless. Positive reinforcement for calm, sensible behaviour in frightening situations will enable a dog to face the unknown with equanimity. A quick overview of this breed and its little foibles for the professionals who are going to be dealing with him so that should he show fear or give the odd grumble they don't misinterpret his behaviour. That is all that is needed to avoid people jumping to the wrong conclusions when a dog understandably takes action to protect himself.

PROFESSIONAL GROOMERS

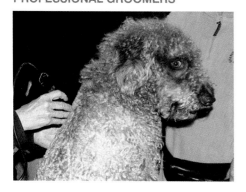

The first visit to the Groomer is, unfortunately, usually smack bang in the middle of the first fear imprint stage at about five months of age. As well as taking on board the advice given in Chapter 4, CARE OF YOUR SPANISH WATER DOG, it would be wise to perform the same preparatory steps suggested for visiting the Vet. So many problems could be prevented with a little forethought. An explanation to the Groomer that the odd growl and the occasional inhibited 'snap' simply means that the puppy is frightened and that 'punishing' him will only increase his fear, might lead them to the view that a little patience and understanding is all that is required.

TRAINERS

The subject of trainers and their various methods has been covered exhaustively in Chapter 12, TRAINING. Often trainers will see an inadequately socialised Spanish Water Dog puppy hiding under a chair and hear him growl if he is forced out. The assumption is frequently made that he is "going to become aggressive" and "needs to be shown who is in charge" when, really, all that is needed is a little canine psychology, a degree of patience and some common sense.

BOARDING KENNELS

This is the big one! Has your dog ever been in Boarding Kennels before? Has he ever been away from you? If the answer to either of these questions is "No" then you should start preparations now to avoid the danger of him being misunderstood. Spanish Water Dogs often react defensively when they feel abandoned and 'out of their comfort zone'. This will be specially so if they are not used to being separated from their family. It is important to choose a Boarding Kennel where your dog will be given every consideration and time to settle.

First of all, you should choose your Kennels carefully. Recommendation by a friend who boards a similar type of dog is the best advertisement but, failing that, you have to start checking them out for yourself. Your Vet **may** be able to recommend a Kennel, but this is not always possible, as many Vets prefer not to commit themselves. Get out the Yellow Pages and start ringing around. Ask if the Kennels are heated during chilly weather and whether they have covered outside runs on every kennel. Ask if they will feed your dog twice a day on the diet he is used to at home and whether or not you can take his own bed and toys. Ask if they are exercised in secure paddocks or lead walked away from public roads and whether or not they have a good Insurance scheme to cover any veterinary expenses that occur while you are away. Ask if you need to produce evidence of annual vaccination and whether or not you need to vaccinate against Kennel Cough. If the answer to any of these questions is "No" – move on to the next Kennels on the list. If the answer is "Yes" to all the questions ask if you may visit, **without an appointment,** anytime during their normal opening hours, to have a look round. If the proprietor is happy for visitors to arrive unannounced it is fairly safe to assume that they have nothing to hide!

Once you have a list of Kennels that have passed the initial test then start visiting. **Don't** take the dog with you! If you are completely comfortable with what you see on your visit, and you are sure you have been shown the entire Kennels, not just the 'showpiece' section, you can then discuss the nature of your breed. Very few kennels will have experience of the Spanish Water Dog but a good proprietor will be prepared to listen, learn and accept your knowledge of your own dog.

Explain that the dog may be withdrawn initially. That he may appear 'sulky' or 'nervous'. Don't be afraid to tell them that he may even growl if approached. During this testing time even the nicest dogs may object to strangers invading their space or wafting brushes and shovels around. They may even refuse to submit to the lead being put on, but this will pass. Reassure them that as long as he is ignored and given some space for the first forty-eight hours or so he will eventually come out of his shell and be happy to get to know them. Tell them how important his toys are and that once he is feeling relaxed those toys will be a great way to get through his reserve. By the time you come back he will be their best friend!

Once you are sure all these criteria have been met you may decide to book your dog in. Remember that the better Kennels will always be booked up well in advance, particularly at Bank Holidays and during August, so don't leave it till the last minute and don't scrimp on the accommodation. The best is never the cheapest. After all, you are going to enjoy **your** holiday, why shouldn't your dog enjoy **his?**

Assuming all is well, and the dates are available, ask if you can book the dog in for a 'trial' about two weeks before you go away. This visit should be for a matter of hours, not overnight. Ideally, the Kennels will be happy for you to drop him off one morning and pick him up in the afternoon. He will not even need to be fed. This visit will show your dog that, although your leaving him may upset him, it is not for long, and you will return to collect him. When he returns for the longer stay the difference in duration will not be a problem for him. He has been there before and you came back. That is all that matters to him. When you leave him at the Kennels don't make a big song and dance about it, no matter how upset you are. Simply hand him over to the kennel staff, give him his toy and **GO!!** Hugging him, making all sorts of promises and crying your eyes out are not going to make him feel better – he will just get more and more stressed because of your behaviour. You have made your choice, now let the Kennels get on with their job and go and enjoy yourself.

A little forethought goes a long way and if you prepare your dog in advance and choose the Kennels well, he will be absolutely fine. Finally, do please be prepared to travel if the best kennels are not the nearest – it will be worth it in the end.

Every opportunity to socialise your puppy prior to its vaccinations will be of long-term benefit. The range of equipment available these days to help with this is truly mind boggling!

11 BODY LANGUAGE

If only they could talk! Wouldn't that be wonderful? How much easier it would be for dogs and people to understand each other. However, dogs don't speak English and we don't speak dog. Of course we can teach dogs what certain words mean through correct training, and clever dogs, especially those as intelligent as Spanish Water Dogs, are capable of picking up the meaning of many more words and phrases. Some remarkable dogs may even understand that we sometimes use the same word to mean different things! We, of course, believe that we know what our dogs are trying to say to us. But do we, really?

All animals employ some means of communication, mainly through the interpretation of body language. We humans, however, have developed the spoken word to such an extent that body language has become less important. Of course, we still read it subconsciously, but we rarely think about it. To truly understand how to communicate with our dogs we need to learn how to 'read' them and to be aware of what our body signals and postures say to them.

This chapter is an attempt to clarify some of the misconceptions on both sides. Some body postures may occur in more than one category. This is because the dog's perception of them may depend upon his confidence levels.

WHAT WE SAY TO THEM

I am being friendly and non-threatening
• Smiling
• Standing up straight
• Arms held loosely by the side
• Squatting down
• Confident eye contact
• Hand outstretched, palm up

I want to play
• Arms raised or waving
• Body twisted with shoulders to the side and ribcage towards the dog
• Running away
• Laughing or screaming

I am feeling aggressive or threatening
• Bending over
• Leaning forwards
• Hands on hips, head thrust forward
• Scowling
• Narrowing the eyes
• Staring

I am being unintentionally rude! (Usually applies to dogs you do not know well)
• Patting or stroking the head
• Hugging
• Leaning over or touching the shoulders
• Face to face contact
• Asking for a kiss

I am angry with you
(Usually applies to your own dog!)
• Head thrust forward
• Bending over
• Leaning forwards
• Harsh stare
• Turning your back
• Scowling
• Strong sigh
• Pointing or wagging your finger

I am frightened of you
• Widening eyes
• Staring
• Raising hands to chest or face
• Squealing
• Hunching shoulders

WHAT THEY ARE TRYING TO SAY TO US

Calming Signals

Most people understand the basics of canine communication but there are some, more subtle, signals known as 'calming signals' that dogs use to express their emotions and produce a calming effect upon one another. If we learn what these signals mean we may be able to understand more fully what our dogs are thinking and feeling as well as increasing our ability to 'talk back' to them in their own language. Our dogs live with us in a combined 'human/canine pack' and it is up to us, the 'intelligent, superior species', to try to understand what our dogs are so desperately attempting to tell us through their body movements and behaviour.

Turning the head

Although turning the head is generally used to denote high status and indicates that a subordinate dog should avoid rude or unacceptable behaviour, it can also be used as a calming signal. Turning the head is a totally non-aggressive body signal and what it may simply mean, in some circumstances, is "chill out".

Squiffy is giving mixed signals: turning her head as a sign of authority but also lip licking, which suggests tension or stress.

Scratching

Puppies scratch, usually with their hind leg in the area of the neck, shoulder or ribcage, when they feel 'pressured' or are stalling for time when they don't understand something that is happening to them. If you have just put a collar on a new pup and he's scratching like mad because it feels funny that is obviously something entirely understandable! If, on the other hand, he is used to his collar and you are trying to teach him something new but he suddenly sits down and has a good scratch he could well be trying to tell you to slow down, you're moving to fast. When this happens go back to something he has already learned, reward him for his success and give him a break. Try the new thing another time and give some thought to how clearly you are communicating what it is you want him to learn.

Stretching

Dogs stretch when they wake up just as we do. However, dogs will also stretch in an attempt to reduce the likelihood of what they see as aggression or a potential threat from another dog. An 'alpha' dog will stretch in front of a young upstart to tell him to mind his manners and not cause trouble. He might stretch in front of two dogs that are threatening each other, to calm them and prevent potential aggression. Our own dogs sometimes feel the need to stretch in front of us if we are behaving in a threatening manner or if we have put them in a situation that makes them feel vulnerable, such as asking them to lie down in front of a person who frightens them, or demanding something harshly rather than asking nicely! A dog who believes he is of higher status than his owner might stretch to say "hang on a minute, you can't make me do that!"

Sneezing

This is another way that your dog may tell you (or another dog) that he is unsure or finding a situation uncomfortable, usually brought on by over–excitement rather than actual stress. A Spanish may issue several small sneezes while dancing around rather foolishly! He is **not** playing! He is signalling that he doesn't know exactly how he is supposed to be behaving and 'acting the fool' might get him out of trouble.

Curving

When you recall your dog does he come as straight as a die or does he seem to curve away and approach you in a kind of semi-circle? If the latter, he is telling you that something is making him uncomfortable and, although he knows he must come to you, he is trying to make sure you don't attack him when he arrives! If you are bending, shouting or glaring that would explain the dog's uncertainty. Try recalling in a nice voice, with a smile on your face, standing upright or crouching right down on your haunches and you will see the dog immediately react by coming in a straight line, all the way up to you, ready for a reward.

Yawning

When a dog yawns what he is trying to say could depend on his position in the hierarchy or the dynamics of the situation he finds himself in. For example, a dog may yawn to tell another pack member (human or canine) that he is feeling stressed or uncertain. An extremely stressed or frightened dog that is panting excessively may intersperse the panting with frantic yawns and whines. Conversely a confident, high status dog might yawn back to say "don't worry, relax, you are not in danger". Your dog could yawn at **you** because you are being bossy or aggressive! He might yawn because he doesn't understand what you want him to do and your voice is expressing your irritation, or he is in a situation that he finds difficult and worrying. He may yawn because you are ignoring him when he is normally used to getting your attention whenever he wants it. If you believe that your attitude is worrying him then change it! Reduce the pressure, don't stare at the dog or adopt an aggressive stance, use a nice voice and don't ask for more than he can give. If it is the situation that is the problem you should consider how to modify it so that the dog is comfortable again. Whatever the reason for your dog yawning at you, or in front of you, the best response is for **you** to yawn and turn your head away. This will tell him that although you are important you are not threatening him, and he should just chill out a little. You are in charge but in a kind, benevolent way.

So next time you are fussing someone else's dog and your dog is stretching like mad you will at least understand what he is trying to say. When recalls are a little shaky look at your own body language and if your dog is yawning during a training session you will know that he isn't trying to tell you he's tired!

The dog on the left has lowered his head and ears to prevent aggression. We would wrongly view this as guilt.

THE BIG MISCONCEPTION

"He knows he's done wrong"
This is probably the area where we humans most often get it wrong when interpreting what our dogs are saying to us. I make no apology for repeating the subject elsewhere in this book since it is one of the commonest, and unkindest mistakes that owners make when punishing dogs retrospectively.

When a dog lowers his head, folds his ears back, puts his tail between his legs and cringes 'apologetically' across the floor to meet his owner he **does not know he's done wrong. He is not feeling guilty. He is not saying "sorry".** He has sensed anger in his owner and is adopting the body posture that is designed, in the dog world, to fend off an attack. In the dog world it works. A superior dog would not attack a dog offering this kind of submissive body posture. A human, on the other hand, sees this grovelling performance as proof of guilt and punishes the dog. The dog, of course, has no idea what he is being punished for because he did whatever it was minutes or hours ago. He becomes even more confused because his body posture, so carefully handed down through his genes to protect him, has failed. Next time he is left alone he will worry about the owner returning and will probably cause more trouble through his increased fear and apprehension. Poor dog.

12 TRAINING YOUR SPANISH WATER DOG

WHY BOTHER TO TRAIN AT ALL?

Many years ago, when Crufts was first televised, a gentleman (who shall remain nameless!) was employed to present the coverage and was portrayed as a 'dog expert'. Year after year he used to extol the virtues of Border Collies. "Born trained", he would say; "Make perfect pets". Half the nation went out and bought a Border Collie expecting a 'perfect' dog. What they got, of course, was a wonderful working machine that they had no idea how to train. Everywhere one went there were harrassed mothers with young children being dragged over the countryside by frustrated collies without a job to do, looking desperately for something to fulfil their working instincts. You can still see the legacy today. Bored collies herding children, ducks, pigeons, bricks. Collies chasing cars, trains, bicycles, children. Collies chained in gardens; collies in rescue kennels in their hundreds; collies put down because of their unacceptable behaviour. **This is not the fault of the collie.** It is the fault of people who think you do not have to train a clever, 'working' dog. It is because people think a working dog is easy. It is the collie that pays the price, often with it's life.

Spanish Water Dogs are very clever and will train themselves. They are also clever enough to train you! These dogs are highly motivated, very independent **and they guard.** Untrained, untutored and allowed to be 'in charge' a Spanish Water Dog is a time bomb waiting to go off. Whether you have already acquired your Spanish Water Dog or are still thinking about it, training should be foremost in your mind. From the moment the puppy arrives in your home training and character shaping must begin in earnest. An intelligent breed such as the Spanish needs direction, boundaries and very clear leadership. Please don't listen to people or trainers who tell you to 'be firm and show him who's boss' if what they mean by that is shouting commands and using forceful, bullying tactics or punishment-based training methods. The Spanish is clever, manipulative and capable of getting it's own way but it is also very sensitive and will not tolerate harsh treatment.

CHOOSING A TRAINING CLASS

There are many different types of class you could attend and your research should be thorough so that you can give your puppy the best start in life. Although there has been a revolution in dog training over the last twenty years there are still trainers using out-dated, abusive methods of training. Whilst most caring owners would refuse to return to such a trainer once they realised what was happening the incredible memory of the Spanish Water Dog would almost certainly result in a single bad experience ruining the puppy, possibly for life. Once the puppy has been subjected to a negative or fearful encounter it is **too late** to walk out without permanent harm, so do your homework and make sure the training is appropriate **before** attending class.

In an ideal world you would search for your training class **before** you get your puppy. First of all, make a list of all the training classes and clubs within your area and be prepared to travel some distance. Ask around friends who have well-trained dogs; ask your Veterinary Surgeon; contact the organisations listed at the end of this book. Once you have your list and have telephoned to enquire when the classes take place get in your car and go visiting, **without** the puppy if you already have one! Sit in on a class, preferably one for puppies, and observe. Watch and listen to the trainer. How does he or she speak to the owners?

Never mind 'spot the ball' – spot the dog!

"Well I've spotted you – gimme my ball back!"

What is their approach to the puppies? Is there a lot of shouting or is the atmosphere quiet and calm? Of course there may be some barking, this is inevitable, but how is it dealt with? Would you feel comfortable in the class or intimidated? If you would feel uncomfortable just imagine how your puppy will feel. Is the trainer confident and knowledgeable without being aggressive, and in control of the class?

What to look for
• All puppies must be under twenty weeks of age on the first day of the course.
• The course should be structured and probably last for six or eight weeks.
• All puppies must be vaccinated and at least one week past their final injection.
• Modern, motivational training methods must be used.
• Food rewards should be encouraged and clicker training would be an advantage.
• There should be no more than eight puppies on the course.
• If puppies are allowed to play off-lead they should be in matched pairs and supervised.

What to avoid
• The use of choke/check chains.
• Refusal to allow food rewards.
• Refusal to allow you to use a clicker even if it is not a clicker class.
• Any use of force or physical punishment.
• Shouting and verbal correction.
• Owners being told to "use a firm voice" or "say it as though you mean it".
• Disparaging, belittling or bullying approach to the owners.
• Large classes .
• Classes where puppies are mixed in with older dogs.
• So-called 'puppy parties' where all the puppies are let off lead at the same time.
• Nervous puppies forced to interact before they are ready.
• Barking or 'aggression' towards other puppies punished by shouting or yanking.
• Puppies being pushed or pulled into position, i.e. sit, down etc.

THE PROS AND CONS OF DIFFERENT TYPES OF TRAINING
As you will see from the two lists above the pitfalls of finding a suitable class for your puppy are many. Let us think about the effects of various aspects of training, the positive results of motivational training and the damage that can be caused by negative, punitive methods.

Modern, motivational, reward-based training
This type of training will involve rewarding acceptable or required behaviour and ignoring unacceptable or unwanted behaviour. There will be no physical punishment and there should be no use of force to obtain a desired position or behaviour. The dog will be lured with food and will then receive it as a reward. In the absence of food the reward will be fuss and verbal praise from the owner.

Clicker training
Clicker training takes reward-based, motivational training to the next level. It changes the food from a lure or a bribe to a 'wage packet'. The clicker is a small, easily held plastic box that produces a sound, when pressed, that is unlike any other the dog is likely to hear in its everyday life. Through conditioning the dog learns that the 'click' is always followed by a treat and, eventually, that the behaviour it was offering when it heard the 'click' is what it is being rewarded for. Clicker training is extremely effective and generally

much quicker than any other method. Dogs of all breeds respond well to clicker training but, due to their superior intelligence and excellent memory, Spanish Water Dogs that are being clicker trained will learn with such speed that it will take your breath away! Once a dog is 'clicker-wise' it will offer behaviour in order to get you to 'click&treat' so you will need to understand the different ways in which it may be used.

- Luring—this is the way that clicker training is generally introduced. The puppy is lured, with food, into the position the trainer wants to teach i.e. a tit-bit held in front of the puppy's nose and lowered to the floor will eventually induce it to lie down. At that instant the trainer 'clicks' and gives a tasty treat. Eventually, through gradually reducing the amount of luring the puppy learns the behaviour and, once it is learnt, the trainer will tell the puppy what it is called, i.e. "down". This method is described in much more detail later in this chapter.

- Shaping—this is the method used to teach more complicated behaviour such as tricks or household tasks like closing the door. To begin with the dog gets a 'click&treat' for the first part of the behaviour i.e. lifting a paw towards the door. This stage may well be lured. After a few successes the 'click&treat' is withheld until the dog tries a bit harder and hits the door with a little more force. 'Click&treat' again a few times. The trainer then witholds again until the door is hit hard enough to close it—'click&treat'. Once the dog is closing the door automatically at a simple signal from the trainer the cue "close the door" can be introduced.

- Capturing—this method is useful for behaviours that cannot be 'lured' or for things the dog finds difficult, e.g. some dogs will not be lured into a lying down position. The trainer will simply wait for the dog to lie down of it's own accord, say the word "down" and 'click&treat' while the dog is in that position. Several repetitions will convince the dog that lying down is a good thing and it will learn what it is called. Eventually it will go "down" on a verbal cue.

- Target training—this method involves the use of a 'target stick' which is simply a stick (nowadays, probably telescopic) with some sort of smooth, often coloured, blob on the end of it. The dog is taught to touch the end of the target stick with its nose, for which it receives the 'click&treat'. After a few repetitions the dog will willingly follow wherever the target stick leads and is no longer required to actually touch it. It can be used for all manner of training and is invaluable for Agility and Heelwork To Music (HTM) as well as competition obedience and tricks for fun. Mary Rae is the most famous exponant of this type of training; she can be seen each year on the last day of Crufts amazing the world with her wonderful dramatic routines.

- The Rules of Clicker Training
  1. The 'click' tells the puppy he has done the right thing and is about to receive a reward.
  2. 'Click' **always** means a treat will follow—don't lie to your puppy!
  3. **Never** 'click' to tell your puppy to do something—only to tell him he **has** done it right.
  4. 'Click' means the exercise is over—it is OK for the puppy to move or do something else.
  5. Do not point the clicker at the puppy—it is **not** a remote control device!
  6. **Never** 'click' near the puppy's ears. The clicker is quite loud and may frighten him. Click it close to your own ear so you never forget how awful it is and then think about the fact that your puppy's hearing is four times better than yours! You want your puppy to love the clicker, not fear it, so keep it away from his head.
  7. The clicker is a training tool. When a behaviour is established you no longer need to use it so please don't think that you will be welded to it forever! You will only need to use it as your puppy gets older when you want to teach a new trick or behaviour.

Books, DVDs and videos on all aspects of clicker and target training are readily available and some are listed at the back of this book.

'Stamp & Pull' and 'Yank & Yell'

As mentioned earlier in this chapter there are still old fashioned trainers of this variety involved in the business of 'training' dogs. If your Spanish Water Dog is 'trained' by these methods it will be ruined and may possibly become aggressive in order to defend itself. It may develop a fear of people that will be very difficult to cure, so be warned! Many Spanish are a little wary when they first attend classes, sometimes even hiding under the chair. Dragging the puppy out and 'insisting' it takes part is a recipe for disaster. Pushing and pulling the puppy into position will result in a distinct distrust of strangers as well as a lack of confidence in the owner. Using shouted commands and yanking with the lead to correct unwanted behaviour will result in the puppy crawling into a shell from which it may never emerge. Allowing people to continue to approach or bend over a sensitive puppy before it has gained confidence will only serve to convince it that people outside of the family are bad news. Avoid these trainers and their classes like the plague. Your puppy will be a fine, confident member of society as long as people like this do not get their hands on it. **Remember, one bad experience is enough to put a Spanish off for life!**

How Puppies Learn

Once you have found your trainer and decided on the type of class you are going to attend you need to think about how puppies learn. Puppies are 'situational' learners, and they learn 'in pictures'. This means that they learn things in the situation in which they were taught a particular exercise and have a mental picture of the surroundings in which they were taught it. For example, if you teach your puppy to "sit" in your living room, with the T.V. in the corner and the family sitting on the sofa watching intently it will certainly learn to "sit" but it will think that "sit" only happens in **that particular situation**. The puppy's 'picture' of "sit" will include the T.V. in the corner and the family on the sofa! When you go outside and ask it to "Sit!" the puppy will look at you in amazement and say to itself, "Sit? What's that?" The puppy is not being naughty or stupid—it simply doesn't understand! You need to teach the same exercise in lots of different places and situations before the puppy realises that the word "Sit" means "put your bottom on the floor, no matter where you are". The same will apply to training classes. If you teach your puppy something in class you will need to re-teach it at home in different rooms as well as the garden and during walks before the behaviour is truly learned.

Puppies also learn by realising what 'works' and what 'doesn't work'. For example, if jumping up results in the owner pushing the puppy down and saying "Get off" whilst looking at it, the puppy will think to itself "Oh, great, I got stroked, spoken to and looked at—I'll do that again!" Conversely, if jumping up is greeted by the owner folding their arms and turning their head away until the puppy sits, at which point it gets a 'click&treat', that puppy is more likely to think "Oh, right, jumping up doesn't work so I will sit on the floor instead. That worked for me".

Behaviour that is rewarded will be repeated and behaviour that is ignored will die out. That is the golden rule of dog training. If you apply this rule to all your training procedures you will eventually have a dog that has good manners, great social skills and is well trained. If you shout and scream and get cross you will end up with a confused bundle of nerves that has no idea how you want it to behave.

BASIC TRAINING EXERCISES

The following pages are devoted to training specific exercises. The use of a clicker is recommended throughout. However, if you have no wish to try clicker training please follow the advice and reward with a treat anyway. The principles are the same—it will simply take a little longer!

SIT
This is the easiest cue word to teach if you do it with food. It is even easier if you employ a clicker:

- Hold a piece of food slightly above the puppy's nose and slowly move your hand upward and backwards over his head.
- As his head comes up and back to follow the food his bottom, as if by magic, will go down!
- **At the instant his bottom hits the floor** you say, "Sit!" in a really nice voice and, at the same time, click and pop the food into his mouth. In this way he quickly learns that his bottom on the floor and the word "Sit" are connected and result in a juicy tit-bit. Within a very short time he will learn what the word means.

- Once he knows what "sit" means, and will respond immediately, you can reward just once in a while with food to keep him keen.
- Within a couple of sessions you should no longer need to lure with food—a simple raising of your hand will do the job.
- You should also start to wait a while before you reward so that the puppy learns to sit for longer periods, rather than just one second! While the puppy is in the sitting position you can repeat the "sit" cue whilst giving some quiet, verbal praise. This will reassure him that he is doing the right thing and may, eventually, receive a reward.

- Eventually the dog will fully understand what the word "sit" means and you will no longer need any hand signals.
- However, when you are asking him to sit it is imperative that you only say the word once. If you repeat words over and over again what the puppy will actually learn is that the cue (or command) for "sit" is really "sit, sit, sit". You will get angry and frustrated and the puppy will be totally baffled because he can't understand your attitude. After all, it was you that taught him that three words were the norm!

DOWN

To teach "Down" easily, first wait for the puppy to sit of his own accord. It is very much easier to get a puppy to go into the "down" position from a "sit" but if you ask for "sit" every time you teach "down" your pup will think it has to sit and then go down. He will become very confused about which is which and will do neither properly!

- Get a piece of food and hold it under the puppy's nose. Lower your hand to the floor so that he follows it down. As soon as his chest is on the floor 'click&treat'. **Do not say "down" at this stage.** If he stands up don't get cross with him – simply start again from the sit.
- Repeat several times using the food but don't always give the treat from your hand– sometimes throw it so he has to move to get it. Then you can start again!
- If the puppy gets up again before you have chance to give him the treat don't worry. It only matters what he is doing when he hears the 'click', i.e. lying on the floor. It doesn't matter at all where he is or what he is doing when he gets the treat.
- After a few repetitions, when he is lying on the floor readily, start to lure him to the floor with an **empty** hand and then, after you have 'clicked' give him the treat from the other hand. This will teach him that even though the food wasn't there he will still get it after he has heard the 'click'.
- The next step is to lure him with an empty hand and then try to stand up a little bit before you 'click&treat'. This will teach the puppy that lying on the floor is not dependent upon you bending over to help him. Remember the 'learning in pictures'? You want your puppy's 'picture' of 'down' to include you standing, not bending.
- Eventually you will be able to stand up completely before you 'click&treat'. Now your puppy will move on in leaps and bounds!
- As he gets the idea you can reduce the amount of help you are giving him by not taking your hand all the way to the floor. Your aim is to be able to point at the floor without bending down so the dog is not relying on your body signals but is working out what you want. Some dogs are very quick; some take much longer – whichever yours is be patient and don't rush!

- Eventually your dog will drop into the down position as soon as you point at the floor. The first time he drops without help is 'jackpot time' which means that he gets a fantastic reaction from **you** plus a jackpot of several treats instead of just one. This will help him to remember what he did to achieve such a great reward.

- As soon as he is 'offering' the down position every time, you are ready to teach the cue word as follows:
- **Now** you can start to say "Down" as a cue word! Instead of clicking as soon as he drops say "Down! Good boy!" then click and give him the treat. If he gets up before you have chance to 'click' don't correct or scold him. Simply try again.
- As he gets better you can teach him to stay in the 'down' position by waiting for a few seconds before you click and treat. **Don't rush** – if you expect too much too soon the puppy will get frustrated and make mistakes – it will not be his fault, but yours! Gradually increase the time you expect him to wait before you 'click&treat'. Move away a little, then return to him, 'click&treat'.

- Eventually the puppy will learn that "Down" means "Lie down until I tell you to do something else or tell you we have finished".
- To tell the dog you have finished you should use a 'release word' such as "Go play", "Off you go" or whatever you prefer. It must always be the same and should be used whenever you want to let the puppy know he is no longer working and can go and do his own thing.
- Once the puppy is responding to the word "Down" instantly and staying there for as long as you decide, you no longer need to use the clicker – the job is done!

STAND

Many owners feel that they have no need to teach their dog to 'stand' unless they are intending to take him into the show ring. Whilst this is probably true, 'stand' does have merit as part of a training programme because it enables you to make a distinction between 'sit' and 'down' in the dog's mind. A lot of people get into the habit, when training, of asking the dog to 'sit' and then 'down' so that he learns that the two positions are interconnected. One never happens without the other. The result is that the 'sit' will never be maintained for more than a few seconds and the 'down' will not happen unless preceded by the 'sit'. Teaching 'stand' enables you to rotate the positions randomly so that a pattern never develops and the dog clearly understands what each one is in isolation from the others.

Conversely, many people who show their dogs will not teach "sit" because they fear the dog will sit in the ring. Let us credit our dogs with enough intelligence to know the difference! A properly trained dog will do whatever it is asked to provided it receives the correct information from the handler. Clicker training allows the dog to learn exactly what the verbal cues mean but this does not mean that you cannot also use hand signals. It is up to you.

Clicker training is the quickest and easiest way to teach the 'stand':

- First of all decide what hand signal you want the puppy to associate with the 'stand' and be sure it is different from any other that you use. Hand against your tummy is a good one.
- Hold the clicker in one hand and a treat in the other.
- Hold the treat against the puppy's nose and lure him into a standing position. At this point, even if you intend to show, the actual positioning of the feet is not important.
- Click instantly and give the treat.
- Repeat several times but do not introduce a verbal cue ("stand") yet.
- Start to remove your hand a little bit before you 'click&treat'.
- Then start to do the same with no food in your luring hand.
- Click and give the treat with the other hand.
- After a while the puppy will begin to offer the behaviour. 'Click&treat' immediately.
- When he is offering a 'stand' reliably you can begin to wait a second or two before clicking.
- At this point you should say the cue word "stand" in a nice, quiet voice just before you click.
- After a few repetitions you will be able to use the cue word "stand" to ask for the behaviour.
- Now you can begin to ask for a 'show' stand that will be held for as long as you like.
- Ask for 'stand' but don't click unless the pup is standing foursquare. Don't correct or manhandle him—simply wait until his feet are where you want them. 'Click&treat'.
- Remember that the clicker signals the end of the behaviour; so don't expect the puppy to maintain the 'stand' after you have clicked.
- From now on you will only click perfect stands and, gradually, longer ones.
- Eventually, you will dispense with the clicker and reward with fuss or praise as you see fit.

LEAD WALKING

Basic puppy lead training
In preparation for lead training accustom your pup to wearing a flat, buckle collar around the house. The collar should be fitted so that you can fit two fingers underneath. If it is any looser it may slip off, and any tighter it will choke him! Remember to loosen it as the pup grows! **Please do not use a choke chain.**

- Before attempting to put a lead on a young puppy encourage him to follow you by holding a tit-bit in front of his nose as he walks alongside you, giving plenty of praise and the occasional 'click&treat' as he is walking.
- Don't go too far as he will soon tire. Around the house or garden is far enough.
- When he is quite happy to walk with you a light, flat lead (not a chain) may be attached to the collar. Let the lead drag as you walk with the pup. 'Click&treat' whenever he is in the right place.
- When he is quite happy for the lead to drag behind him you can pick it up as you are walking, keeping it very loose, and drop it again after a few paces.
- Gradually build up until he is walking happily at the side of you with the lead in your hand. 'Click&treat' whenever the lead is loose and the pup is walking nicely, preferably looking up at you.
- If, at any time, he starts to pull, hang back or tries to walk in front of you **stop everything!** Don't move, don't pull, don't speak. Wait for the pup to slacken the lead and look at you, then start to walk, praise him, and after a few paces 'click&treat'.

Using this method your pup will never learn to pull in the first place, and a pup that never learns to pull never will! Teach him that, as soon as he pulls, the walk stops. He'll soon get the message! Keep these lessons very short - two or three minutes at regular intervals throughout the day would be ideal.

Teaching the 'Heel' or 'Close' cue

Before your dog can learn to walk properly on the lead he needs to learn that there is a word that means "be by this leg" and that when he is doing that he will be rewarded. You should decide what you want the word(s) to be and whether you want him to learn to walk on either side. If you do, there **must** be a different word for each side. Your dog cannot understand that one word could mean two things. The following guidelines assume you want to do both. If you only want to teach one side then ignore the references to the side you do not wish to train. I have used the words 'heel' and 'close' but you can use whatever words you like. It doesn't matter to the dog if you say 'rhubarb' and 'custard' as long as you teach him what they mean!

This exercise teaches the dog to associate the word with 'joining up' with the relevant leg. He will learn that whether you are walking, standing or running the word means he should be by the relevant leg, staying next to it. He will also learn that if he is in front of you or a long way away from you it means the same thing.

In the early stages the dog **must** be on the lead.

- Stand facing your dog with him sitting, and your feet close to his.
- Hold the clicker in the same hand as the lead, the left hand at this stage.
- Have a plentiful supply of treats that you can reach with the other hand.
- Decide which word applies to which side (e.g. "heel" for left, "close" for right).

- Slide your left leg back and **lure** the dog past it with the food in front of his nose. Do not move your right leg.

- Still luring, turn him in towards your leg.

- As you bring your left leg forward lure him along with it and say, "heel".
- The aim is to get the dog to follow the left leg as it goes back, and to continue to follow it as it comes forward again to join the right one, which doesn't move.
- Keep your left hand far enough back so that the lead prevents the dog moving any further forward than your leg.

- As soon as your feet are together raise your right hand above the dog's head and say "sit".
- If the dog is sitting **by your left leg** ....'click&treat'.
- If the dog is sitting in front or too far away, simply start again.
- Remember you must click **before** you lower the treat hand.
- While he is still sitting, step in front of him and repeat the exercise.
- Randomly repeat, reversing the instructions for the right leg, saying "close".
- As the dog gets the idea you can stop luring, but still use your leg to guide him.

- Eventually you can dispense with the leg movement and just use the word.
- Remember, as with all training, to teach the exercise in lots of different places and, eventually, off the lead as well as on.

Reliable Lead Walking

To teach your dog to walk nicely he needs to learn, ideally as soon as he starts to wear a collar and lead, that pulling **doesn't work!** If you continue to walk when your dog is in front and pulling he will think that is what he's allowed to do. If you pull him back he will think pulling is part of the game! If he's allowed to pull **sometimes** he will think he can decide when he should pull. If he pulls and is then let off the lead he is being rewarded for pulling! To teach nice lead walking you **must** be consistent and the dog must realise that pulling **never works!**

The exercise above prepares your dog for lead-work and the following instructions explain how to include it during lead training. **Remember**: every time your dog is on the lead he is being trained, not just during classes or training sessions!

- Make yourself comfortable with the clicker in the same hand as the lead.
- Make sure the treats are accessible to the other hand.
- Start with the dog sitting quietly by your side.
- As you move the leg the dog is sitting next to, say the appropriate word (e.g. "heel" for the left, "close" for the right).
- If the dog is by your side, the lead is loose and he is looking up at **you** (not the treat!) 'click&treat'. Keep walking as you give the treat.
- If he is still in the right place repeat the cue word then 'click&treat' again.
- If he goes ahead or pulls, **stop!** Do nothing to correct him.
- When he stops pulling and looks at you, slide your leg back (left if he's supposed to be on your left side and right if he's meant to be on your right).
- As soon as he joins up with this leg start to walk, using the correct cue word and 'click&treat'.
- If he is over-excited ask him to sit each time before moving off.
- Initially you may have to 'click&treat' every step but gradually you will be able to expect a little more.
- Eventually you will be able to phase out the clicker altogether, but don't be in too much of a hurry, especially if your dog is easily distracted.

Why Do Dogs Pull?

As stated previously, the reason most dogs pull is that they learn very early on that pulling works and they get some kind of reward for it. Many dogs pull as soon as they leave the house because they have become over-excited by the very thought of going for a walk. The dog picks up on various 'triggers' in the owner's behaviour. 'Triggers' are the signals perceived by the dog as a sign that something is going to happen. The triggers arouse the dog and as his excitement builds, so do his levels of adrenalin. Dogs produce adrenalin when excited in the same way that we do but, whereas our levels drop to normal again quite quickly, dogs take much

This dog has learned that, because the walk continues, pulling works.

longer to revert to a calm state. This can contribute to problems on the walk because the dog is already 'high' when he leaves the house! His being taken out for the walk then rewards this behaviour! This makes life unpleasant for him as well as you, especially if there are things out there that worry him. Adrenalin is the 'fight or flee' hormone and, as such, may make a dog react more fearfully or aggressively to situations he is not comfortable in. When 'pumped up' and 'high' on adrenalin dogs do not act rationally! To prevent this we need to 'desensitise' his reaction to the lead and other triggers.

The triggers that tell him he's going for a walk will vary from dog to dog: it may be the lead; the shoes you wear; a particular coat or simply some little thing you do just before leaving, such as checking how you look in the mirror! Only you can identify the first trigger so watch for the point at which he begins to get excited and then you can start to de-sensitise him as follows:

- Set aside a day when you have nothing else to do and be prepared to persevere without going for a walk until you have achieved your aim: a dog who waits patiently for the lead to be put on!
- Approach the first trigger then, **as soon as** the dog reacts, completely ignore him and sit down again. Every few minutes approach it again and you will find that you get a little further each time before the dog becomes excited. For example, if the trigger is the lead, initially you will only have to put up your hand to touch it but, after a few attempts you will be able to pick it up and eventually you will find the dog will give up and wait until you are ready to put it on. Don't look at him while doing this!
- Apply the same principle to each trigger in the order in which it affects the dog until you can get all the way to the door, with the lead on, and leave the house in a calm, controlled manner!
- During the course of a normal day pick up the lead from time to time and then put it down again so that the dog never knows when the lead signals a walk.

RECALL
Problems regarding getting your dog to respond quickly and easily when you call him usually arise for one of two reasons - the dog getting his wires crossed during training or the dog believing he is more important than you so that you do not have the 'right' to call him away from whatever is taking his attention! To prevent the problem occurring in the first place the correct training procedures, as outlined here, need to be applied. To correct an existing problem you would need to go back to basics and teach the dog that you **do** have the right to expect an instant response and that when you call him he will be rewarded in such a way that he is left in no doubt that coming to you is the best thing in the world!

Voice
First you need to understand how important your voice is, both the tone of it and the words you use. Here are a few simple pointers:

- Always use a nice, friendly, soft and inviting tone to call your dog. Or use a whistle!
- Do not shout at your dog and **never** use his name as a reprimand.
- **Smile.** This improves the tone of your voice and your dog will feel confident to approach you.
- If you have trouble making your tone soft, whisper! The dog will listen more carefully.

Are you valuable and important enough? Are you giving the right signals?
Think about life from a dog's point of view for a moment. Here are a few common scenarios:

- The dog is having fun in the garden when the owner decides it is time to go to work. The dog is called but is having too much fun to notice. He has also learned from past experience that the only time he is called from the garden to go into the house he is immediately left all on his own. The owner, realising he is going to be late for work, goes out and starts to chase him, red-faced, steam coming out of his ears! What a great game for the dog, and the incentive to win the game is enormous because if he loses he's going to be left alone.
- The dog is out for a walk. He's having a great time. He knows that when he's called the lead goes back on and the fun is over. The owner calls him but he carries on sniffing. Well, wouldn't you? The owner becomes irritated and starts to shout. Eventually the owner manages to persuade him to come but is so fed-up and frustrated he tells the dog off. Why would the dog want to go running up to someone who gets angry and punishes him?
- All day long as the owner potters about the house they are talking to the dog, using his name repeatedly and talking to him as if he was a child. Then suddenly they decide to call him so they say his name. Over and over again. He doesn't come and they wonder why. What does his name mean? His name has become the equivalent of a dripping tap and he has learned to completely ignore it.
- Whenever the dog wants a fuss he trots over, puts his head or a paw on the owner's lap and they respond by giving him what he wants. When they call him he can't be bothered to respond. Why should he? He can have their attention for free whenever he wants it!

All of the above can be avoided by correct **early** recall training and following some simple rules about household privileges. The importance of the dog's position in the family and the giving and withholding of certain privileges are covered in depth in "A Dog Is A Dog" which can be found in Chapter 7, EARLY DAYS.

Teaching Recall
Begin the moment your puppy arrives home. Feeding time is a good place to start. Only use his name to call him to you, not every time you speak to him or tell him to do something, and never in an angry tone! His name needs to be a special word that makes him want to pay attention to see what you want him to do next. In the early stages **always** reward the puppy in some way for coming when you call. Later on we will talk about variable rewards and phasing out the rewards, but not yet!

A recall can be broken down into three stages—the point at which you tell him you want him, his approach and his arrival. Each stage needs to be addressed and reacted to differently:

Stage One

- Attract your puppy's attention by saying his name in a lovely, happy voice.
- Persuade him to start coming towards you by doing something attractive and exciting such as clapping your hands, throwing your arms out to your sides or, if all else fails, running away.
- The **second** he starts to move towards you say "Come" and get in some really encouraging verbal praise—it is important to tell him that **thinking about coming** is a good thing.

Stage Two
- Repeat the word "Come" and alternate with verbal praise all the while he is approaching you.
- Do **not** bend over (bending is 'aggressive' to a puppy—see Calming Signals, Chapter 11, BODY LANGUAGE).
- Keep smiling!
- If he stops half way get more excited and call then praise again.
- Never use a harsh or angry tone, no matter how long it takes to get the puppy to move.

Stage Three
- As the puppy arrives at your feet **stay upright** while you click.

- Bend down to give him the treat and lots more praise. Bending **after** you have clicked will de-sensitise him to this scary body posture as he learns that the treat is going to be the result.
- If your puppy comes in at 30mph and is likely to jump at you, click when he is a few feet away then bend very quickly to give the treat. This will teach him that stopping at your feet is good and will prevent him bouncing off you!
- If your puppy is coming very slowly run backwards and get even more excited so that you can reward him for being more enthusiastic.

Developing **Reliable** Recall

Having worked hard to teach your puppy what "Come" actually means you now need to make it work in all situations, no matter what the distractions. This is often easier said than done!

Random Rewards

While teaching a puppy something new it is necessary to reward every time until he is clear what is expected of him. However, dogs work on something called the 'Jackpot Principle'. Once a dog has **thoroughly learned** a behaviour receiving a high value reward **occasionally** will make him try harder than if he is rewarded every single time. For this reason, when calling your trained dog, you should offer random, varied rewards. Let us say that out of five recalls you 'click&treat' only one of them using a special treat, on three of them you give him a fuss and on the other one you simply say "Good boy". This is 'random rewarding'. There should be no special order but you could decide how to react based on how hard he has tried.

WHISTLE TRAINING

The best kind of whistle for your dog is the type you can buy from a Gun shop. Ask for a 210 1/2 or 211 whistle. Keep it on a cord around your neck so that it is always easily accessible. If you see a difficult situation on the horizon hold the whistle in your mouth, between your teeth, so that you can blow it without wasting time.

There are two good reasons for whistle training your dog: he will hear it better, when distracted, than he will hear your voice and, more importantly, he will never know if you are getting irritated, angry or panicky!

Recall to the whistle

- To condition your dog to the whistle you should start at feeding time. You need two people to start with. One of you holds him in another room, with the doors open, so that he can hear his food being prepared.
- Call him, in a nice voice, followed by two or three short blasts on the whistle: pip, pip, pip. Blow the whistle again once he has been released and is on his way, then give him his food **immediately**, accompanied by loads of praise. Don't make him sit or wait; his food is the reward for coming.
- Practice at other times in the house and garden: call, in a nice voice, pip, pip, pip, and then 'click&treat' or lots of praise.

- In this way the whistle will be associated only with nice rewards, voices and tit-bits.
- Once the dog is responding quickly to the whistle use it to recall him to you; to get him away from the window if he is barking; or if he is barking in the garden.
- Once his response is immediate and consistent, the whistle can be used when out for a walk if you want to call him to you or if he chases or barks at another dog. Again, 'click&treat' on arrival.

Stop on the whistle
- Your dog must be conditioned to 'sit' on a hand signal, so, every time you ask your dog to sit raise your **right** hand, facing the dog. Don't forget to praise immediately and release the dog.
- Then begin to walk the dog at heel on a loose lead and, every now and then, ask him to sit as you halt, using a clear hand signal.
- As his bottom hits the floor, give a single pip on the whistle. Praise well. 'Click&treat'.
- When the dog is sitting reliably each time he hears the whistle you can start asking him to 'sit' at a distance using the whistle, reinforced by the hand signal to begin with.
- Once you are sure the dog is consistent in his response, you can remove the hand signal. If using a clicker, 'click&treat' as soon as he sits **after** he has heard the whistle.
- The sequence is: - "Sit!", at the same time raise your hand, then immediately give one pip on the whistle. 'Click&treat'.
- If the dog starts to come towards you, go to him and gently place him on the spot where he should have sat, whilst giving another pip on the whistle. Then praise him well or 'click&treat'.
- If he responds immediately, go to him, praise him well, 'click&treat', release him and play.

This exercise will be very useful in future to stop the dog when he is running off after his own interests and is already a long way away. The single loud blast will attract his attention and although he may not actually sit (and it doesn't matter if he doesn't) it will give you the chance to use the recall whistle while he is paying attention and get him to return successfully. If you are training your dog to the gun you will also be able, at this point, to redirect him to the right or left as desired.

STAY
This extremely easy way of teaching 'stay' can be taught with or without a 'stay' or 'wait' command. The dog can be taught that "Sit" and "Down" mean that he doesn't move until you say he can by giving either another command, such as "Heel" or "Come" or, if you have finished, your release word. A release word is what you say when the dog is no longer required to work for you e.g. "Go on", "Off you go", "Go play" etc. It is usually the word or phrase you use when you take the dog's lead off. **If you use a clicker don't 'click&treat' until the last time you perform the exercise and reward your dog.** Remember, the 'click' says it's over and, with 'stay' it's not over until the last one.

To teach this exercise you will need some pieces of tasty food, a stool or something similar and your dog on a longish lead and his normal collar. It will help enormously if you have someone to help who can tell you if the dog moves so that you are not tempted to look behind you to check on him. Eye contact is an invitation so if you look at your dog he will surely start to follow you!

- Show the dog that you are placing the tit-bits on the stool.
- Take the dog a short distance from the stool, within easy reach of the lead.
- Turn him to face the stool.
- Ask him to "Sit" or "Down". Use a nice voice and ask only once.

- If you choose to use the word "Wait" or "Stay", say it in a nice voice.
- Without looking at him or giving any hand signals walk away from the dog towards the stool.

- As soon as he starts to follow (which he almost certainly will at first) take him back to the spot he was on **without** speaking to him or touching him – using the lead. **Do not show any signs of displeasure.**
- Ask him to "Sit" or "Down" again (whichever you had asked for).
- Say "Wait" or "Stay".
- Walk to the stool again.

- Keep repeating until he doesn't move, then pick up one treat.

- Return to the dog without speaking or staring at him.
- If he moves as you return put the treat back **before** replacing him exactly where he was before.

- If he hasn't moved by the time you reach him give him the treat.
- Pick up the lead and give him your "Heel" or "Close" command. If he moves before you can do this ask him to "Sit" or "Down" again.
- Walk to a different position the same distance from the stool and repeat the exercise.
- Gradually increase the distance you place the dog from the stool until he is far enough away for you to drop the lead.
- When the dog is steady and understands what he has to do to get the reward you can take the lead off and, initially, leave it on the ground near him.
- Practice in lots of different places and, after a while put the food on different surfaces rather than using the stool all the time.
- After very few training sessions your dog will understand what is expected and you can start to leave him for longer periods, go out of sight sometimes, and once in a while call him instead of always returning to him.
- Once he reaches this stage you can dispense with the visible reward (the stool or whatever else you have been putting the food on) and simply reward from your pocket when you return to him.
- Don't call him in the early stages, as this will unsettle him.
- Never get cross, no matter how long each stage takes. You are teaching him **how to get the reward**, not telling him off if he gets it wrong! The 'punishment', if you want to call it that, is the withholding of the treat.
- When you are ready to progress to 'out of sight stays' it would be a good idea to return to using the stool. Now it will be essential to have a person who can watch the dog from a distance and let you know if he moves so that you know when to return and reposition him.
- When you feel the dog is confident enough to be 'recalled' from his 'stays' remember to do it randomly. In other words, don't call him to you every time otherwise he will start to pre-empt you and his stays will become rocky.

TAKE AND LEAVE

This exercise is to reinforce your status as pack leader, by the giving and taking of food. It also teaches the dog to release an article on command and to take one only when you tell him to. It will also teach him that the word "Leave" means "stop what you are doing and come to me for a reward" so it can be used to prevent your dog eating something harmful on a walk, bothering people or other dogs and stealing your possessions!

"Leave" is the **only** word you should ever use with a firm voice, so make the most of it!
You do **not** need your clicker for this exercise.

- You will need a pile of small tit-bits and one bigger one.
- Sit your dog facing you.
- Offer your dog a small tit-bit saying, "Take it" in a soft voice, followed by verbal praise.
- Do this four or five times.

- Now you need good reflexes! Try to put the **big** tit-bit on the floor. Say **absolutely nothing** until the dog attempts to take the food.

- Snatch the tit-bit away and, as you do, say, "Leave", in a **firm** but not harsh voice **before** the dog touches the food.
- Do not say, "leave" as you put the food down—it is not a command until the dog has learned what it means! Saying, "leave" as you **remove** the food teaches the dog to associate the word with the loss of the reward if he doesn't stop what he is doing at the time.
- The dog may sniff around the floor looking for the tit-bit so wait until he is paying attention again. Then repeat the process of putting the food on the floor and snatching it away, saying "leave" at the same time as you remove the food.

- **As soon as** the dog stops trying to get the tit-bit give him another one from your **other** hand or the table and say "Take it". **Do not give the one off the floor.**
- This teaches the dog that he will be rewarded for not attempting to grab the food whilst learning that "leave" means "stop what you are doing and come to me to be rewarded for stopping".
- Repeat several times.
- When the dog makes no attempt to touch the food as you put it on the floor you should say "Good leave" in a **nice** voice before giving him the reward and saying, "Take it".
- Practise in lots of different places both inside and outside until the dog makes no attempt to take the food from the floor no matter where you are.
- Now you can practise using the word in everyday situations.
- Nonchalantly drop something interesting, such as a tissue or empty crisp packet, as you walk across the room.
- **As soon as** the dog approaches the item say, "Leave" in a **very** firm voice.
- **The second** the dog looks at you praise him and call him to you in a really nice voice.
- 'Click&treat'.
- Repeat with ever more interesting distractions until he is reliable in every situation.

WATCH

This is a very useful word to teach your dog as it can be used to attract or distract your dog's attention in many situations. It is useful in the show ring when the dog is being presented to the judge; it can be used to ask the dog to look at you instead of something he would prefer to bark at or pull towards when out on the lead; you can also use it to get his attention during training when you want him to concentrate.

- Have your dog in front of you, on the lead, in a place with no distractions.
- Hold a tit-bit in your right hand and the clicker and lead in your left.
- Hold the tit-bit close to the dog's nose.

- Bring your hand up towards your eyes so that he looks up at you.
- Look through your fingers (of the hand holding the food) at the dog.
- As soon as he looks into your face say "Watch!", 'click&treat'.
- Say "Watch!" in a whispery, hissy sort of voice!
- Only say the word and reward him if you have eye contact. If the dog has looked away try again.
- Be careful not to lower your hand until after you have clicked otherwise he may be looking at the food instead. You are rewarding **eye contact,** not "gimme"!
- Repeat in lots of different places, gradually increasing the distractions.

- We don't want the dog to learn that "Watch" is a new word for "Sit" so encourage him to do this exercise when he his standing, lying down and walking as well as sitting!
- Practice often until the dog looks at you as soon as you say the word.
- Once you are sure the dog understands the word as a cue, click at the end of longer periods of eye contact. Eventually, he should look at you for as long as you want him to, no matter what the distractions.
- Use the word to distract the dog in difficult situations.

RETRIEVE

Spanish Water dogs are natural 'retrievers' and love to carry things around so getting them to want to pick items up is not usually a problem. Teaching them to actually come and give them to you can be a different matter altogether! The best way to teach a reliable, solid retrieve is something called 'back-chaining'. This means teaching the **end** of the behaviour first. For example, if the dog learns that a word you have chosen, such as 'hold' means that he sits in front of you with the retrieve item in his mouth, that will be his **picture** of 'hold'. If you then toss the item a little way away and say 'hold' what would you expect him to do in order to achieve his picture of 'hold'? Yes, that's right, run and fetch it then sit in front of you with it in his mouth! Clever dog! In this way you never have to teach the actual retrieve—just the presenting of the item. The word you use is unimportant as long as it is a word you feel comfortable using in retrieving situations. If you prefer, you could use 'fetch' or 'give', it is entirely up to you. Use an item the dog likes to hold but **not** one of **his** toys. I shall refer to the item as a dummy for ease of writing!

Teaching Basic Retrieve

- Organise yourself with the clicker in one hand, the dummy in the other and plenty of treats within easy reach.
- Ask the dog to sit in front of you. Do **not** 'click&treat' the sit.
- Hold the dummy in front of his nose and wait for him to touch it. 'Click&treat'. You must **not** say your chosen word yet but you can give some verbal reward and encouragement.
- Repeat several times.
- Once the dog is confidently touching the dummy withhold the 'click&treat' until, in frustration, he opens his mouth a little around the dummy then 'click&treat'.
- Repeat several times.
- Once the dog is happily putting his mouth around the dummy wait until he actually holds it before you 'click&treat'.

- As you click he will let go of the dummy to take the treat. This is quite all right.
- Do not let go of the dummy yourself at this stage.
- Once the dog is holding the dummy without mouthing (chewing) it for a couple of seconds you can begin to let go of it.
- If at any point he gets up, spits the dummy out or mouths it simply take it from him, withhold the reward and quietly start again.
- Do **not** get cross with him at any time.

- When the dog is calmly holding the dummy for several seconds you can introduce your chosen cue word just **before** you 'click&treat'.
- Gradually extend the length of time he will hold it before you 'click&treat'.
- Practice in lots of different places.
- Eventually, when the dog understands the cue word to 'hold' you can also ask him to let go of the dummy by saying 'leave' (or whatever your word is for this) in between the click and the treat.

- Once you are confident he knows what to do, place or throw the dummy a little way (not far) and say your cue word.

- In order to fulfil his 'picture' of your cue word the dog will have to fetch the dummy!

- As soon as he sits in front of you say your 'hold' word then, when you are ready, say your 'leave' word, take the dummy from him and 'click&treat'.
- Gradually phase out the clicker over a period of time.
- If ever the dog starts to mess around go back to basics.

Directional retrieving and hidden retrieves are beyond the scope of this book. Once you and your dog have mastered the basic retrieve you will be able to seek out a trainer in your chosen field if you wish to progress further. Gundog and water training are two areas where you will need to extend your dog's retrieving ability.

SIT TO GREET

When your dog meets people in the street or the park etc. it is vital that he learns that pulling on the lead or jumping up to say "Hello" doesn't work. If your dog is unhappy or unpredictable with people it is essential that he learns these situations are rewarding as long as he is sociable and well-behaved and 'Saying Hello' may be more appropriate to begin with. If you intend to show your dog it would be advisable to teach him to 'Stand to greet', as this will prepare him for examination by the Judge.

To teach your dog that good manners pay off you should teach him that sitting quietly is the only way to get what he wants:

- First, you must c**ontrol the person.** This can be easier said than done! Ask them to ignore the dog and not give him any eye contact.
- Ask the dog to sit.

- Give the person a treat in view of the dog so that he knows it is **your** treat. This will prevent him believing that people carry food and are therefore worth mugging!
- Ask the person to give the treat to the dog, **after** you have clicked. You may need to explain what the clicker is.

- If the dog is still sitting, click and allow the person to give him the treat.
- If the dog has moved **start again,** don't let the person give the treat.
- If the dog is likely to bite, ask the person not to bend over at all as this will be perceived as 'aggressive' by the dog. Ask them to drop the treat on the floor in front of him. (See "Saying Hello")
- If the dog is afraid or unfriendly make sure the person does not stare, raise their hands or try to stroke him. (See "Saying Hello")
- If the dog is friendly invite the person to stroke him under the chin or on the chest. Don't allow them to rub his ears, as this will over-excite him!
- If the dog gets up, lifts a paw or starts to jump up ask the person to wait for him to sit quietly again before continuing to stroke him. 'Click&treat' as appropriate.
- Repeat with as many people as possible every day.

SAYING HELLO

If your dog is fearful or apprehensive when he meets people in the street or the park etc. it is vital that he learns that showing fear or backing off doesn't work. You should never reassure him for this type of behaviour, as you would be rewarding him for it and ensuring that it gets worse! If your dog is unhappy or unpredictable with people it is essential that he learns these situations are rewarding as long as he is confident, sociable and well behaved.

- Speak to the person first. Ask them not to look at the dog or bend over him. Bending is 'aggressive' to a fearful dog. Please stress that they **must not** try to stroke the dog.

- If the dog will not approach freely **lure** him towards the person with the food. You may need **very** high value treats for this, such as cheese, chicken, ham or fish.

- Give the person a treat so the dog can see that you have given it to them. This will stop him mugging people for food later when he has gained confidence.
- At **no** stage should the dog be cajoled, forced or reprimanded.
- As the dog **approaches,** click.

- Ask the person to give the treat, (or drop it on the ground if the dog can't cope with them bending) as he approaches, **after** you have clicked.
- If the dog has moved away or backed off, start again. **Don't** click **or** let the person give the treat.
- If the dog barks at any point completely ignore him and persuade the person to stand still with their head turned away. Turning the head is calming and non-aggressive. Ask them not to turn their body.

103

- As your dog becomes more relaxed and confident you can start to say a greeting word, such as "hello", in a really nice, soft, upbeat voice, as he is about to take the food from the hand. Remember to click just **before** he takes the food.
- If your dog is likely to bite, **always** ask the person to drop the treat on the floor in front of him. Ask the person not to give the dog eye contact.
- When your dog is happy, and confidently approaches people, you can begin to ask him to 'sit' before clicking and allowing the person to reward him. Sooner or later they will be able to stroke him. When that time comes you can dispense with the clicker!
- Repeat with as many people as possible every day, but only people you can trust to behave!
- It is possible that once the dog is confident he may try to manipulate people and become 'bossy'! He is Spanish, after all! If so, return to 'Sit To Greet'.

GOODY JAR

If your dog has a problem with visitors due either to over-exuberance or fear, the Goody Jar is an effective, non-confrontational way of teaching him that he will be **rewarded by the visitor** for good, quiet behaviour. Most Spanish love visitors and want to leap all over them, asking them to play! Some are less comfortable with people entering the house. **All** of them may guard in certain circumstances. Control of the dog when people enter the house is essential. The Goody Jar is a visual cue that tells the dog he needs to think about his behaviour in order to obtain the reward. It also tells him that it is **you** making it possible for the visitor give the reward, not him. Treats from the Goody Jar should not be used for any other form of training. The Goody Jar is reserved **solely** for visitors.

Follow these steps to teach him a new pattern of behaviour:
- Put some small, tasty treats (**not** his normal food but something of greater value to the dog) into a small pot or jar that has a lid. Place your clicker on or near the Goody Jar.
- Keep the Goody Jar as near to the front door as you can.
- Divide your visitors into two categories: people he knows and is comfortable with and those he doesn't know or is afraid of. This is especially important if your dog is likely to bite a stranger.
- The first group can meet the dog in the doorway.
- The second group should be brought into the house and instructed on how to use the Goody Jar while the dog is kept outside or in another room. You may need a child gate to give nervous visitors confidence.
- Hand the Goody Jar to the visitor and ask them to completely ignore the dog by folding their arms and turning their head away from him. Make sure you tell them not to turn their body or the dog will be confused and, if he is friendly will jump up or, if afraid, might nip!
- If your dog is afraid it is vital for the visitor to understand that eye contact and bending towards the dog will imply a threat and may result in a bout of barking or, in extreme circumstances, a bite.
- Once the visitor has the Goody Jar **you** ask the dog, very nicely, in a soft voice, to "Sit". **Don't** ask for a "Down" as this may make the dog feel vulnerable.
- Once the dog is sitting quietly 'click' and allow the visitor to drop a treat from the Goody Jar onto the floor near the dog. **Don't** allow them to bend and give it to him at this stage.

- If the dog will not respond when you ask for the sit don't argue with him! Take the Goody Jar away from the visitor and put it down. Try again after a few seconds.
- Gradually, as the dog realises what the Goody Jar means, his behaviour will improve and eventually become automatic. As his confidence grows you can allow the visitor to hand the treat to the dog or even ask for the 'sit' themselves. Don't rush to do this, as it will involve eye contact that your dog may not be ready for. However, be careful about allowing them to use the clicker in case their timing is off.
- Don't allow visitors to give their own food as this may teach your dog to 'mug' them!

Eventually you should be able to phase out the Goody Jar once your dog has learned that visitors do not present a problem for him or, in the case of 'bossy' individuals, are not on this earth to entertain him!

CORRECTION

Throughout this book emphasis is constantly placed upon kind, reward based, motivational training with no punishment. Frequent reference is made to the sensitivity of the Breed and also to the manipulative, bossy side of the character. An interesting mix! You may be wondering what to do if your mature, **trained** Spanish Water Dog is really being a so-and-so and steadfastly ignoring you or choosing to do his own thing. How do you correct this whilst complying with the theory of non-punitive training? There is **no** excuse for 'punishing' a dog during training. Punishment will **not** help him to learn. However, all a **trained** dog needs is a sharp change of voice tone, a fierce look or the lead being put on and the dog excluded for a while. A **properly** trained dog knows what is expected of him so it is perfectly reasonable to let him know if you are displeased as long as he knows what he has done wrong. More than three seconds after the event is **too late.**

TRAINING AIDS

There is such a myriad of dog-related equipment available these days, particularly on the Internet, that it is not possible to cover everything. What follows is a guide to the best and the worst of the most commonly used training aids. They are listed in alphabetical order, **not** order of importance!

Anti-bark collar

This is a battery driven anti-barking device that relies on a microphone lying against the dog's throat to activate it. It ejects a squirt of either odourless or lemon-scented spray in front of the dog every time he barks. In theory it is not a bad idea providing the reason for the barking is known and preventing it will not cause distress to the dog. In practice, it is useless in a multi-dog environment because it is likely to be activated by a neighbouring dog. It also tends to react to a dog that shakes its head in response to the first spray so the unfortunate animal is then squirted for shaking its head! It can also be activated by mobile phones.

Calming band

This is a very useful piece of equipment that can help with barking problems, stress and aggression. It is worn on the head and consists of a webbing strap round the neck and an elasticated band that sits over the nose. It is not designed to be used as a muzzle or to keep the mouth closed. It is based on the Tellington Touch principle that while a dog is thinking about what is happening on an area of his body he cannot think about whatever is worrying him. It is kind, effective and easy to use. Some breeds respond better than others and the Spanish reacts remarkably well, especially where barking is concerned.

Calming t-shirt and body wrap

These, too, are innovations from the Tellington Touch stable and can be very useful. Once again, the concept is one of kind, comforting distraction with an added calming effect. The t-shirt is self-explanatory. The body wrap is a little like a soft, broad bandage that fits around the dog's body in a figure of eight fashion. They are worth considering for dogs that lack confidence.

Choke chains

These are, unfortunately, still readily available, even in such 'enlightened' times. They are both harmful and unnecessary. Need I say more?

Clickers

The use of clickers has been covered fairly exhaustively throughout this book. Suffice to say that they are readily and, usually, cheaply available in many forms wherever you care to look. They are produced in many variations from the original box with a metal tongue through to digital versions that make a variety of sounds. Some have a switch to vary the volume and there are those that have a plastic button which can be much easier to use for people with arthritis or who are wearing gloves. There are many, many books on the subject of clicker training, the best of which are listed at the back of this book.

Collars

The main concerns when choosing a collar for your dog are his comfort and the length of his coat. A great many collars will damage or matte a longer coat. A plain, flat, buckle collar is all that is normally required but, if leather, it needs to be of the highest quality. Once 'worn in' it will serve well and should last a lifetime. The same would apply to rolled leather collars. Be aware that in some cheaper leathers the dye may run and stain a white coat, which can be quite unsightly. Some webbing collars tend to 'grab' the coat and spoil it as it gets longer, the quality and texture of the webbing is the key. The smoother it is the better it will be. Ideally, once a Spanish Water Dog has a long coat he should not wear a collar but, in a public place, a dog must wear a collar with an identification tag to conform to the Law. Occasionally one can come across collars made from flat curb chain, especially in Spain. As long as it is a fixed collar and not a choke chain this can be an ideal choice since it tends not to ruin the coat. However, it can stain a white coat black, so beware!

Electric or Shock collars

There is, at the present time, a movement afoot to get these collars banned in the United Kingdom but at the time of writing they are, unfortunately, both legal and available. There is no justifiable reason to use an electric collar on a dog, no matter what the problem, because the harm that can be caused may well outweigh any short-term 'benefits'. If used on an aggressive dog the aggression will almost certainly become worse. If used on a fearful or nervous dog that dog may well **become** aggressive. As a cure for sheep chasing etc. they rarely work because the thrill of the chase is usually strong enough to outweigh the pain of the collar. It is a poor trainer, in my opinion, who feels the need to resort to this type of barbaric, outdated equipment.

Harnesses

The range and variety of harnesses is enormous and selection will depend on the reason for needing one. If a harness is required to help in teaching a dog not to pull the best one to chose is the 'Kumfi Stop-pull' which is comfortable and effective. A 'Kumfi' harness is the best training aid for dealing with dog-to-dog aggression as it gives complete control whilst allowing the dog to feel safe, and still have the freedom to use his head and neck for communication. For water training there are many harnesses that will suffice, the best of which would be a slightly longer harness with two body straps for comfort and a handle for lifting the dog out of the water. If training for flyball advice should be sought from the trainer.

Head collars

There are several types of head collar that are worth considering for dogs that have learned to pull, are dog aggressive or have an injury that prevents the use of a collar or harness. Finding the one that will fit your dog best is a matter of trial and error. What is comfortable for one dog may not be for another, depending on head shape and coat length. The head collar must fit so that the nose-band does not rub the eyes, usually an inch beneath them is ideal. Some head collars tighten uncomfortably if the dog pulls backwards so it would be wise to consider the problem you are trying to cure and try different designs.

Leads

If you are using a collar your choice of lead will depend on your taste to a great extent! All I would suggest is that it should **not** be made of chain and should be around four feet in length. Longer leads are available for training purposes, with varying places to attach the hook so that you can vary the length. Retractable leads have their uses for dogs that cannot be let off the lead but they are potentially dangerous when used in public places and should be viewed with caution. They also teach dogs to pull! Slip leads, usually made of rope but, sometimes, leather are great if you have a well trained dog who needs to work without a collar. There is, however, a right and a wrong way to put them on so please seek advice before using one if you have no experience of them. For the show ring you could choose an all-in-one nylon or rolled leather lead that has a sliding adjustor to vary the size of the loop around the neck.

Remote Control Spray Training Collar

This is generally accepted as the 'humane' alternative to the electric collar. It is battery operated and remotely controlled by the handler. When activated, it squirts a jet of either odourless or 'citronella' spray in front of the dog in an attempt to 'interrupt' the behaviour. If used correctly it is indeed effective in curing certain problems but to be 'humane' the dog **must** understand what it is being used for. It must be used with care and the timing of the handler is paramount. If used willy-nilly without thought for what the dog is being expected to learn it could prove just as inhumane as one that causes pain. It should not be used for anything other than the curing of unacceptable behaviours that occur at a distance from the handler.

Pinch or Prong collars

To the best of my knowledge these types of 'collar' are illegal in the United Kingdom but I mention them because they are very popular in the United States and can probably be obtained on the Internet. They have sharp or not-so-sharp prongs on the inside that, when the collar is tightened, press into the dog's neck, causing varying degrees of pain or discomfort. I hope that no one who is reading this book would consider such an instrument of torture as a shortcut when all that is required is correct training.

Poo Bags

These are an essential part of every dog owner's kit! In this day and age of anti-dog propaganda it behoves each and every one of us to show that we are responsible and will always have the wherewithal to clean up after our dogs.

Rewards

Most dogs will work for food. You need to choose a treat that is tasty and valuable to the dog but is not going to fill him up or make him fat. One of the best, I find, is 'Puffed Jerky', which is dried lamb's lung. Sounds awful, I know, but most dogs love it. It is far better to use in quantity than liver because it has little or no food value, and no vitamins, whereas liver is full of vitamins A and D which are stored by the dog's own liver and are harmful if taken in excess. There are so many commercial food rewards available that it would be impossible to list all the good ones. However, James Wellbeloved make two worth mentioning: Crackerjacks and Minijacks. I would advise against the use of 'biscuit' treats as these are fattening, 'heating' and boring to the dog! Always check the ingredients on commercial treats to see what you are putting into your dog. Keep treats as natural as possible.

Training Discs

These little brass 'cymbal-like' discs, held together by a ring and attached to a red loop, are designed to 'interrupt' or 'cure' certain behaviours that happen when the handler is at a distance or out of sight. They are not missiles that can be thrown at the dog any old time it does something wrong! A dog needs to be properly 'conditioned', according to the instructions in the booklet that comes with them, so that it understands that a tiny 'chink' of the discs tells him to stop what he is doing in order to be rewarded. The booklet must be read and followed carefully. As with any 'interruptive' training aid it is essential that the dog understands what his options are.

Treat Bags

Some sort of clip-on or belted container for all your training equipment can be very useful and the choice is endless. However, please bear in mind that it will be a signal to your dog that he is 'working'. If you always use one during training sessions but not at other times your dog may refuse to believe that 'work' happens all the time, but only when the treat bag is evident!

Whistles

The best type of whistle is the gundog whistle, either 210½ or 211. I suggest you avoid the 'blaster' type that has a pea inside as it is not so clear over a great distance and, in my opinion, the 'silent' whistle often found in pet shops is worse than useless. If you have a whistle you will also need a lanyard to hang it around your neck but, to be honest, a boot lace or bit of string will do just as well.

With basic training firmly in place the world is your oyster when progressing to other activities that Spanish Water Dogs so enjoy. In his youth Miguel had issues that were dealt with successfully because of the training regime which had been established early on.

13 PROBLEM SOLVING

Many of the normal everyday problems that you may encounter as you live and work with your Spanish Water Dog are referred to and have solutions offered elsewhere throughout this book, especially those associated with the troublesome 'teenage period'. There are, however, one or two particular issues that require much deeper understanding in order to reduce their impact.

BARKING AT HOME

First of all you need to consider why your dog is barking. Some barking is acceptable, even desirable, but barking for no reason is definitely not called for! Barking because someone is at the door is probably desired behaviour, as long as it stops when you want it to. Barking at passers-by, neighbours on their own property or birds flying through your garden is not legitimate 'guarding'. It is not only a nuisance but is potentially a cause for complaints against your dog.

If you shout at your dog when he is barking inappropriately he will believe that you, as a pack member, are joining in and backing him up. He will not learn anything positive but will, in fact, probably bark all the more because his behaviour is being reinforced! Instead, stay calm, ignore him completely and wait for him to stop. Once he is quiet make a soft 'shushing' sound, tell him he's good and 'click&treat' or reward in some other way, but quietly. Repeat this pattern every time he barks unnecessarily until he learns to associate the 'shush' sound with being quiet. You will then be able to use it as a cue to stop barking. Because it is a sound rather than a word he will not think that you are barking too!

If the barking is excessive and it is not possible to ignore it this could be a job for the 'Training Discs' mentioned in Chapter 12, TRAINING. It must be stressed that training discs are not intended to be thrown at the dog willy-nilly. You must read and thoroughly understand the 'conditioning' instructions before trying to use them. They are not meant to frighten the dog but to tell him that he should stop what he is doing in order to be rewarded. The reward may be actual or it could be that the discs are not thrown, depending upon the circumstances.

BARKING IN PUBLIC

There are two aspects of barking in public places that can be problematic: **on** the lead at dogs, passers-by, traffic etc. and **off** the lead when it may or may not involve 'herding' behaviour.

On the lead

Dogs may bark on the lead because they are excited, frightened or because their barking has been accidentally reinforced. If barking is ignored and quiet behaviour is rewarded from the very beginning the problem should never escalate. If a dog grows up realising that barking doesn't pay off in any way he will never bark excessively. Certainly he may bark when startled or worried but if he is ignored as usual he will realise it is more effective to stop! If he has been taught the 'shush' sound when barking in the home you will be able to use it to ask him to be quiet when he is outside.

   Teach your dog to be calm when having the lead put on and leaving the house. See Lead Walking, Chapter 12. This will help to prevent barking caused by over-excitement. Teach him to "Watch", also in Chapter 12, TRAINING, so that you can reward him for looking at you instead of what he is barking at. Any punishment or yanking on the lead will only serve to 'fix' the barking behaviour and will never cure it. If the barking is due to fear or apprehension turning around, walking in the opposite direction and asking for "Watch" may work very well. Allowing the person or dog that your dog is barking at to walk away will reinforce the idea that barking 'drives way' the problem. If your dog is barking at someone you are trying to have a conversation with ask them to avoid eye contact and **both** of you ignore him. When the barking has stopped use "Say Hello", Chapter 12, TRAINING. **Never** stroke, speak to or reassure a dog that is barking through fear. **Never** get cross, either!

Off the lead

Barking that occurs when a dog is off the lead is potentially dangerous because he could be described as being 'dangerously out of control', especially if the subject of his attentions is a child. Do not let your dog run loose in a public place until you have developed a strong, reliable recall. Make sure that he has learnt 'Leave' and that he knows for certain that when he returns to you he has done the right thing!

   If your dog has already developed a desire to charge up to people or dogs barking his head off, and your training is all to no avail then you may need to use training discs. Timing is of the essence and the dog **must** understand why the discs are being used. Please don't wait until he has reached whatever or whoever he is barking at. As soon as he starts to rush in or bark tell him to "Leave" and, if you get no response immediately rattle the discs. At the moment that he hesitates call him, in your best, most inviting voice, then 'click&treat' when he arrives. If, on the other hand, he should ignore the rattle of the discs you must throw them between him and his 'target' or, if really necessary, **at** him. Once again, if he halts momentarily, call him and reward him for responding. You will realise from this that you should not let an unreliable dog get too far away from you!

   Occasionally this type of behaviour can be too difficult to cure with training discs and, if this is the case you may need to use a Remote Control Spray Collar. The signals given to the dog before activating the collar should be the same as if you were using discs. Timing is paramount. Be very careful never to activate the collar once the dog is looking at you or he will be totally confused and will not know where he should go to be safe. Although situations like this can be very worrying and embarrassing you must **never** be cross with your dog if he has returned to you.

"Who needs sunglasses when you have a fringe like mine?"

"Mind you, if it wasn't for the fringe the dumbbell wouldn't need to be bright orange!"

STEALING

Spanish Water Dogs are agile, intelligent and resourceful. Many of them make successful thieves! Trying to punish or correct stealing after the event is pointless and cruel. Lying in wait and punishing at the time will prevent future theft occurring in the owner's presence but will not cure the problem permanently. The culprit will simply become more careful!

PREVENTING THEFT

This method of teaching a dog not to steal is effective because the punishment occurs **at the moment** the 'crime' is being committed, rather than afterwards, as would be the case if you told the dog off. Also, reprimanding the dog yourself will confuse and upset him as he will become frightened of you entering the room and will not actually be learning what you want him to learn.

- First of all, collect together a large quantity of empty aluminium cans, such as Coke cans, place several small stones inside each one and seal the hole. Alternatively, if your dog has already been conditioned to training discs you can use those in the same way.
- Make sure the dog is **not** in the room when you set the trap.
- Place a piece of food on the work surface, or wherever the dog is stealing from. Tie the cans together with string and attach the end of the string to the food bait so that when the dog grabs the food he brings the cans crashing down!
- Once the bait is set let the dog into the kitchen (or wherever) and then **leave the room.** It is vital that you are not present when the cans come clattering down, as the dog must think that he has been 'punished' by his own actions. It is an **Act of God** and must not be associated with you in any way.
- Throughout the whole proceedings you should **ignore** the dog completely, even if he comes running out of the room and straight to you for reassurance.
- It should only be necessary to do the booby-trapping once in each place to affect a cure, but if the dog is particularly persistent or there are several places from which he steals, you may have to repeat it a few times. For example, in a large kitchen you may need to booby trap several different areas of work surface. You will probably need to disguise the cans so that the dog does not realise what is happening. A tea towel or plastic carrier bag should do the trick!
- Variations of this method can be applied to anything the dog is stealing from, such as the rubbish bin (by stacking the cans on the work surface above and attaching the string to the lid of the bin) and the fridge (by attaching a piece of string to the cans and the door handle).
- **Please** make sure that when you tidy the cans away afterwards you do not make a noise with them or the dog will react at a time when he is doing nothing wrong and the point of the exercise will be lost. He must **never** hear them if he is doing nothing wrong.

CHASING AND HERDING

This type of behaviour, which is perfectly natural to the Spanish Water Dog, can be a problem, especially during adolescence. Dogs that have a desire to 'herd' or 'chase' hardwired into their psyche will suffer greatly if the behaviour is 'trained out' by punishment and nothing is put in its place. Imagine that you love jogging. In fact you are addicted to it and if you can't go out for some reason you feel awful. It may not be jogging, of course, it could be dancing, reading, eating chocolate or even smoking! How would you feel if someone 'punished' you to stop you doing it? Wouldn't you feel awful? Wouldn't you want something equally rewarding to do instead? So does your dog. If your dog is chasing or herding because it is in his genes he has a **need** to perform the behaviour. Preventing it without offering an alternative that is of equal value is not only pointless but could actually be cruel. Jogging makes a jogger 'feel good'. Herding makes a dog of a herding breed 'feel good', too. Punishment will not prevent the behaviour; the dog will simply find a way around the problem. Herding people makes the dog feel good. Punishment makes the dog feel bad. Being caught is the problem. Herd people, avoid owner. Simple!

If a puppy is suitably trained and stimulated from an early age there should never be a problem. Teach good recall. Teach 'Leave'. Teach constructive play and a good, solid retrieve. Easy! What to do if the problem already exists? That is another story altogether.

So you want to chase? Chase this!

First of all you should make yourself more important than the dog by following 'A Dog is a Dog' in Chapter 7, EARLY DAYS. Go back to basic training and reinforce sit, down and recall with a really high value reward. Teach the dog that you have control of the good things in life, such as toys and food, and that he has to **earn** them. Let him know that nothing comes for free! Develop a really good retrieve in places with **no** distractions. Make sure that the chosen retrieve item is **yours** and that the dog only sees it when you bring it out. Be sure that he will **always** give it to you when you ask.

Once you have these things in place you can begin to offer an alternative to the dog's chosen pastime. You need to teach the dog a word that he will associate with having more fun chasing your chosen item than he does herding people or chasing sheep or rabbits.

Train new 'chase this' word

Choose a word that you have never used before and one that you can call easily in an exciting voice. I shall call it the 'chase' word but that does not mean that I am suggesting what the word should be! It will be a word that the dog associates with the arrival of his favourite toy. **He will not have to earn this toy while you are teaching the word.** He will learn that as soon as he hears the 'chase' word he will be allowed to chase the favourite toy. In play situations, every time the dog **looks** at you show him the toy, say the 'chase' word and throw the toy. After a few repetitions the dog should recognise the word and associate it with the toy.

In the unlikely event that your dog is not interested in toys you could try making it more exciting: soak a tennis ball or a rolled up sock in gravy, attach it to a string if necessary so you can make it move erratically. If your dog is obsessed with birds you might use a shuttlecock, but make it smell strongly of something else such as cheese or aniseed so that he doesn't think it is actually a bird! Eventually you are going to need **two** identical versions of this favourite toy; more on that later.

Train chase recall

This exercise will teach your dog to come back to you when he is **already** chasing something. It must be carried out in a place with no distractions that has no connection with anything the dog has enjoyed chasing previously.

• Select two of **your** toys, including the favourite one mentioned above. Throw the less important toy.

• As soon as he starts to chase it call the 'chase' word and throw the favourite toy in the other direction.

• Play with him with the favourite toy and make it **really** exciting and fun.

- In the early stages you may need a second person who will pick up the thrown (less important) toy before the dog reaches it if he has not responded to you calling the 'chase' word.
- Repeat until you can wait a couple of seconds before saying the 'chase' word, in other words until the dog is closer to the thrown toy, but he still responds by turning to chase the favourite toy.
- You may, once you are getting a positive reaction every time, try throwing a more interesting toy but still using the favourite toy as the reward.

Now you will need two **identical** favourite toys. You are going to teach the dog that no matter how interesting his chosen 'prey' is he will still get a wonderful game with his favourite toy if he responds to the 'chase' word and stops chasing.

- Throw the favourite toy a long way.
- When it stops moving release the dog **without a command,** just your release word. This is **not** a retrieve exercise!
- Immediately call the 'chase' word.
- Throw the second favourite toy in the other direction.
- Play enthusiastically with the dog and the second favourite toy.
- Eventually you will be able to progress to releasing the dog while the first toy is still moving.

When you feel sure that the 'chase' word has become really important to the dog and he is reacting reliably by turning to chase the favourite toy instead, you can progress to using it in a 'real life' situation. Don't make it too difficult to begin with. Choose a place where your dog has chased before but at a time when there isn't actually anything to chase! Practice the exercise in that situation until the response is reliable.

Now you will need to work when the 'prey' is visible. To begin with the dog must be on a long line so that he cannot possibly succeed in chasing his previously chosen 'prey'. Within sight of the 'prey', but not too close, call out your 'chase' word and throw the favourite toy in the opposite direction. Play **really** enthusiastically if the dog responds. Gradually work closer to the 'prey' but don't overdo it too quickly or all your hard work will be wasted if the dog decides that the favourite toy is no longer exciting enough. If he doesn't respond use the line to bring him to you and repeat the exercise at a greater distance from the chosen 'prey'.

If, after weeks of work, you have not succeeded in convincing your dog that chasing and playing with the favourite toy is preferable to the old chosen 'prey' you will need to introduce aversion to the 'prey'. This is a subject that needs to be fully understood and approached with caution. It is not possible to cover this type of training in a book. Expert advice should be sought but I would like to stress that it **must never** involve the use of an electric collar.

NEUTERING

A great many people see neutering as the cure for all manner of problems. Sometimes it can be of help; often it makes no difference whatsoever.

Castrating males

If castration is being considered for purely 'social' reasons, i.e. to prevent unwanted pregnancy, straying, leg lifting and territorial marking, the only question is when to present the dog for the operation. It has been a widely held belief for many, many years that castration should be carried out at around twelve months of age so that the dog has reached his full growth potential. Unfortunately, from a behavioural point of view, this could be erroneous as, at around a year old, a young male is at the peak of his testosterone production. Sometimes dogs that are castrated at this age remain hormonally driven thugs for the rest of their lives. Castration **before** this time, at around seven months, normally results in the dog failing to attain this level of sexual maturity, never learning to lift his leg and never becoming a 'lager lout'. However, early castration does carry with it a possibly undesirable side effect in that other males frequently think that the dog in question is female. Early castration may certainly prevent 'sexual dominance' or 'sexual aggression' (two very different things!) towards other males, which can be very useful for a dog that lives in a highly social environment. It will normally prevent leg lifting and other territorial behaviour. Should you not wish to castrate early it may be wise to wait until after puberty and castrate when the dog has reached sexual and mental maturity, usually around eighteen months of age. The veterinary profession are in no doubt that castration reduces the risk of prostate cancer in later life and, without wishing to state the obvious, it will prevent testicular cancer, which is a common cause of death in many older dogs.

Castration performed to 'solve' such problems as wild and unruly behaviour, 'dog to dog' aggression or aggression towards people is much less likely to be affective. Destruction of the home and separation problems almost never benefit from castration. These types of problems are much more likely to be 'learned' behaviour or result from lack of social skills and adequate training and, as such, will be unaffected by clinical castration. Discussion with a behaviour counsellor would be a much better route to take.

If a dog is 'cryptorchid', i.e. having one or both testicles retained within the body cavity, castration would be considered essential to prevent the retained testicles becoming cancerous at a later stage in the dog's life. This problem is inherited so breeding from such a dog would be out of the question.

If castration is being considered in an attempt to cure hierarchy problems between two males great care must be taken to assess which dog should be neutered. Castrating both dogs will **never** work. There is no such thing as 'equality' in the dog world. It is essential to castrate the **lower** ranking dog to widen the gap between the two, thus allowing the higher-ranking dog to take over the top spot. If there is some doubt as to the status of the two dogs it might be advisable to 'test' which is the lower ranking dog by asking your Vet to prescribe a drug that simulates castration to the dog that you **think** is the right one. If you are wrong very little harm will be done, as the effects will wear off after a few weeks.

Spaying females

Generally bitches are only neutered to prevent them having puppies, although the mess and inconvenience associated with their 'seasons' is a consideration to some owners. Again, the question of when to perform the operation will provoke varied responses. Until a few years ago it was always considered essential to allow a bitch to have her first 'season' but many Vets today prefer to spay before that time. Early spaying has been shown to drastically reduce the likelihood of mammary tumours later on in life and, of course, it completely removes the risk of pyometra, which is a serious threat to a great many bitches of all ages and is often fatal. Take advice from your vet.

Spaying may also be considered where there are hierarchy problems but, as with males, it is essential to spay the lower ranking bitch so caution is advised when deciding on surgery.

Early spaying does carry a small risk that the bitch may suffer from urinary incontinence but as this condition is easily treated it should not be cause for too much concern. Discussion with your Vet should put everything into perspective.

Anaesthetics

Modern anaesthetics are very much safer than their predecessors but there is always a small risk so discuss this with your Vet. Something that **must** be addressed beforehand is the type of anaesthetic to use. It has been shown that some Spanish Water Dogs, especially those that are extremely fit and competitive, have a very high muscle to fat ratio, which puts them at risk if a barbiturate type of anaesthetic is used. It may be necessary to explain to your Vet that this breed can sometimes react in the same way as greyhounds and lurchers. If a dog has very little body fat and a high muscle mass the barbiturate will not leave the body as quickly as it should, resulting in a delay in the recovery process.

TRAVEL SICKNESS

"Are we there yet, Mum?"

Dogs suffer from car-sickness for a variety of reasons, but the most common one is association of the car with unpleasant experiences at a very early age. If their first journey by car is into the great unknown, away from Mum and siblings which, for most pups, is a fearful experience and the second one is to the Vet's to be jabbed with a needle, it is hardly surprising that the car becomes something to fear. If, as often happens, they are cuddled on the lap of the caring, new owner, who reassures and pets him, thus reinforcing their fear by rewarding it, the problem may soon escalate into a phobia. If the breeder has taken the time, as some do, to take him out and about in the car between four and seven weeks of age he will think nothing of it. It will be just another situation he has learnt to deal with as he goes along. If your pup seems to dislike the car and now hates travelling, and if he slobbers, vomits, howls or barks all the way to your destination, you won't like it much, either!

117

To cure the dog's car-phobia, because that is what it is, you need to de-sensitise him to the car and his fear of it, and teach him completely new associations with it.

To begin with, make up your mind to spend considerable time and effort for the next two to three weeks, and be prepared not to make any journeys with the dog until he is cured.

Park the car in a safe place, as near as possible to the house, with the door open and the radio on. **Do not** start the engine. Put the dog's food down as near to the car as he will tolerate in order to eat it. If he will eat it inside the car, all well and good, but don't shut the door. Then go away and leave him to eat on his own. Don't make any fuss or try to encourage him, just put the food down and go! If your dog panics as soon as you leave him you can sit quietly in the car, **but you must ignore him.** Split his daily food ration into several small meals so that you can practice throughout the day. Once the dog will eat happily in the car you can close the door. This stage may take from one to several days, depending on the level of his fear, **don't try to rush it.** When he will eat happily in the car with the door closed you can start the engine. Only start the engine and leave it running, **do not try to move the car.** At this stage it may be necessary with some dogs to go back to feeding beside the car - don't worry, you will soon make progress. **Never at any time should you try to force the issue or all your work will have been in vain!** After the dog has eaten happily in the car, with the engine running, for a couple of days, it is time to begin moving.

Now you will do things a little differently. Take the food to the car, and give the dog a piece as soon as he gets in, but keep the rest out of reach. Drive the car about twenty yards, stop, leave the engine running and give him half the food. When he has eaten it drive back the way you have come, stop, leave the engine running and give him the rest of his food. Provided that the dog is still happy you can now progress on a daily basis, increasing the distance you travel before feeding him. After a day or two you can cut out the feeding of half the food in the middle and just feed when you get back. **Do not be tempted to go too far too quickly.** If, at any time, the dog shows signs of distress, go back to the last stage you were at when he was happy. After a couple of weeks the dog will realise that the car is a source of good things, instead of an object of fear, and should be happy to travel anywhere.

Remember this: never make a fuss of him if he is showing fear, only if he is happy and relaxed. Don't try to rush the job!

SEPARATION ANXIETY

If a puppy is taught from a young age that being left alone is not a problem, as described in 'Teaching your puppy to cope alone', Chapter 7, EARLY DAYS, separation anxiety should never develop. However, there is a possibility that something could happen in the life a dog that might 'trigger' such a problem: inappropriate punishment for something that happened while the owner was out; illness resulting in twenty four hour a day care from the owner; family bereavement or the loss of another pet causing distress for the owner and over attention to the dog; burglary; accident in the home; family break-up resulting in the 'disappearance' of a beloved owner; the family moving house and, in the case of 'welfare' dogs, being rehomed. There are many more but these examples give an idea of the changes and traumas that could affect a dog deeply and result in him feeling afraid to be left alone.

If separation problems are being nipped in the bud the advice in Chapter 7, if followed carefully, should suffice. However, where the behaviour has become established and the dog is seriously distressed, possibly with house soiling and destructive tendencies, a more in depth approach may be needed.

Desensitisation programme for established Separation Anxiety

This is a four-week programme designed to help a dog cope happily with isolation from the owner. It is essential to understand that the dog must **never** be punished in **any** way for lapses that might occur from this point onwards. 'Punishment', from the dog's point of view, does not have to be physical. A scowl, a sigh of frustration or an exasperated "Oh, not again" may set the programme back days or even weeks!

The purpose of the programme is to teach the dog, gradually, that no matter what frame of mind he is in when the owner leaves the room (and, later on, the house) he can cope and all will be well in his world.

First week:
- Twice a day, give your dog your full attention by playing with and/or fussing him for between ten and twenty minutes.
- Follow each of these periods with ten to twenty minutes of absolutely **no** attention at all.
- Don't even look at him.
- If he whines or barks during this period get up and walk away, sit elsewhere or go into another room.

Second week:
- Continue with the contrasting periods of attention/no attention but with the dog on the other side of a child gate, tied on his lead somewhere a little away from you **or** in his cage.
- Only use the cage if the dog is **completely** happy in it and preferably after discussion with a behaviour counsellor.
- Stay within sight of the dog at this stage.
- When you release him or let him back into the room with you, **completely ignore him.**
- As he becomes more relaxed about what you are doing start to increase the distance between you, **but still within sight.**

Third week:
- Continue as before but with the dog in another room and yourself sitting just the other side of the door.
- As you put him in the room place a special chew item (stuffed Kong, bone etc) in the room with him.
- If he whines or scratches on the door, tap the door with your hand but **do not say a word.**
- After **five minutes** of good, quiet behaviour, go into the room, ignore him for the first minute or two then greet him and allow him back into the room with you.
- **Remove the chew toy.**
- Repeat twice a day for a few days then gradually increase the time he is away from you until he can be left for thirty minutes without making a fuss.
- Once he has reached thirty minutes you can do it just once a day.

Fourth week:
- Half an hour before you are due to go out give the dog five minutes attention **at your invitation.**
- Just before you leave, place a worn item of clothing near the door and give the dog his chew toy.
- Always remove both items when you return.
- Remember to ignore him when you re-enter the room and only greet him after a couple of minutes.
- Practice this routine in a random way, i.e. don't always leave the house, just pretend that you are!
- Do this several times a day to de-sensitise the dog to your movements.

N.B. If your dog is too stressed to accept this routine try recording your voice on a tape recorder and leave it playing when he is left alone.

BIRTH OF A BABY

Preparations for the birth
When an established dog is faced with the impending birth of a baby there can be some issues that need to be dealt with beforehand to prevent problems later on, after the birth. The whole family needs to be involved in this.

First of all, if there is any possibility that your dog could be a little 'spoilt' be honest with yourselves and face the issue! You will need to distance yourselves slightly from your dog and teach him that he is still a very important member of the family but not 'top of the heap'!

Make a point of ignoring him when he is demanding attention by folding your arms and turning your head away and teaching visitors how important it is that they should do the same. You and your visitors should also make the point that no one will play with the dog when he is demanding attention from them.

Make a really determined effort to reduce any lingering dependency upon you that the dog still has by leaving him in another room sometimes when you are at home. If possible do this by leaving him in the cage (if you are using one) sometimes and at others leaving him loose so the cage is not an essential part of his being left alone. Make sure he is not allowed to follow you about by simply shutting the door behind you whenever you leave the room. Don't make a fuss when you leave him or when you return so that your absence is of no great importance to him.

Try, if possible, to put the cage in different places in the house so that no one particular area becomes his "territory".

Do not let the dog have access to any squeaky toys as the squeak could awake a primeval desire to 'stop the sound' and may cause him to react in the same way to the baby crying.

Make a point of spending a little less time with the dog and paying less attention to him before the baby arrives so that your preoccupation with the baby will not have so great an impact on him.

Remind all your visitors between now and the birth that they must ignore the dog when they first come in so that he is used to being calm now when people arrive before all hell breaks loose afterwards!

Get the dog used to the sound of a crying baby by purchasing a 'Sound CD', available through the Internet, and following the instructions in the accompanying booklet. It is very important that the dog learns to expect nice things when the baby is present, but also that only calm behaviour will be rewarded.

After the birth

When you first arrive home try to get someone else to actually carry the baby in so that, once you have ignored the dog as usual, you can give him some attention before he sees you with your arms full!

When the dog is out of the cage and the baby is around carry on ignoring him in the same way as usual by turning your head away. Provided you have followed the previous advice there will be no need for the arm folding when you are holding the baby as long as the head movement is clear. Don't shout at the dog or push him away with your spare hand! If he won't go away, shove him with your elbow and immediately turn your head away. When he is sitting quietly near you and the baby, 'click&treat' so that the good behaviour is rewarded, and the baby is associated with nice things.

Make sure that your millions of visitors who come to admire the baby all use the proper body language when they arrive so that the dog doesn't start to leap all over the place in excitement and risk upsetting you. Tell them how to behave before they come into contact with the dog so that there is no initial period of chaos. It is much easier for everyone to stay calm if the dog is calm and he will be calm if he is ignored as usual until you decide it's time to give him a fuss.

Don't put the baby on the floor initially unless the dog is in the cage because once the baby is at ground level he will think it is a subordinate member of the pack, i.e. a puppy! Once you know he has accepted the newcomer you can play it by ear.

If the baby is unsettled and crying a lot this may upset the dog, especially if you are dealing with the baby personally, so quietly put him (the dog!) in the cage, reward him (with verbal praise or a tit-bit) once he is in and carry on dealing with baby. Gradually he will realise that he can cope with the noise and will start to relax.

Remember that a dog finds the contents of a dirty nappy appealing to a degree that we would find distasteful! This may result in him trying to grab the nappy in order to eat the contents, which could result in an accident. Always put the dog in the cage until the dirty nappy has been disposed of.

Now then - I am going to suggest something that you may not find acceptable and if so I quite understand! However, it is a very good idea if you can bring yourselves to do it! If you were to put the baby inside the cage for a moment or two from time to time it would make the point to the dog that he doesn't 'own' the cage and would prevent him becoming territorial about it. By doing this you would reduce the risk of him objecting to the baby being inquisitive later when the crawling stage is reached.

Never make going into the cage feel like a punishment to the dog or he will associate that punishment with the presence of the baby. You are using the cage as a safety measure, not a punishment or a way of excluding the dog, so make sure he understands this. Always make going into the cage a pleasure for him and remember to **ignore** him for a few moments when he comes out so he doesn't become over-excited.

Finally, don't worry! Take a deep breath, relax and enjoy your baby and your dog! Keep everything calm and the dog will be calm.

Oh, one last word of caution! No matter how good your dog may seem to be with the baby **never leave them alone together unattended!** Accidents can happen for the most unexpected of reasons and it is simply not worth the risk of possible harm to the baby and almost certain death for the dog, even if it was not his fault. Take reasonable precautions so that your dog and baby can grow up to be firm friends.

HIERARCHY ISSUES
(aggression between dogs that live together)

Dogs that share the same space have a 'hierarchy' within their canine pack that enables them to live peaceably together. This hierarchy can be 'fluid' and may change over time or in certain circumstances. As mentioned elsewhere in this book, all dogs are not equal and, if we try to treat them as such we are doing them a disservice and making life very difficult for them.

When aggressive behaviour develops between pack members the reasons must be addressed before attempting to cure the problem.

- The arrival of a new puppy may cause an established dog to feel 'demoted' if the puppy receives too much attention. See 'A Dog is a Dog', Chapter 7, EARLY DAYS.
- The dog that has always been 'top dog' may be getting old and there is a 'young pretender' waiting to take his place. If the old dog is accepting this but the owner is not fights could well occur because, in the dog world, it is perfectly normal for a younger, stronger dog to knock the old King off his throne. It is essential to respect what is happening and support it by giving precedence to the younger dog. Change the feeding pattern so that the younger dog is given his food first; call the younger dog first; play with him first; fuss him first etc. etc. Many owners find this very hard to do but it is much kinder than forcing an old dog to fight to stay in a position he no longer feels able to maintain. This applies to both dogs and bitches.
- When there are two or more bitches in a pack, problems can arise when a subordinate bitch is approaching her season. She may become 'pushy' and cause a higher-ranking bitch to feel inclined to 'put her in her place'. If fights develop at this time it is important to support the higher status bitch, even though she may be the one that is showing obvious signs of aggression. If this type of hierarchy problem is not handled with care bitches may fall out irreconcilably, resulting in permanent separation or one of them needing to be rehomed.
- When two pack members of the same sex have been separated, even for a short time, there may be some 'niggling' between them when they are reunited. Interference should be kept to a minimum but, where it is essential to intervene, support must be given to the higher-ranking animal.
- Where aggression between pack members cannot be resolved neutering may be an option. See 'Neutering', earlier in this chapter.

DOG-TO-DOG AGGRESSION
('aggression' to dogs outside of the home)

Spanish Water Dogs are generally very sociable. It is rare for them to be genuinely aggressive but they are assertive and they like to be 'in charge'. Differentiating between true 'aggression' and 'aggressive behaviour' is where the misconceptions arise.

A dog that is aggressive will attack in any situation without a thought for his own safety and will almost certainly cause much physical damage to his victim. He will not waste time posturing or checking the sex and intentions of his target. This book is not the place for discussions on how to deal with such a dog; consulting a specialist in dog-to-dog aggression would be advised.

Aggressive behaviour is part of normal canine communication. Humans, unfortunately, do not often consider this fact and are inclined to 'punish' the behaviour, which usually exacerbates it.

Reasons for 'aggressive' behaviour
• Lack of proper socialisation at the right age.
• Fear (of other dogs, of the handler, of the collar, of the surroundings, of impending punishment)
• Inappropriate 'guarding' (of personal space, of the handler)
• Signals from the handler (tight lead, tension in voice and body)
• Over excitement (too much adrenalin)

On the lead

Most dogs that exhibit aggressive behaviour towards other dogs, especially when on the lead, have been 'taught' that the behaviour works or is the only option available.

This dog is showing clear signs of apprehension: ears back, eyes wide, mouth slightly open.

When a dog is unsure how to behave in a given situation he has three choices: freeze, fight or flee.
• Freezing means that the dog is terrified, totally unable to deal with the problem, is keeping completely still and praying that the cause of his fear will go away. Very few dogs resort to this extreme behaviour and, if they do, they need specialist help.
• Many dogs, if feeling threatened, would choose to flee but, if they are on the lead, that option is removed.
• With the option to flee unavailable the only one left is to fight. Showing aggression, lunging out and looking big, strong and dangerous, is a good way to get rid of a perceived threat. At least, it is if you are a dog!

Since option three, fight, is the one that causes all the problems, that is what needs to be discussed. When dogs meet they use body language and ritualised postures to say "Hello, who are you?" size each other up, invite play, decide which dog is the stronger and whether or not they need to fight about it. If a dog is restricted by a collar and lead his ability to use the correct body signals is limited. What most owners fail to understand, because they are not dogs, is what the other dog is saying. Their own dog growls, (because he feels threatened or the other dog is 'rude') so they immediately think he is 'aggressive' and punish him in some way. The dog then has two things to worry about: what the other dog is going to do and what the owner is going to do. He is caught between a rock and a hard place and, just to add to his problems, he can't flee! The more the dog is punished (shouted at, yanked back, held on a tight lead, smacked on the nose) the more 'aggressive' he will appear because the owner is teaching him that there is a problem. Eventually, the very sight of another dog will cause an explosion of barking and growling in the hope that it can be driven away before the punishment comes. In the dog's mind the other dog is causing the punishment so to him the solution is obvious: get rid of the dog, get rid of the punishment.

Before working in close proximity with other dogs some basic training will need to be reinforced in a very positive manner: reliable lead walking, sit, recall, 'watch' and 'leave'. If the dog is over excited when going for a walk follow the advice in Why do dogs pull? All of these can be found in Chapter 12,

TRAINING. There is absolutely no point in trying to teach something new and difficult to a dog who has no boundaries or guidelines and is high on adrenalin as soon as he gets outside. It must be possible to walk with the dog on a loose lead so that there is no tension running down the lead from the handler. Then, because the collar and lead can have a negative impact on the dog's behaviour it would be advisable to use a Kumfi Stop Pull harness. This type of harness gives kind, comfortable control if the dog lunges but sends no negative messages to the neck area. It allows the dog to use his head and neck to communicate without restriction. All this work should be carried out at home and in places where there will be no other dogs until the response is reliable.

When the dog is ready to work around other dogs try to arrange for a friend to walk a quiet, well-behaved dog, on the lead, in a place with no other distractions. Ask your dog to watch you and, every time he does, click&treat. Whenever he reacts negatively to the dog turn quickly around and walk the opposite way. Ask him to watch and click&treat as soon as he does. Ask your friend **not** to turn away if your dog reacts negatively otherwise he will think he has been successful in driving away the other dog. The principle you are trying to teach your dog is that paying attention to you is more valuable and rewarding than barking or showing aggression towards another dog. Gradually reduce the distance between yourself and the other dog but do not try to get too close too quickly or you may set your dog back and knock his confidence. Keep yourself between the two dogs to act as a buffer and make your dog feel safer.

Another useful ploy is to teach your dog to walk behind you on cue so that when you meet a dog in a narrow space you can put yourself in front until you are level with it. You will then be able to bring your dog back to the side furthest away from the other dog. This achieves two things: it shows your dog that you are in control of the situation, rather than him and it allows you to shield him if he still lacks the confidence to walk so close in a confined area.

Off the lead

A dog that is showing aggressive behaviour towards other dogs when he is off the lead may need specialist help from someone who understands canine aggression and has dogs that are experienced in teaching other dogs how to behave. However, some perceived aggression is simply a dog putting another in its place and should not be over-reacted to. If a dog is being 'rude' and putting its chin or paws on your dog's shoulders it is perfectly reasonable for him to tell that dog to stop. He will, if

Tonto, aged nine months, is being very 'rude' to the Shepherd bitch. If she is a confident, dominant bitch he will simply receive a 'telling off'. However, if she had social problems of her own she would almost certainly attack him.

necessary give a growl or maybe even a snap but there should not be a bite. Although it can be embarrassing and the owner of the other dog may not be very happy about it there is no reason to assume that your dog is doing any more than communicating in his own language. Nevertheless, it is essential to be seen to have control of your dog so 'leave' and recall must be reinforced, using a very high value reward, convincing your dog that when he returns to you he will be rewarded amply. Shouting at him will actively encourage him and telling him off when he comes back will make sure he doesn't return quickly next time!

'AGGRESSIVE' BEHAVIOUR TOWARDS PEOPLE

A genuinely 'people aggressive' dog is very rare and, as with dog-to-dog aggression, this book is not the place to discuss methods of dealing with such a problem. Giving advice without knowing the dog is fraught with danger, and should only be undertaken by a behaviour counsellor who can discover the reasons for the behaviour and offer a properly structured behaviour modification programme for that particular dog.

However, apparently 'aggressive' behaviour can occur for many of the reasons mentioned earlier with regard to other dogs and the principles of dealing with it are virtually the same, so there is no need to repeat it here. The dog needs to understand several things: there is nothing to fear; the owner/handler is in control of the situation; the person is not going to 'invade his space'; the person will not 'run away' because the dog has 'threatened' them; there will be **no** punishment; there **will** be valuable rewards for **not** exhibiting the behaviour and, most importantly, there will be no 'reward' for the unacceptable behaviour! This last statement may seem illogical. Whoever would 'reward' a dog for growling or barking at a person? Actually, an awful lot of owners do, quite inadvertently, by touching the dog, speaking to him, pulling him away and even, from the dog's point of view, by shouting at him! Any response from the handler can be interpreted by the dog as reward or

This dog has absolutely no desire to bite! He wants to get rid of the problem, not attack it. In the first picture he is clearly saying, "I would rather not be here". Since this strategy has failed he increases the severity of his barking, picture two, but is leaning back, clearly indicating he has no desire to attack. Finally, in desperation, he leans forward, draws his lower lip back and says "Look how big my teeth are, I could use them if I wanted to, but I would rather you just went away". If he were genuinely 'aggressive' or intending to bite he would have drawn his top lip back to show his upper teeth. This dog is asking for his handler to help him, not punish him!

encouragement.

A not uncommon problem with Spanish Water Dogs, especially during adolescence, results from the 'herding', 'guarding' and 'second fear stage' all combining at the same time. This problem is their inclination to rush up to a person, barking, and then slip behind them and have a 'go' at the back of their legs. Generally a 'head butt' is all that will happen but it is not unknown for them to actually 'nip'. This behaviour cannot be tolerated and must be dealt with quickly, efficiently and without any 'mixed signals' for the dog. If the dog has been thoroughly trained it should be very easy to tell him to 'Leave' in no uncertain terms, recall him and reward him for responding. If this is not sufficient to regain control then, once again, it may be a job for the Remote Control Spray Collar. The timing must be perfect, the commands clear and the reward very valuable. Should this fail then professional advice must be sought, quickly, before the behaviour becomes habituated.

All in all, Spanish Water Dogs are good-natured and friendly but with independent natures that can, occasionally, get them into trouble. A trained dog is a happy dog and an owner with a trained dog is a happy owner.

"Hi, Sweetie, fancy a night out?"
"Oh, please, it takes a man, not a shirt button!"

14 WORKING WITH YOUR SPANISH WATER DOG

INTRODUCTION

As has been stated in previous chapters, in its country of origin the Spanish Water Dog was bred to work. The breed was primarily used as a working dog until it received full recognition by The Spanish Kennel Club in the mid '80s and is still, even today, used for a variety of purposes in rural areas of Spain. Asking a relatively 'primitive' breed such as this to adapt and settle into family life as a household pet in just a few generations is expecting a great deal, especially when you take into account its strong guarding instinct. These dogs can and do make excellent companions but the basic inherent trait to 'think and do' cannot be ignored by the owner without expecting unwanted behaviours to manifest themselves. This does not mean you have to find a field of sheep or goats to round up or take your dog to the nearest port in order for it to pull a boat in!

In the UK we have a variety of canine pursuits that this breed is already involved in and which you too can join in with your dog. Alternatively, you and your dog can just enjoy activities of your own making. Either way, it is of the utmost importance that your dog is suitably stimulated and exercised in accordance with its emotional and physical needs. If, however, you cannot commit yourself to doing justice to these needs because you work long hours, enjoy the TV too much or don't like going out in cold or wet weather then you need to question whether or not this is the breed for you. On the other hand, if you enjoy the company of your dog and appreciate an active lifestyle, then you will get immense pleasure from shared activities and your dog will reward you with love and devotion.

Tas enjoying heelwork. Training should always be fun.

Organised canine activities will give you the opportunity not only to stretch your own and your dog's abilities but also to socialise with like-minded doggy people. The Spanish Water Dog Club runs a number of different types of event throughout each year but, if you are not able to get to these, there are always the local clubs that you can attend. Very often, you will find that once you have got involved with one particular activity it often leads to joining in with others. Of course, you will have the added advantage of having a breed that is highly motivated and quick to learn so the chances are that, as long as you can keep up with your dog, you will tend to be 'top of the class' in a lot of activities.

BASIC OBEDIENCE FOR WORKING

"A trained dog is a happy dog." This is a quote from the Kennel Club's Good Citizen Dog Scheme. Obedience training has been covered more fully in Chapter Twelve but there are several points which need to be considered and cannot be emphasised enough. Once you have committed yourself to including a dog as part of your family then it is only right that you also accept the responsibilities that go with it. You have an obligation to ensure that your dog is not a nuisance to others in any way. It should not be out of control, running loose without supervision, toileting in public places without the results being cleaned up, or persistently barking and causing upset to neighbours.

Through obedience training you are aiming to produce a companion that is dog and people sociable and under control at all times. Not only will your dog be a pleasure to live with but it will also be a joy to own and you will achieve a great deal of satisfaction from the fruits of all the work you have put in.

You may or may not decide to become involved in the other activities dealt with in this chapter but basic obedience with your Spanish Water Dog is a must for the reasons already pointed out. The main requirements for a contented dog and happy owner are sit, stay, heel, recall, walking on a loose lead and greeting dogs and people in a controlled manner. By following a course in basic obedience your dog will have a sound understanding of where it fits within your family, will feel secure and confident and, be a companion that you can be proud of!

Obedience training begins as soon as you bring your puppy home. Details of this have been covered in an earlier chapter but as soon as your pup is vaccinated you need to enrol it in a puppy training class. As pointed out previously, choose your training club carefully, ensuring that the training methods recommended in this book are the ones being used.

If you find that you have enjoyed the basic training and have achieved success in this discipline you may decide to take it a step further and aim for Competition Obedience. There are various types of obedience competitions to enter depending upon your and your dog's ability.

A 'straight' sit

Competition Obedience

Companion Dog Shows are a lot of fun and a good place to start. You will be able to turn up and enter on the day and your dog does not need to be registered with a breed society or particular club. The classes often range from a beginner to an advanced level. Limit Shows are restricted in some way. They may be limited to a specific breed, members of an organisation, or residents within a particular area. Open Obedience Shows are open to anyone who wishes to enter. However, your dog must be registered with the Kennel Club either on the breed register or the working register. You must enter and pay before the closing date for entries. Championship Obedience Shows have the same rules as open shows and anyone can enter but the Championship Show offers the Kennel Club's top obedience award – Obedience Certificates (known as tickets). These awards can only be given to dogs winning the highest class, the Championship Class C.

If you feel that you would like to compete in obedience with your Spanish Water Dog a degree of precision is required of you and your dog. A Spanish Water Dog will probably never work quite as closely as a Border Collie, which often leans right into the handler's leg. This is of no great importance as long as he works reasonably close to you and doesn't weave, maintaining a position that is consistent throughout. The rules state that your dog must work in a happy manner and that will suit a Spanish Water Dog, as they are generally cheerful dogs. As long as your dog is not forced or put under pressure, he will work with a happy demeanour.

Competition Obedience is made up of a number of classes, each one more demanding than the previous, and in each class the handler and dog are required to perform a number of exercises that are judged for accuracy and are scored accordingly. As your dog becomes more proficient and wins his class he will become overqualified for that class in the future. He will then progress to the next level. The exercises in the lower classes are often shorter and easier with allowances made for the level at which the dog and its handler are working. In higher classes the standard is more exacting and errors are consequently penalised.

In the lower classes of Pre-Beginner, Beginner and Novice, you will be allowed to speak to your dog as much as you like. However, you are not allowed to take toys or food into the ring, so at this stage you will have to rely on your voice for encouragement. In the more advanced classes you will not be allowed to speak but by the time you have reached this level you and your dog will be working as one, your dog taking its cues from your body language.

There are a number of exercises that you must teach your dog. Heelwork is both on and off the lead, including left, right and about turns, and a number of halts where your dog must sit at your side. The recall requires you to leave your dog and call it to you when asked and the dog must sit in front of you so that its body is straight. Retrieves begin with an article of your choosing, progressing to a dumb-bell in advanced classes. Scoring will depend on how cleanly and carefully the dog brings the object for you to take hold of. Your dog will be required to do sit-stays and down-stays which will progress from a relatively short time with you still in sight of the dog, but not looking at it, to extended stays with you out of sight.

In the more advanced classes your dog will also be tested for correct temperament by being handled by the judge. Heelwork becomes more exacting, recalls are to your side as you are moving in a given direction and other exercises are introduced. These include scent discrimination with scent cloths, send away and distance control.

Competitive Obedience is fun and very addictive. As you can see, the sky is the limit because there is always something to work towards. Whether you excel in Beginners or make it to Advanced level, you will have some lovely days out meeting lots of people all enjoying the same sport.

Kennel Club Good Citizen Scheme

If the prospect of competition obedience seems daunting you may wish to consider working towards the Kennel Club's Good Citizen Scheme. A number of basic obedience clubs incorporate this into their programme and provide training towards the awards. These awards are at three levels; Bronze, Silver and Gold and certainly the first two are well within the capabilities of the average Spanish Water Dog. The third award is more of a challenge, which, if you have successfully completed the first two, is one that you will most probably wish to accept.

The awards are made up of basic training tests balanced with exercises that are designed to establish that a dog is controlled and manageable in social situations.

AGILITY

Spanish Water Dogs are naturally agile and well suited to this sport, whether competitively or just for fun. Be aware, however, that they will use this ability to jump up, over, on and off whatever presents itself from a very early age and while the body is developing this can lead to injuries and sometimes long term impairment. The puppy's bones, tendons and muscles grow quickly during the first few months and do not necessarily keep up with each other, nor are they strong enough to withstand the pressure that jumping, landing, twisting and turning can exert on them. It's not unusual for youngsters to have a recurring limp; having at some stage sustained an injury that never has time to heal before it takes another battering. Basically, it's a 'Catch 22' situation. Your puppy needs to rest an injury but try limiting its exercise! It isn't that easy! Once your dog has more or less reached maturity the chances of injury will lessen and regular balanced agility training will strengthen the body. It is important always to remember to keep the training within your dog's capabilities and to warm your dog up prior to using the equipment. This is where an experienced trainer can help and advise.

This does not mean that your youngster cannot do agility until it reaches maturity. There are all sorts of simple exercises that it can learn which will stand it in good stead for when it is ready for the big stuff. Ruth Hobday, an experienced dog handler and agility expert, has written a very useful book called 'Agility Fun-The Hobday Way' and Volume 1 is Agility Training For Puppies. She introduces puppies to some essential obedience exercises before they are six months old. These include basic commands of 'sit', 'down' and 'stand', 'recall', 'send-away', 'retrieve', turning left and right and, most important of all, socialisation. At six months of age, along with developing already learned obedience skills, the puppy is introduced to some equipment. The tunnel is simple to teach and is quickly mastered. It can be squashed up to make it short to begin with and fully extended when the skill is achieved. Weave poles are arranged in two parallel lines creating a pathway down the middle along which the pup runs. At this stage, bending round them is not advisable. Contacts for the full height equipment are frequently taught using hoops placed at the end of the contact and at this stage the pup can be taught to go through the hoops without the equipment present. A puppy dog-walk that is lower and wider than the standard dog-walk is frequently used. I taught my pups to walk along a builder's plank raised on bricks, firstly set against a

Perdi, a mature bitch, showing how to weave.

wall then with open spaces on both sides. Jumps can be set up with the pole laid on the ground between the wings. Initially introduce your pup to one jump and build up to a short row of three or four.

As your puppy approaches twelve months of age the equipment can be made slightly more challenging but still well within the puppy's capabilities. Weave poles can be drawn nearer together to introduce minor bending, jumps raised a few inches off the ground and the tunnel set up with a bend in the middle.

Having reached twelve months your dog is ready to go on to training on standard equipment but, again, I

Taffle at twelve months gaining confidence on a low A-frame

"So far, so good. Oh, what do I do now?"

"I believe I can fly!"

"I'd rather dance."

would emphasise the need for professional help here to build up the skills gradually, increase the strength and aptitude of the dog and avoid accidents.

You do not necessarily have to train to compete and numerous agility clubs have classes for pet owners who just want to have a bit of fun and to see what their dogs are capable of. When you know how to handle your dog round an agility course you may wish to put a few pieces of equipment together in the garden at home. All sorts of bits and bobs lying around could come in useful for this task. Take into account some basic safety factors like making sure there are no nails sticking out and the pieces that are walked along don't wobble. Kiddies' play tunnels make good substitutes for the real thing, garden canes for weave poles and jumps and an old motorcycle tyre to jump through for example. If you have a DIY expert in the family, perhaps you could be a little bit more ambitious.

Miguel showing how it is done

Agility requires a great deal of stamina from you but, as children seem to have boundless energy, this is a great way to exercise both dog and offspring, at the same time creating a strong bond between them. A final word of advice here, though.......try to avoid becoming a competitive parent screaming commands from the sidelines and ticking off dog and handler for not performing to perfection. Perhaps that reminds you of junior football or gymkhanas!

FLYBALL

Flyball is a relatively new canine sport compared to agility, but is becoming increasingly popular. As with

Perdi returning with the tennis ball

agility, this breed takes to it very easily but if you plan to introduce your Spanish Water Dog to Flyball I would recommend that playing with tennis balls becomes very much part of your daily routine. Dogs that are ball-focused are much easier to train and will learn the procedure much more quickly. If your dog is not interested in playing with a ball, no matter how many hours of trying you have put in, I suggest you find another pastime for it.

For those of you who are not familiar with Flyball, it is a frenetic and noisy dog sport that requires a team of four dogs to compete against a similar team. Each dog has to go over four jumps in a straight line, push the front of the Flyball 'box' with the fore-feet to release a tennis ball, catch the ball and return to the handler by jumping over the four jumps again. Once all four dogs have done this in a run, the fastest team wins that run. That is Flyball in its simplest terms but serious racing requires training for speed, accuracy, fast change-overs between dogs and various other permitted tactics. The fastest teams in the country are completing runs at around 16 seconds, four seconds per dog!

Again a youngster has to be introduced to Flyball carefully so that it is not over-stretched or injured. Basic training can begin with puppies to accustom them to the equipment and commands but use of standard equipment does not begin until the dog is at least a year old.

As mentioned earlier, the dog must be very focused on tennis balls and these can be thrown or rolled in a variety of ways for your dog to catch or retrieve so that it keeps its eye on the ball. The two basic lessons that your dog has to learn are how to operate the box and going over the jumps. These are generally introduced separately so that when your dog reaches the box after going over a jump or several jumps it has already met it and knows how to trigger it. Again, an experienced trainer will show you how to teach your dog these procedures.

Very often a process known as 'backward chaining' is used to introduce a dog to Flyball. This method requires the dog to learn the last thing it does in the process first. The very last thing your dog will do is jump over the last jump when returning to you so that is where you start. Someone will hold your dog in front of the jump and you will stand at the other side and call your dog to you. Having a favourite toy in your possession helps to encourage your dog to come back quickly. When the dog reaches you it gets the toy as a reward. The next stage is to introduce a second jump, then a third then a fourth. When your dog has successfully achieved all four jumps without running out to the side it can then be held with its back feet on the box while you stand at the end and call your dog to you again. It is essential that your dog has been taught to accept strangers holding its collar or harness before this happens. If successful at this stage, and you are sure your dog will return to you jumping all four jumps on his way, then triggering the box can be added to the sequence followed by the four jumps going towards the box. Further training to increase speed and perfect the 'swimmer's turn' on the box will come as the dog gains experience.

There are two sorts of Flyball, 'British Flyball Association' (BFA) and 'Crufts', the difference being the type of box used. In BFA Flyball, the ball comes out of a hole in the front of the box and in Crufts Flyball it is released from the back, requiring the dog to jump in order to catch it. Views and preferences vary on which is better but I will leave that for you to judge if you decide to pursue this sport.

Whether you decide to carry on enjoying Flyball as a fun exercise or to take it more seriously and compete will depend on how much you wish to make that commitment, the expertise of your dog and, possibly, how much noise you can tolerate! However, earplugs are sometimes provided! Competitions involve full days or weekends away and are often some distance apart. They are very noisy and manic but great fun, especially for your dog.

WATER WORK

Spanish Water Dogs are, as the name implies, very much at home in the water and, given the opportunity, will excel at water-based activities. This may be with your family as part of a day out to the coast, a river, a lake, a hobby such as sailing or canoeing or an organised activity with a club. Whilst the Spanish Water Dog is, for its size, a strong swimmer, it is nevertheless quite a small dog with a very big heart. For this reason it is advisable to be very cautious when swimming your dog in the sea or very fast flowing rivers.

Ellie enjoying a free ride with JB and demonstrating how all the family can become involved

Spanish often refuse to give up when they have lost something and may be carried away by a strong crosscurrent or undertow while searching for a retrieve item that has long gone.

As the activity will include either your dog, yourself or both going into the water it is vitally important that safety precautions are put into place and hazardous conditions are avoided, especially if children are involved. Taking part in a club based water training session is the safest option where exercises are kept within the limitations of the dog's ability and are designed to increase its confidence and expertise in small stages, at the same time ensuring that everyone taking part is not put at risk. The Spanish Water Dog Club runs water training sessions throughout the Spring and Summer where you will be able to learn how to have fun with your dog in a safe environment. All activities are covered by insurance, life jackets are worn and trainers are present at all times to ensure that the dogs are trained within their capabilities. To enjoy water work and be fully involved you may choose to invest in a wetsuit. This is as much for your protection against the dogs' claws as well as keeping you warm when the weather is unkind.

Spanish Water Dogs can be taught a number of exercises in the water that involve entering the water in a confident manner, swimming short distances away from the handler then back again, retrieving an article that floats, an article that sinks and working from a boat if the opportunity arises. In more advanced work the dog can be taught to enter the water from a boat and pull it to the shore by means of a length of rope attached to the bow with a dummy on the end for the dog to hold. These dogs can also be trained to ride on a surfboard or pull one along. Dogs that are confident at diving can be asked to retrieve an article at the depth of several metres but this comes after the dog has achieved a high standard of working in the water. During training of underwater retrieves a dog may lose the item he is seeking. In order to lead the dog to the correct location, it is standard practice to throw a stone to indicate where the dog should dive. It has been known for an excited dog to catch the stone, resulting in a broken tooth. In the heat of the moment a dog might also manage to swallow the stone. Careful aim is required to avoid an incident such as this!

Ben Egginton being 'saved' by Pardo!

MIGUEL WORKING IN WATER

Underwater Retrieve

"I see it!"

"Another breath and…"

"Here we go"

"Got it!"

Look before you leap………..

…………oops! No brakes

Is it a bird?

Is it a plane?

When working with your dog in water two potential hazards that you need to be aware of are:

Blue-green algae is a form of bacteria that thrives in warm, shallow water and appears during the summer months when the water is slow moving or still. As the 'bloom' dies off it releases toxins that can be harmful to humans and dogs, causing illness or even death. If you choose to swim your dog in lakes or slow moving rivers you will need to check for the likelihood of a blue-green scum on or near the surface of the water but it can be present without being visible. If in doubt, do not allow your dog to swim.

If you think your dog has been in contact with the bacteria and may be affected by the toxins these are the signs to look out for:
• Fever
• Diarrhoea
• Abdominal pain
• Nausea and vomiting
• Eye and skin irritation
If your dog is experiencing any of these signs, take him to the nearest Vet immediately.

Weil's disease, also known as Leptospirosis, is transmitted through the urine of infected rats, both in water and on land where rats are present. It can enter the system either through the mouth or cuts and grazes on the skin. Once the dog has become infected the bacteria multiply and spread through the body, causing damage to the liver and small blood vessels. After approximately seven days death may occur but if the dog survives the liver and blood vessel damage will present as jaundice and there will be widespread haemorrhaging.

The initial signs of infection are:
• Dullness
• Loss of appetite
• Fever
• Vomiting
• Black diarrhoea

Your dog can be vaccinated against Leptospirosis as part of the annual booster regime. However, should you prefer not to have annual vaccinations and your dog is regularly in water, it is imperative to vaccinate against Leptospirosis on a yearly basis. Single vaccines are available for this disease. Be aware that you can catch it, too. If, following contact with contaminated water, you experience flu-like symptoms, see your doctor immediately.

Anything you do with your dog in water will show its strength and dexterity in this environment and the sheer joy of doing

Water training is fun

something that comes so naturally. It will also give you, the owner, a great amount of pleasure to see how talented your dog can be. Out of all the activities that you and your Spanish Water Dog are involved with, this has to be the most rewarding.

WORKING TRIALS IN SPAIN

In their country of origin Spanish Water Dogs have, for hundreds of years, worked for a living and the breed nowadays still retains strong working traits. Today in Spain, where Spanish Water Dogs may not necessarily be used in the traditional way, the desire to work may be channelled towards working trials. These are a group of specially designed exercises to test and challenge the dog, at the same time, simulating some of the activities that these dogs were originally bred for.

Working trials regularly take place in Spain and we now have owners travelling over from the UK to participate. In order to take part it will be necessary to have a 'Pet Passport' for your dog, familiarise yourself with the travelling procedures and research the various tests so that you can prepare your dog prior to going.

Spanish working trials include exercises in water and on land during which your dog will be tested for its ability to do the following:-

• Retrieve an object in water from the surface
• Search and retrieve an object from under water

A Test of Agility, Spanish Style

• Pull a boat to shore
• Search for an object hidden on land
• Search for a person hidden out of sight
• A memory test that requires the dog to search for an object thrown a short distance, the dog walked to a specified point and sent to search for it
• A test of agility where the dog negotiates obstacles and apparatus raised off the ground on scaffolding
Ultimately, these working trials will be standardised and used in other countries, so that there is a common element throughout. The UK's water training is based on the Spanish equivalent.

GUNDOG WORK

Spanish Water Dogs are genetically predisposed to being easily trained and to respond readily to positive, non-confrontational methods. Traditionally, gundogs have been trained by methods that could be considered too harsh for this breed, although these are changing. Training your dog for gundog work requires a great commitment on your part and if the dog is going to enter trials or be taken out into the field with other handlers and dogs it has to be taken seriously from the outset. It is not a hobby that can be 'dipped into' occasionally then left for weeks or months.

It is as well to decide this while your dog is still a puppy, and use training methods and basic exercises that it will require later on, at the same time avoiding allowing it to learn behaviour that could be considered undesirable for a gundog.

Already your pup will possess natural instincts for hunting and retrieving and these need to be channelled in the right direction early on. Serious training will start later, but in those early months your pup will need to learn basic obedience and be introduced to a variety of situations that will help build its self-confidence and ability to cope with the requirements of working in the field.

You may be interested in training your Spanish Water Dog to work as a gundog to go on shoots, compete in trials or just for pleasure. Spanish Water Dogs are very versatile and naturally excel at retrieving, so they make an excellent partner on shoots.

Depending on the type of shoot, different sets of skills will be required from both the dog and handler. Although, at the time of writing, the Kennel Club has not decided which gundog group the Spanish Water Dog belongs to, the breed is eligible for The Gundog Working Certificate. This certificate is to test both handler and dog as a competent partnership by demonstrating control, obedience, temperament, hunting and retrieving. There are two stages, the preliminary stage being a series of exercises on land and in water using dummies, and the more advanced stage taking place on a shoot where both handler and dog are observed for the day and assessed according to how they coped with the various tasks. Assessment is either a 'pass' or 'not ready'.

As with any discipline you must start with the basics. Do not be tempted to rush and always remember to have fun with your dog, because it is amazing how much can be taught as just a game! You will need to join a gundog group where you can be taught and your dog can be trained. Formal obedience is not required but good control of your dog in the presence of others is essential, so your pup will need to know how to walk correctly on a lead, walk to heel off the lead, sit and stay on command, return to you when called and stop to a whistle. As your dog matures it will need to learn how to retrieve a dummy in a steady fashion and give it to your hand when asked. From the dummy the dog progresses to 'cold' game, which it must carry without damaging it. Your dog must learn to sit quietly by your side until given a command, and needs to be taught how to run out to the left or right from your hand signals.

An important requirement of a gundog is that he must very steady therefore you will need a solid stay. Recalls are also very important, so if all else fails you can at least call your dog back! A gun dog must also be quiet, so do not encourage barking in excitement, as it may be difficult to stop later on. Always remember it is quite easy to teach dogs new habits, but it is much more difficult to correct bad ones. Do not allow your dog to do something in the early days that you will not want him to do later. Most Spanish Water Dogs naturally love to retrieve. However, never throw sticks, as this is a very dangerous practice. There is a very real chance of the chasing dog becoming impaled on the stick if it finishes stuck in the ground. Equally hazardous is the poor dog ending up with a mouth full of sharp splinters. A small solid ball may well slip down the back of the dog's throat, blocking the airway. If this cannot be swiftly removed or you cannot get to a Veterinary Surgeon very quickly, you may well lose your dog. Have fun with your retrieves but do not do too many in one session, as the last thing you want is the dog losing interest. It is best not to introduce dummies until you have accomplished a reasonable retrieve, since a dog with a quick and accurate return is less likely to 'mouth' the article.

Always encourage the pup to give you the article and not to just drop it. If he does drop the article, move away and ask him to fetch it again. When he comes near take the article from him with the "give" or "dead" command. At this stage do not worry about asking him to sit, as long as he gives the article to your hand. Even when competing in Gundog Trials it is not necessary to get your dog to sit when he brings the dummy or bird back, but he must not drop it on the ground. It must be delivered 'to hand'.

Tas retrieving 'to hand'

Introduce dummies when he is retrieving cleanly. Later on you can get a dummy covered in feathers or rabbit skin, or even make one yourself. This will get him used to feathers and fur. Following such an introduction, moving on to game shouldn't present too much of a problem. Start with a small cold bird, such as a pigeon, and then work up to larger, freshly killed game. Once you have a good fast retrieve you are well on the way.

A gundog will need to be trained to the whistle. As with verbal commands, it does not matter which you use as long as you are consistent. However the main ones of **stop** and **recall** are the most important initially. The recall should be easy but stopping your dog at a distance may be more difficult. This is very important because most of the work will eventually be done at a distance. The specifics of how to train your dog to come to the whistle and stop at a distance will be taught at your training sessions and can also be found in 'Chapter 12 TRAINING.' The next stage will be directional control, which, like most exercises, should be taught with the dog close to you at first.

With him sitting facing you, throw your dummy a few yards to his left. He will initially watch where it goes, but when he turns to face you again extend your right arm in the direction of the dummy, then put your arm down again. Repeat this movement getting him to watch your arm, but this time give him the verbal command to fetch the dummy. Repeat this exercise using both left and right retrieves. Once learnt, you can progress to two dummies, one to the left and one to the right. Next, throw a dummy to the rear of the dog so he has to go backwards. Some handlers use a 'Back' command or 'Out' combined with the arm stretched out to the front of you.

When your dog is confident with 'seen' dummies he can be taught to search for 'blind' ones, i.e. dummies that he did not see thrown. The dog will gradually grow in confidence as he learns there is always something hidden out there; he just has to find it by listening to your commands of redirection and using his nose. You will soon learn how to read your dog's body language and know when to stop and re-direct, or to allow the dog to continue.

Fine-tuning these disciplines takes time and patience, but you must make sure that you and your dog remember to enjoy yourselves. Spanish Water Dogs do not learn readily if being forced and certainly will not work in a relaxed and happy manner. If things go wrong and you feel yourself getting agitated then stop, perform a simpler exercise, such as a straightforward retrieve, then praise and end your session. In your next session, start with a simple exercise and work your way up again. This way the dog will not get confused and you will not get frustrated.

A gun dog must be able to sit quietly beside you whilst other dogs are working in close proximity. It is therefore essential that some of your training sessions are undertaken with other dogs. Your dog will also need to retrieve in water, and sometimes swim to the far bank to search for the game. As before, when teaching a new task, start with simple water retrieves. Then throw the dummy on to the far bank where he can see it, and retrieve from that position. He will soon get used to the fact that the dummy may not always be in the water, and he must listen to your commands.

Introduction to the gun must be done very carefully by using a starter pistol. You need someone to help with this so that you can remain with your dog while they fire the pistol at least 30 yards away. This should be fired into the air with the arm extended high. Have your dog sitting by your side before the gun is fired, then praise and reward with play. This should be repeated regularly with the gun gradually being fired nearer and nearer. It is very important not to rush this process. If your dog should "startle" initially, remember to ignore him. Any attempt at reassuring him will have completely the opposite effect.

If you would like to teach your dog to hunt, then he must learn to quarter the ground. This is generally introduced by facing into the wind, before casting your dog to either the left or right. When he has gone approximately thirty paces, give two pips of the whistle to signal a turn of direction. When he turns to look back at you, command him to go in the opposite direction for a further thirty paces, and then repeat. As you progress very slowly walk forward. If your dog goes too far in front, so does not cover all of the ground, you must walk backwards so that he comes with you. This will encourage him to keep a line just in front of you, and not advance too rapidly.

Incorporated into your training will be opportunities to meet penned animals such as rabbits and your dog must learn to completely ignore them. A stage on from this is the introduction to a simulated 'bolting rabbit' which again must be ignored so that your dog learns not to be distracted by something suddenly leaping up in close proximity but keeps its mind focused on the task.

Part of the training will include teaching your dog to jump obstacles and fences and to enter water without hesitation.

In due course your dog will be introduced to flushing and retrieving in a real situation and this is hopefully where all the previous training will pay off. In order to achieve this, as expressed earlier, you will need to join a gundog group or club and take part in regular training sessions where you can be trained along with your dog.

SEARCH WORK

All dogs have a heightened sense of smell which is far more effective than our own, around a thousand times stronger. Spanish Water Dogs, like other gundog breeds, have a particularly keen sense of smell coupled with the drive to follow and remain on a scent. This makes the breed ideal for search work.

You may have a picture in your mind of search and rescue dogs being given an item of clothing to sniff, following a ground scent and leading the handler straight to the missing person. In reality a trained Search Dog is more likely to 'air-scent,' that is pick up traces of human scent in the air. Scent spreads from a missing person or article in a three-dimensional cone shape, or 'scent cone'. The dog works across the scent cone covering a narrower area with each pass, until it locates the source of the scent. This is, in fact, a very efficient way of covering a large area of land far more quickly and effectively than a line of people walking in the same direction and, of course, dogs can be deployed at night. Once it has reached the 'body' the dog will have been trained to give an indication to the handler and the last part of its job is to make sure the handler reaches the place where the find is located, safely. The preferred indication may vary from dog to dog or group to group but it may be in the form of barking or possibly running back and forth between handler and 'body', all the while indicating the direction. Once the

Team Talk!

handler and the missing person are together in the same place, the dog has finished its job and is rewarded with a favourite toy, or food—whatever the dog likes best. The dog is not involved in the rescue, which is why they are referred to as 'search dogs' rather than 'search and rescue dogs'.

The circumstances in which a search dog is deployed can vary. It may be a hill walker in a remote

Kaye preparing to send Bramble on a search

upland setting who has not returned to base because he has become lost or injured, a child who has wandered away from home, an old person who has become confused and wandered away from familiar surroundings or even a victim of crime. Dogs may be used to search for missing people in the mountains, in lowland areas, woodland, water, urban areas, buildings etc—anywhere in fact where someone might get lost. Training not only involves looking for the living. Everyone hopes for a happy outcome but in some instances the missing person may have died. Some search dogs will have been trained to find a body as well as a live person, using a synthetic chemical or, in some areas, well-rotted pork—which apparently smells very similar to a decomposing human body.

There are a number of different breeds

used in search work but the advantages of a breed such as ours are that it is highly motivated, naturally agile and eager to learn. There are several Spanish Water Dogs already operational or in training in the UK and they are considered very much an asset to the group that they work for.

You may find that this sort of activity is one you would very much like to become involved in. Apart from being well worthwhile by providing a useful service, it is a rewarding and enjoyable way to spend time with your dog, although you do need be aware that you, as handler, are one half of the operational team—and it takes considerably longer to train a handler than it does a dog. It does require a major commitment in terms of time spent training, practising, being assessed for the various stages of expertise and being ready at the drop of a hat to go on a 'call-out' when required. In the event that a search results in a sad conclusion you need to consider the emotional effect this may have on you. Instruction will be given to prepare handlers for such eventualities and counselling would be available after the event, should it be required. If you wish to consider this then you would need to find a group local to yourself and make some enquiries. Most groups are pleased to consider new recruits and will advise you as to what is required from you and your dog.

THERAPY DOGS

It is a proven scientific fact that contact with a companion animal can lower the heart rate, body temperature and stress levels of an individual simply through stroking it. So many people, adults, children, the aged, physically and mentally handicapped find themselves in a situation where owning or having full time access to a pet is not possible. It may be that the person is in a hospital, nursing home, or being cared for where pets are not permitted. There are groups of volunteers who take their own pets to visit people in this situation and dogs seem to be the easiest and most popular animal used for this purpose. A number of organisations now welcome visiting dogs with their handlers and regular visits can be very therapeutic for patients and residents.

So often, people who have been hospitalised for some considerable time or who spend day after day with little change to their routine, can feel isolated and lonely and this often leads to them becoming depressed or withdrawn. It is amazing how quickly people in this situation respond to a visiting dog.

Ripple is a registered 'Pets as Therapy' Dog and works in a residential home for the elderly

The dog does not make any judgements and will treat each individual the same, asking for no more than a hand to stroke it or to be cuddled. People with poor or no communication skills seem to quickly relate to a dog and bond with it. Others who are well aware of their own physical limitations but are mentally astute look forward to a regular visit and will spend a few happy moments telling and retelling stories about pets they have had in the past.

Not all Spanish Water Dogs are suitable for this task, as I have found through experience. Because of the naturally reserved temperament of this breed it is not unusual for them to be wary of strangers, and therefore reluctant to meet new people or to be touched by them. Also, some establishments can be daunting to a dog with all the hustle and bustle and myriad of strange smells. This, fortunately, is not the case with all of them and a large number of Spanish Water Dogs are friendly, outgoing and confident. Couple this with some solid basic training, good manners and a desire to be touched and stroked by children, adults, old and infirmed alike and you have the perfect therapy dog.

If your dog fits this picture and you have some spare time available then why not consider having it registered as a therapy dog? As long as your dog is quite happy to travel in the car and enjoys going to different places then nothing else is required in terms of special skills, but there are certain procedures required of you and your dog before you can begin visiting. It is necessary to become a member of a group that organises visits and this has the advantage of you being covered by insurance. PAT (Pets as Therapy) is probably the most well known organisation and several Spanish Water Dogs are already members. In order to become a visiting member it is necessary for a police check to be done which is currently standard procedure for everyone coming into contact with children or vulnerable people. Once cleared, you will be asked to take your dog to be assessed by a nominated person who has been trained for this task. The assessment takes the form of a number of simple exercises to test for the correct reactions in certain situations and to see whether the dog displays the desired temperament. If successful then the paperwork is forwarded to the organisation and arrangements are made for visiting to commence.

Another aspect of this work is the use of dogs to help dog-phobic people overcome their fears of seeing and meeting dogs. We accept that not everyone likes dogs and if it is simply a dislike then contact can be avoided without too much difficulty. A genuine fear of dogs can have an entirely different result in that the fear is so great it seriously affects that person's life. A phobic person may avoid going out into public places or, on coming into contact with a dog, become immobilised by extreme panic. If help has been sought in order to deal with this problem then

Abigail was dog-phobic but, with patience, Ripple is helping her to overcome her fear.

meeting a dog may be part of the treatment. Having contact with a dog in a none threatening situation and being within a comfort zone will help the person to rationalise and begin to control their fear. It is a special sort of dog that is needed for this work, one that is very calm and quiet and with plenty of patience in order to wait until the patient feels confident enough to approach and eventually touch. There are at least two Spanish Water Dogs in the UK that have already worked with phobic children. One of them has the added advantage of having a beautiful golden coat, giving it the appearance of a cuddly teddy bear rather than a dog.

Regular visiting with a therapy dog is very rewarding for the handler as well as the clients. It is an opportunity to meet and talk to some very interesting people who have led full lives and enjoy the opportunity to talk to someone who can take the time to listen. The presence of a dog often helps them communicate more freely and being able to caress it brings them so much pleasure.

BREED SHOWING

Some time after the Spanish Water Dog was introduced into the UK, the breed was accepted by the Kennel Club onto the 'Imported Breeds Register' followed by its inclusion onto the 'Breed Register' in January 2008, which allows the breed to be shown in a greater variety of classes at shows.

The showing of Spanish Water Dogs is becoming more popular as the numbers in the UK increase. Certainly, those that have been shown have attracted a great deal of interest from both owners of other breeds and judges alike.

Showing your dog can be an expensive hobby, requiring a substantial amount of travelling, but it can be a very rewarding occupation, especially if your dog does well in the ring.

However, it must be pointed out that Spanish Water Dogs were **not** bred specifically for the show-ring and, if that is all they do, they will lead a very limited existence and never reach their full potential. This breed does not take kindly to a life of confinement in a kennel or cage only to be brought out for shows. Showing needs to be balanced with other activities, such as those described in this book, in order to keep the dog stimulated, fit and, above all, happy.

Correct presentation of your dog for the show-ring has been covered in Chapter 4, CARE OF YOUR SPANISH WATER DOG but it cannot be emphasised enough that the natural, rustic appearance is paramount. This does not mean to say that your dog's coat should be dirty and unkempt. The natural look can still be achieved after bathing or preferably swimming and hand grooming. The finished product presented before a judge should give the impression of a dog that can do a full day's work which, in reality, it is exactly what every example of the breed is still capable of doing.

Regular 'ring-craft' training will accustom you and your dog to show-ring etiquette. How you choose to handle your dog in the ring is up to you. However, it is worth noting the words of the late Harry Baxter, former president of The Spanish Water Dog Club, "The taut lead lifts the leather on the ear of a Poodle, a short-faced breed gags and snorts for breath. It may cause the dog to raise its head up and in toward the handler, and the forelegs to be lifted in a high prancing movement."

A good show dog will have been taught to 'show' his teeth to the judge

In my experience, a Spanish Water Dog that has been trained and allowed to move freely round the ring on a loosely held lead will step out with style, purpose and enthusiasm, giving the judge the pleasure of seeing it move as nature intended.

A well-presented dog will catch the judge's eye, as Lastar is doing here.

CONCLUSION

Owning a Spanish Water Dog will never leave you wondering what to do with it. Because of their trainability and enthusiasm for work there is always some activity for you to consider having a go at and it may well be one not covered here. What you will find is that, given the correct training and advice, and adapting it to your dog, you will not only have a happy dog leading a full life but also one that you can be proud of. All members of your family can be actively involved. You don't need to worry if your dog is taking part in more than one discipline, as this breed understands what is required for each and adapts accordingly. Obedience, for instance, requires a steady dog but agility and flyball are more frenetic. Provided you are not asking the dog to perform in a venue where both activities are happening simultaneously there should not be a problem.

15 BREEDING

INTRODUCTION

Whether or not to consider breeding from your Spanish Water Dog is entirely up to you. If there are restrictions placed on your dog as part of your contract then the decision lies with you and your Breeder. Once you have clearance to breed then it is not a step to be taken lightly, especially in a numerically small breed such as ours and, in particular, giving consideration to some very important points made in the previous chapters of this book. Spanish Water Dogs are still quite rare in this country and, because of their cuddly looks and unusual, non-shedding coat, they attract a great number of people. Some of these, for many reasons, may not be suitable to take one on, especially in light of the strong guarding instinct and the problems this may cause. Consider what your reasons for breeding a litter are before you take the plunge. Looking at it from the worst scenario, if your remit for breeding litters is to meet a demand and make a handsome profit into the bargain you may well be successful but be prepared for this to back-fire on you. Be warned, you could end up having to take dogs back that have not been suitably homed, have temperament problems or health issues. If you have laid out a large amount of money with the intention of getting it back with interest then do not be surprised by the possibility of your bitch having a small litter or even no puppies at the end of it. We are not dealing with a commodity here but with live animals that do not always perform to the blueprint we have put in place for them.

If, however, you enter into breeding with honourable intentions then, in order to rear a litter correctly, you need to take into account the equipment required, your time, nutrition, socialisation and a whole host of other factors as well as finding suitable homes for the puppies. All this requires great commitment on your part; cutting corners or compromising on standards will not produce good quality, well adjusted puppies that will bring pleasure to their new families for many years to come.

Flooding the market with large numbers of puppies from bitches bred as frequently as possible does not do the breed any favours either. With a small gene pool such as ours it is vital to widen it at every opportunity by introducing new lines that compliment those already established in the UK. Quantity can never improve on quality.

It is essential that, before considering breeding with your dog, you educate and familiarise yourself as much as possible with all the factors that influence the quality and well-being of the planned pups and in this chapter we will endeavour to give you as much of this information as we can.

If you were to compile a list of desirable traits to breed for and put them in order of importance, it would be interesting to see what will be at the top. Would it be working ability, show quality, health or something else? As this breed is not without its temperament problems, perhaps this ought to be at the top of the list. Timidity is a trait that presents itself frequently and, in a feral situation, it is desirable in that it is necessary for survival but is not so acceptable in a family pet.

Behaviour is never wholly inherited nor wholly acquired but develops as a result of a combination of influences of heredity and environment. The Breeder has the ability to modify behaviour by choosing to select for desired hereditary factors along with providing the optimum environment in which to rear the puppies.

Perhaps also high on the list of factors to breed for should be workability or trainability. Some may consider that this could be regarded as 'intelligence' but any correlation between intelligence in humans and in dogs should be avoided. Dogs use whatever capacity they have to problem solve in order to take from their environment all they need for survival and, ultimately, comfort. Spanish Water Dogs, being a relatively primitive breed, have a comparatively strong workability trait which is heritable, therefore can be selected for.

Before you even consider mating your Spanish Water Dog take a good look at her and decide if you consider her to be a good example of the breed, not too big or too small, well proportioned, muscular, active, of sound temperament and with the ability to work. If you feel you need a second opinion then ask your Breeder or someone with experience of the breed who can make an unbiased and sound judgement. If you are seeking the opinion of a show judge then be sure that he or she knows the breed equally as well as some of the more established Spanish Water Dog owners. A good judge will be able to assess a dog for its ability to do a full day's work from 'hands on' and from its movement rather than how attractive it can look in the show-ring. Keep in the forefront of your mind that what you are dealing with is essentially a working breed that can also do well in the show-ring. As such, breeding specifically for the show-ring is not what this breed should be about. If this is your main criterion for breeding have you considered a breed that is well established in the show ring, thus leaving this one to those who wish to keep it as it was originally intended?

HEALTH ISSUES

When Spanish Water Dogs were first introduced into the UK owners were unaware of any health problems in the breed and those that were imported appeared to be sound and healthy, so matings went ahead with emphasis on bringing together suitable lines. Since those early days of establishing the breed in this country three known inherited health problems have been diagnosed. These are Hip Dysplasia, Glaucoma and Demodex. Although, at time of writing, the incidences of affected dogs have been small (less than 1% of the breed in each case) it would be irresponsible of any breeder of Spanish Water Dogs to ignore the fact that these diseases exist. To carry on breeding without doing everything within their power to educate themselves about these issues and so reduce occurrences in future generations would be detrimental to the breed. The Kennel Club keeps a list of current breed-specific health checks for each breed and most Breed Clubs will ask that these are carried out by members prior to mating. There are two on the list at the moment for Spanish Water Dogs: Hip-scoring and Gonioscopy. There are sufficient dogs now tested for predisposition to glaucoma (gonioscopy) for the Kennel Club to put the breed on 'Schedule A'. Schedule A lists the known inherited eye diseases in the breeds where it is considered that there is enough scientific information to show that the condition is inherited in that breed. The Kennel Club has produced the list as a recommendation for breeders to test, unless you are registered as an 'Accredited Breeder', in which case eye testing for predisposition to glaucoma is a requirement, as is hip scoring. As these health problems are already in the breed surely it makes sense to follow KC guidelines and test!

With Hip Dysplasia and Glaucoma there are tests available which will indicate the status of an individual dog. Once testing has been carried out, and a result produced, the Breeder is then in a position of making an educated judgement about whether or not to proceed with a mating. Without such testing, matings are no more than a lottery.

In the case of Demodex, there is no way of knowing whether or not affected pups may be produced prior to mating by doing a specific test. However, there is an inherited factor that causes predisposition to Demodex and only by knowing and understanding the mode of inheritance can an informed decision be made.

Hip Dysplasia

In simple terms the hip joint is made up of 'ball' at the end of the upper leg that fits into a 'socket' within the hip-bone. The ball is supposed to match the socket by fitting it snugly with no slipping or moving outside of the socket. A snug, correct fit allows the dog to run, jump, twist and turn without any effort or ill effect.

Hip Dysplasia (HD) is a term for abnormalities with the ball and socket joint and the extent of the abnormality can vary from a small deviation from the snug fit right through to the ball not fitting in the socket at all. The amount of pain and disability that a dog suffers depends on the extent of the abnormality.

Hip Dysplasia itself is a complex subject, the causes are numerous and inter-dependent, being the result of a combination of genetic inheritance and environmental factors. These include feeding regimes, exercise during the growth period and injury. There is an argument put forward that bedding materials in the first few weeks can influence hip development.

How much is dependent on the inheritance factor as opposed to environmental influences is a subject of much debate and is not fully understood but, in order to reduce the incidence of producing stock with hip abnormalities, testing is the way forward. If the parents are carrying genetic material for HD there is a very high chance that their offspring will as well. The greater the genetic contribution from the parents the greater the chance of the offspring inheriting the same. In my research of the subject I came across an interesting statement by one vet, 'HD is 100% genetics and 100% environmental.' What he meant by this is that before birth the level of HD has already been established 100% by inheritance but after birth the further development of the hips is then 100% dependent on how the dog is fed, exercised and possibly even injured.

The environmental element of this problem can be put down to the methods of individual breeders in rearing litters and owners in feeding, exercising and protecting their dogs from injury.

The genetic element needs to be considered before mating takes place. In order to ascertain the quality of hips of an individual dog it needs to be presented for hip scoring. The method that is readily available to all in the UK is the BVA/KC scoring system. This requires an x-ray of the pelvic region taken under anaesthetic, which is then sent to a panel of four Vets for assessment prior to scoring. There are nine criteria that are measured with six levels of degree of abnormality. Each criterion is then given a number from 0 – 6, first for one hip then for the other. The numbers are added up for each hip and then the totals for both hips are added together to give an overall score. The lower the score, the better the quality of the hip. Generally speaking, if one hip has a substantially different score from the other this is most probably an indication of injury on the higher scored side.

Views and opinions vary on subjects such as the quality of the x-ray, the ability of the Vet to set the dog up correctly, the scoring system, environmental influences etc so the current system does receive some criticism. You need to place a great deal of trust in your Vet, his expertise and his opinion of the x-ray.

The current system of hip scoring is not the definitive solution to the problem but it is a starting point. Recently introduced into the UK is another system of scoring hips, which is considered more detailed and accurate. This is the PennHip System, introduced from the States. If you are fortunate enough to live within reasonable travelling distance of someone who can offer this service then it is worth considering but it does cost more. Whichever system you choose to use it is recommended that you should view the x-ray in the presence of your Vet before it is sent for scoring where the subject can be fully discussed and his expert opinion of the quality of the hips can be given.

Squiffy has a high hip-score and confirmed hip dysplasia. By following a regime of correct diet and exercise she has continued to suffer from few problems relating to hips well into middle age and remains fit and active

The procedure of hip-scoring under the BVA/KC scoring scheme is done once for each dog from the age of twelve months onwards, (three months onwards for 'PennHip') and when you have received the score it is only then that an informed decision can be made whether or not to go ahead and breed from that dog. If you choose to use your dog for breeding without having it scored, how can you ever know what you are breeding from? You may be lucky and have a dog with good hips that passes this on to its progeny. On the other hand, you may be dealing with something entirely different, passing on potential problems that will not only cause the affected dog to suffer excruciating pain for most of its life but also untold misery for the family who own the dog, who will also be faced with a substantial financial outlay in vet's bills. If it is later proved that you were aware of hip dysplasia in the breed but still opted not to test your breeding stock you could also leave yourself wide open to litigation.

Glaucoma

A very small number of incidences of Closed Angle Glaucoma and the closely related eye disease of Primary Lens Luxation have been diagnosed in Spanish Water Dogs in the UK.

In a normal eye the interior is filled with fluid that is continually produced and drains away naturally, creating an environment of stable pressure within the eye. The fluid drains through a narrow pathway (the iridocorneal angle) designed for this function. If this pathway is restricted in any way the drainage of the fluid cannot take place and the result is that pressure builds up within the eye. Not only does an increase in pressure cause great pain to the dog but it also damages certain parts of the eye, which then leads to impairment of vision and blindness. One cause of pressure building up within the eye is that the dog has been born with a drainage pathway that is too narrow.

Whether or not the pathway is narrow or wide is already predetermined; it is inherited. The mode of inheritance has not yet been fully determined but it is believed by experts to be the result of a polygenetic trait. This is where several genes work together rather than one gene working on its own.

Once the first case of Glaucoma had been diagnosed in the breed a small group of owners presented their dogs for testing and, as a result, it has been found that a significant number of them had a predisposition to Glaucoma. Predisposition does **not** mean that the dog will suffer from the condition. However, a mildly predisposed or 'clear' dog is less likely to develop the condition than a moderately or severely predisposed dog. The major problem with this condition in terms of breeding programmes is that the disease does not usually develop until middle or old age, by which time an affected, untested dog may already have produced offspring, and its progeny could well have inherited the trait and passed it on to their offspring. Without knowing the status of a particular dog's eyes before being bred from, predisposition to the condition may already have become entrenched in that line before you become aware of it.

The only foolproof way to be sure that this trait is first of all minimised and then totally eradicated in the future is for breeders to test prior to breeding and not to breed from significantly predisposed dogs. The test used to determine predisposition is called a Gonioscopy. This is done separately from the basic eye test for PRA under the KC/BVA/ISDS testing scheme and only needs to be done once in a dog's lifetime. It can be carried out on dogs from five to six months of age onwards and involves a specially adapted lens being

Azor, who was affected by glaucoma and eventually became blind

placed on the outside of the eye after the administration of anaesthetic drops. The specialist can then see a magnified view of the drainage pathway and will be able to determine the width of it. The whole procedure is painless and quick. In the case of one particular eye specialist, Professor Peter Bedford, a scoring system has been adopted. He gives a score from 0 – 5, 0 being clear and 5 being severely predisposed. The advice from this particular Vet is to breed only from those dogs with a clear result or mild predisposition. Due to the size of our gene pool it is felt that to breed from clear-eyed dogs only would limit the number of dogs available for breeding. If a particular dog is mildly predisposed it is recommended that it be bred to one that is clear.

The aim of caring, responsible breeders is to ultimately produce stock that does not inherit or pass on this trait. In order to do this we, as owners of this breed, need to test for this painful and hideous condition, keep and share records of the results and avoid breeding from moderately or severely affected stock. We have a small gene pool compared with many breeds and the smaller the gene pool the easier it is for an inherited trait such as this to take hold.

Surely we have an obligation, in our aim to protect the breed as a whole, as well as to potential owners, to take every precaution we can to produce stock that will not develop this disease in the future. Each dog that we breed and sell will be a companion animal for a family who will become emotionally attached to it, so we must aim to provide them with the best that we can produce.

Progressive Retinal Atrophy (PRA)

Although no cases of PRA have been diagnosed in the UK at the time of writing, it is common practice in this breed, as in many others, to have your dog tested on an annual basis, especially if you intend to breed from it. The test is supervised by the British Veterinary Association, the Kennel Club and the International Sheep Dog Society (BVA/KC/ISDS). It is a quick and painless procedure that is carried out by specialist Vets who hold testing clinics all round the country, particularly at canine events. These sessions are regularly advertised in the dog press. Current clear PRA eye certificates are often requested before a mating can take place and this is a prerequisite to breeders who are members of the Spanish Water Dog Club.

As the disease is progressive, which means that it gets worse with time, it is not unusual for some breeders to carry on having a dog tested annually, even after it is no longer being bred from, in order to ascertain whether or not PRA has developed in a particular line. Future breeding plans could be dependent on this information.

Demodex

Cases of Demodex or Demodectic Mange, a skin condition, have now been confirmed in the breed and, although the condition is treatable once diagnosed, it is both unpleasant and unsightly but, most importantly, it can be avoided. Although Demodex itself is not inherited, the lack of immunity to the demodectic mange mite is, so it is of great importance for breeders to understand the workings of this condition if it is to be eradicated from the breed. Demodex, a mange mite found in the hair follicles, is present in controllable numbers in all dogs that have been raised by their mothers. The mite is transferred from the bitch to her pups in the nest. In a dog with a normal immune system the mite does not cause a problem and is kept under control so you are not aware of it. It cannot be passed on to other dogs, except by the method already mentioned, or to people. However, in a dog with a compromised immune system, the immune system is not able to control the spread of mites as it would in a normal dog, and they increase in massive numbers and cause skin lesions. This can manifest itself as localised or generalised. 'Generalised' means that it spreads over the body as opposed to 'localised', which may be just around the eyes. The inadequacy of the immune system is an inherited recessive trait that can be carried by dogs that will never, themselves, suffer from the disease, but could pass it on to their offspring.

When two carriers are mated there is a one in four chance that the condition will arise, a one in two chance that carriers will be produced and a one in four chance that the puppies are neither affected, nor a carrier. If a puppy from a litter develops Demodex then you can automatically assume that **both** its parents will be carriers. There is no physical or external evidence to show that they are carriers, as they will appear normal. This will only come to light after they have been bred from and have produced offspring that develop Demodex. Because there is no test readily available to pinpoint carriers the advice of geneticists is that once it has occurred, both parents, and any siblings of affected dogs, should be removed from the gene pool in order to ensure that line does not continue to produce further potential carriers and affected dogs. Taking only one parent out of the gene pool will not solve the problem because the other is still carrying the trait and can produce further carriers in future litters, even if the mate is free of the gene. There is a one in two chance that a carrier parent can produce puppies bearing the affected gene even if the mate does not have the gene.

As a carrier does not show symptoms of the disease it would be easy to assume that it is clear of the condition and so could be used within a breeding programme. The disease may not affect the offspring, suggesting they are also clear. The danger here is that you cannot know whether the offspring are carriers or not, as there is no test for the trait, but ultimately it will become apparent if, further down the line, two carriers come together and produce offspring that later go on to develop Demodex. The chances of this are heightened if you choose to line breed on a regular basis, especially in a gene pool as small as ours, even more so if you favour inbreeding.

If any of you are thinking about breeding from your Spanish Water Dog it is vital that you research this disease further, acquaint yourself with the facts and aim to understand the mode of inheritance. Find out if any of the dogs in your dog's pedigree have produced offspring with Demodex, and study pedigrees very carefully before deciding which mate to use. If you find this a daunting task then ask for assistance from someone who understands lines and inheritance.

At the time of writing, there are no other known inherited health problems in this country but there are two conditions that have come to light on the Continent. Cases of severe hair loss have been reported in Finland, both dogs sharing the same mother but having different fathers. The hair has dropped out and never grown back and, although there is no confirmed diagnosis, Vets are tending towards follicular dysplasia, which is also to be found in Poodles and Portuguese Water Dogs. Cases of shortened or missing toes have also been found in some Finnish dogs and it is believed that there is an inheritance factor governing this trait too. This problem may not be confined to Finland but evidence of examples in other countries is not available at the time of writing.

Although we have not experienced either problem in the UK it is important that we are aware of any health issues in the breed regardless of where they are found. It is also imperative for owners and breeders throughout the world to be open and honest with their findings and share the information internationally. By doing this we can limit the spread of unwanted or damaging traits.

TAIL LENGTH

If your Spanish Water Dog was born when docking was still legal then you most likely will own one that was docked soon after birth. It is quite common for tail lengths to vary, even in the same litter. Lengths can vary to include full, three quarter, half, short and 'natural bob' where no tailbones exist at all. Although an attempt at keeping records of tail lengths at birth has been made, the information is not comprehensive and, unless your Breeder has informed you or you have obtained a dog that is not docked, you may not even know what the length of your dog's tail was at birth. This piece of information is vital before you consider breeding. In other breeds where 'natural bobs' occur there is evidence of problems arising if a dog with a natural bob is bred to another dog with a natural bob. There have been incidences of pups from these matings being born with spina bifida. Although we know of no such matings in Spanish Water Dogs, so cannot say whether such a mating would produce affected pups, it is better to err on the side of caution and not take the risk. Such a mating would be an interesting experiment but who would be prepared to accept the consequences if spina bifida where to occur?

CONCLUSION

Having decided that your dog has the desired temperament, conformation and working ability that are the hallmarks of this breed the next stage is to test for those health problems where tests exist and to take the others into consideration. We all wish for good results and for our dogs to be perfect in every respect but sometimes a result comes back that signifies a problem to a greater or lesser degree. This does not mean that the dog cannot be bred from. What is required is for you to look at the whole dog from all aspects mentioned in this chapter. If your dog is basically sound in most areas but is less than perfect in one, this is where your educated decision of whether or not to go ahead and breed needs to be made. In a gene pool as small as ours we cannot exclude all dogs with one fault, especially if it is perfectly sound in every other aspect. We are assuming, of course, that the fault is not a major one and the degree of the fault can be balanced by using a mate that has good qualities in that area. If, however, you have not bothered to test in the first place then you cannot make the same educated decision and you could be playing 'Russian Roulette' with your puppies. There has been enough publicity within the breed to make all breeders and potential breeders aware of the risks. There are DNA tests that have been developed to establish if a dog is a carrier of certain inherited health problems but unfortunately none of these, at time of writing, apply to Spanish Water Dogs. Some experts in the field of breeding will advocate the use of carriers within a breeding programme, especially in a very small gene pool, but this is on the assumption that the breeder knows and understands fully the inheritance of the trait, the lines and pedigrees of both mates and their status. The procedure is then carried out as part of a long term breeding programme and doubling up on the fault is to be avoided at all costs.

There may be other health issues that we are not yet aware of, but we are certain that these will be dealt with as they arise as, generally speaking, owners of this breed tend to be open and honest about health problems that they have encountered. We consider that to ignore those we already know about and to carry on breeding regardless without testing could be considered as callous and even irresponsible.

SELECTING A MATE

There is no such thing as the perfect Spanish Water Dog, although we would all like to think the ones that we own are better than everyone else's! To find perfection you need to go to the Breed Standard, which is the blueprint for the perfect specimen. Ultimately, in our breeding plans, this is what we should be aiming for. We will never attain it, but we should attempt to get as close to it as possible. We also need to remove those 'rose-tinted spectacles' when we are judging our own dogs and assessing for strengths and weaknesses. In the search for a suitable mate, if we can **honestly** assess the weaknesses, and then balance them with the other dog's strengths, we are doing our best.

The starting point for choosing a mate should be the pedigrees of both dogs in order to study the 'lines'. There are three possible methods to consider: - Inbreeding, Line Breeding and Out crossing. Different breeders have varying views about which is best but the most important factor to consider, in such a small gene pool as ours, is the width, or lack of it. In a breed where hundreds of stud dogs are available from many different lines we can consider that as wide. In our breed we are currently limited to a very small number of stud dogs and most of them are inter-related.

Inbreeding occurs when the sire and dam are very closely related and have pedigrees that are similar. Matings from half brother and half sister, uncle and niece, first cousins, for example, are close enough to be considered as inbreeding. Unless you know the ancestry of your dog in depth, and have a good working knowledge of every dog in its pedigree, their good points, faults, temperament and health status, then inbreeding is something that should be avoided. If there are any deleterious genes in such close lines you can almost guarantee they would be 'doubled up' through such a mating and will certainly express themselves at some stage in future litters.

Line breeding generally involves breeding together a dog and a bitch with a common ancestor, i.e. one dog or bitch that appears on both pedigrees. The remaining dogs or 'lines' in the two pedigrees would be unrelated. You would choose to line breed to a particular dog because of its exceptional qualities but it must always be remembered that if it had any faults, obvious or hidden, there would be a risk that these could be magnified as well as the good points. Therefore it is essential that the common ancestor is a dog about which you know a great deal.

An 'outcross' is a mating of two dogs that have completely different pedigrees. Out crossing can strengthen your line by bringing together the 'vigour' from both lines. However, the result can be an unknown quantity and it is not so easy to predict what you are going to get. It may be worth considering using a mate that has already produced progeny and to have a good look at what the offspring are like. This will give you a guide.

Assuming it is a bitch that you wish to breed from, and having researched which stud dogs are available, you will need to decide which dog has the most desirable attributes that you want to bring to your kennel, and which one will best suit the attributes of your bitch. Look at all the points discussed already: temperament, conformation, health, working ability, pedigree and previous offspring then choose the dog that will compliment your bitch, avoiding any exaggerations or weaknesses. The temptation may be to go to the one that lives nearest for convenience, the cheapest stud fee or the number of champions in the pedigree. This may not be the most suitable mate for your bitch if all of the above have been taken into account. Becoming a champion does not necessarily guarantee that a dog has the ability to pass his qualities to his offspring.

In order to become a champion a dog must have won its title on the show circuit (under FCI rules but not in the UK). This does not take into account the stud dogs that are not shown but may have excelled in other areas and that have equally as much to offer the gene pool without a title added to their name. Not all Spanish Water Dogs are shown and there are a number of high quality specimens that never step foot inside a show-ring.

If possible, visit the dog and see it in its home environment, watch it at work and in play, satisfy yourself that it has a sound temperament, moves with ease, is free from any obvious ailments, infections or parasites and is happy and relaxed. Also try to see the dog away from its home, possibly in a more stressful environment like a dog venue, and see if the temperament is still as sound. Ask to see evidence of health test results and do not just take the breeder's word for them. Having chosen a suitable stud dog for your bitch ask for photocopies of the health test results so that you can pass them on to potential owners. If test results are not forthcoming, for whatever reason, then reassess the situation and decide whether or not you are prepared to take the risk with an unknown quantity.

If your bitch is a 'maiden bitch', which means she has never had puppies before, it is advisable to use a stud dog that has plenty of experience and can be relied on to do the 'job' without fuss.

Having satisfied yourself that the dog you have chosen is the most suitable one for your bitch the next stage will be the mating.

The Stud Dog

If you intend to use your dog at stud then certain matters need addressing before mating takes place. Your dog should be free from infection and external parasites. It should be fed on an appropriate diet in order to ensure sufficient energy and quality of sperm. The arrangements for payment of stud fee should be made clear to the client beforehand and, in the instance of no pups being produced, an agreement for return of part or the entire fee or the opportunity for a return mating should be offered. Both parties need to agree to these terms before mating takes place so that no misunderstandings arise.

The Brood Bitch

The bitch will generally only come 'into season' twice a year but this can vary from bitch to bitch. If you intend to have her mated on the next due season then it is as well to make certain preparations before mating takes place. Ensure that your bitch is up to date with her worming regime, particularly for roundworms, as these can be passed through the placenta and the milk to the offspring. If your bitch has been wormed regularly throughout her life the chances of this happening are negligible. The worm can lie dormant inside the bitch in the form of a cyst, which is then activated by the change in hormone levels. Even though you have wormed her prior to mating, this will not fully guarantee freedom of worm burden in the pups but will be a step in the right direction. There are worming products that can be administered during pregnancy but I would recommend that once mating has taken place it is better not to interfere unless absolutely essential.

Ensure that your bitch is free of any infections and parasites that can be passed on to the dog, is the correct weight for the breed and is in a fit and healthy condition. Obesity can sometimes cause loss of fertility. Continue your usual daily routine with your bitch but avoid putting her under any unnecessary stress that may affect the outcome of the mating. Pregnancy is more likely to occur if the bitch is calm and generally contented.

WHEN TO MATE?

There are no hard and fast rules about the time that a bitch will be ready for mating, i.e. the time that she ovulates. In a normal season the first stage, usually accompanied by bleeding, lasts approximately ten to twelve days. However, this can vary enormously from one bitch to another. Rarely, a bitch may show no signs of bleeding at all. This is usually referred to as a 'blind' season and can make it very difficult to assess her readiness for mating. In the second stage, the flow of red blood will slow down and change to a brownish or pinkish colour and the swollen vulva will soften. This is the point at which ovulation occurs and is usually around day ten to twelve but in some extreme cases can be as early as day three or as late as day twenty-five. Ovulation is the releasing of the eggs, which then require a further forty-eight to seventy-two hours to mature and can remain viable for another twenty-four hours. This means that generally you have four days during which a successful mating is likely.

Even though the bitch may be more than willing to 'stand' prior to ovulation she is not ready and an experienced stud dog will know this and may show little interest in her. Should you wish to adopt a more scientific approach there are tests that can be carried out by your Vet to ascertain when ovulation has taken place.

Once your bitch has come into season it would be prudent to get in touch with the stud dog owner immediately and plan approximate dates for the visit. It is accepted that the bitch visits the dog for mating to take place and common practice is for there to be two matings forty-eight hours apart. As this may necessitate several visits to get the timing right be prepared for a lot of travelling and possibly overnight stays, or even the bitch staying with the owners of the stud dog for the duration.

THE MATING

On arrival allow your bitch to toilet and acclimatise herself to her new surroundings. It would be wise to discuss all the arrangements, including paperwork and mode of payment for the services of the dog, before the mating takes place. The owner of the stud dog may wish to confirm the identity of the bitch.

If the stud dog is experienced his owner will almost certainly have an established procedure and will advise you as to what is required. Normally, it is a good idea to allow the pair some courtship in a safe, enclosed area. This gives them time to get to know one another and is also likely to lead to a more successful outcome.

When mating takes place both dogs must be supervised and you will be responsible for your bitch as the stud dog owner supervises the dog. When the dog mounts the bitch there may be a period of pelvic thrusts without penetration in the initial stages but once penetration has taken place, firm but gentle restraint of the bitch is required in order that she remains standing in the same place. However, interference with the process should be kept to the absolute minimum. Penetration of the bitch may cause her some discomfort or pain and she may even cry out but this is quite common and no cause for alarm. If the dog has his full weight on the bitch's back she may need to be supported from underneath. It is useful to have a third person available to assist.

Once the dog has achieved successful penetration and ejaculation has begun it is normal for the 'tie' to take place and ejaculation to continue. The 'tie' is the period during mating when the dog is literally held in place by the bitch's vaginal muscle spasms. She is completely in control of this phase and he has no choice in the matter. The dog cannot withdraw until the bitch releases him. This may take from a few minutes to an hour but, usually, lasts around ten to twenty minutes. Once 'tied' the dog does have a choice, however, as to the way he stands! He may choose to turn around completely, lifting one back leg over the bitch, so that they are 'tied' back to back. Alternatively, he may decide to lift a front leg over and stand at her side. As soon as the 'tie' is over and the pair are free the bitch should be removed to a quiet place where she can relax.

Any form of 'forced' mating would suggest the bitch may not be ready so is to be discouraged as this would be detrimental to her and is unlikely to result in a successful outcome.

CARE OF THE BITCH DURING PREGNANCY

On average, the pregnancy will last around sixty-three days. Three days earlier or later is common and normal but you need to be aware that the Spanish Water Dog is inclined to whelp early. During the early days in particular it is imperative that the bitch is kept calm and stress-free wherever possible whilst being allowed to carry on as normal a life as possible. Places where infections may be picked up, such as dog shows, should be avoided at all costs, especially during the first three weeks. Undue stress and certain infections could well lead to absorption or abortion of the embryos. Partial absorption of a litter is not at all uncommon.

The first signs of pregnancy appear from around three weeks onwards. First indications may be changes in behaviour or temperament, such as a more placid outlook on life and a strong desire for more cuddles! Later on you may notice some physical changes that could include a slightly 'flushed' vulva, swelling of the nipples or a subtle change in body shape. However, these symptoms can also be indicative of a phantom pregnancy so you may wish to confirm the pregnancy by having the bitch scanned. An ultra sound scan may be carried out from twenty-eight days but it should be borne in mind that embryos could still be absorbed after this stage.

Feeding the bitch during pregnancy should be approached with caution. She should continue to receive her normal diet, avoiding higher levels of protein and supplements, for the first few weeks. There should be no need to increase the amount of food, or the frequency of her meals, until around seven weeks unless she is showing obvious signs of weight loss or lack of condition. You will need to gradually increase the amount of food you offer the bitch from seven weeks onwards and almost certainly, towards the end, she will require smaller meals more frequently throughout the day. The canine uterus lies above the bladder so do not be surprised if, during the last days of her pregnancy, your bitch has toilet accidents or even some leakage of urine. Please do not scold her. Instead, ensure that any vulnerable parts of the house are either suitably protected or designated out of bounds.

Normal, sensible exercise should continue throughout the pregnancy until the bitch herself chooses to slow down. She should not, however, be allowed to over-exert or strain herself. Allowing the bitch to keep herself fit will facilitate an easy birth.

During the latter stages of the pregnancy preparation of the whelping facilities, i.e. the room and the whelping box etc., needs to be considered. The bitch should be introduced to these in a positive, rewarding manner without coercion. She may choose to ignore your carefully chosen spot at this stage but, with the correct encouragement, she should be happy to move in when the time comes!

WHELPING FACILITIES

The place you choose for the birth should be a part of the house that the bitch has frequently had access to previously. This should be a calm environment where she feels relaxed and secure. The area should be clean, warm (but not too hot) and with easy access to outdoors for toilet trips, which will be frequent!

The whelping box should be large enough for the bitch to lie comfortably stretched out on her side without being so generous that she feels lost in it. There are available good quality disposable whelping boxes, or you may choose to make or buy a more traditional one. Strong cardboard boxes that electrical goods come in can be adapted for the purpose and an off-cut of vinyl flooring provides a hygienic waterproof base. The box should be lined with copious amounts of clean newspaper covered by some comfortable bedding, which should be removed during whelping. Remember that during labour the bitch may shred the available bedding and it will certainly need to be replaced afterwards.

THE BIRTH

Before the great moment arrives please make sure that your whelping 'kit' is complete and includes a bottle of strong spirit. This is **not** for the bitch! Your need will be greater than hers! It should also include a good supply of clean towels or paper towels, a stock of newspapers, a pair of sterilised scissors, a box with hot water bottles or heated pad with some bedding, a bin liner for soiled waste, baby wipes for cleaning your hands and something comfortable to spend a long night on!

Labour is divided into three stages.

Stage One

The first stage commences with a slight drop (37.2°C) in temperature of the bitch that you may wish to monitor by using a sterile rectal thermometer or you may choose to wait until you observe changes in the bitch's behaviour and physical appearance. She will appear restless, possibly apprehensive, attention seeking and will most likely wish to remain in your company. The abdomen will become firm to the touch as it contracts in preparation for the next stage. The vulva becomes slacker and there may be a slight discharge, which is normal.

It is as well to take plenty of time out of your normal routine and move into the whelping room, spending time with your bitch gently reassuring her, but not putting her under any pressure to lie or remain in the whelping box unless she chooses to. Remove the soft bedding from the box, leaving a thick layer of newspapers so that she can begin to 'nest' by shredding and arranging them. Nest making is a response to the discomfort the bitch is feeling and, as contractions get stronger, so may the shredding. This phase may last for several hours or even longer, during which time you will find that your bitch loses her appetite, so offering her food is not necessary, although clean water should still be available at all times. The restlessness is accompanied by a great deal of panting, which is a sign that the next stage is getting nearer. The most important point to remember is that all these behaviours are normal and you must remain calm and patient. It may help to give her a drop of 'Rescue Remedy'. A couple of drops may do you the power of good as well!

Stage Two

An indication that the birth of the pups is imminent is when regular and prolonged contractions occur. It is now time to encourage the bitch to remain in the whelping box so that she is easier to supervise. The bitch will choose to alter position frequently, look uncomfortable and pay particular attention to cleaning the area around her vulva especially if there is a lot of liquid expelled. In due course, all her efforts will be focused on bearing down in order to push the first puppy out. The puppy, sac and umbilical cord usually remain intact throughout the birthing procedure so it will most probably be the sac that is observed first at the entrance to the vagina. Further pushing will deliver the pup, probably still inside the sac and with the afterbirth attached. Do not worry if this is not the case and the pup is outside of the sac as this is also a normal procedure. The afterbirth and its components will follow later. If the bitch is overwhelmed by the whole procedure, especially if she has never had puppies before, she may try to leap out of the box and dash across the room, possibly with a puppy dangling by the cord and in danger of being given an umbilical hernia. You may need to gently but firmly place your arms

A puppy emerging in the sac.

around the bitch's upper body to hold her in place. This will also give her something to push against and expel the puppy. If the process is particularly painful she may cry out but do not be alarmed. You need to remain calm so that she will also be calm.

A confident or experienced bitch will know instinctively what to do next so it is best to let her get on with it, only intervening if you feel she is not coping. She will lick the puppy in what appears to be a vigorous fashion, which will help to stimulate it into breathing. If she wishes to eat the afterbirth, allow her to as the placenta is full of hormones that promote the production and flow of milk as well as taking the place of the bitch's first meal. Only remove them if the litter is large and there are too many for her to deal with. Mum will cut the cord with her teeth but you may wish to place two fingers either side of it near to the puppy's tummy to prevent her chewing too close. If the bitch does not deal with the cord herself, take hold of it between your finger and thumb well away from the pup and squeeze the contents towards the puppy and crush it, simulating the action of the mother's teeth. Try to break it with your fingernails if they are long enough or use the sterilised scissors if not. If you are only going to

Breaking the cord with a thumbnail

use scissors without crushing, tie a piece of sterilised thread around the cord about an inch from the puppy before cutting below the knot. If the bitch is confused and does not instinctively know what to do you may need to assist in removing the 'sac' from the puppy's face and rub it fairly vigorously, simulating the mother's tongue. Offer her the puppy to see if she will take over or put it towards a teat. The pup will know what to do even if mum does not.

Other puppies will follow in due course, possibly minutes later but sometimes there may be a delay of a couple of hours, which is still normal. As each subsequent puppy is born, if the bitch will allow it, it is sensible to gently remove those already arrived to the box which you have prepared and which should have been heated with the hot water bottle covered by a piece of bedding. When the bitch has cleaned the newborn puppy you can pop its brothers and sisters back in with their mother.

If there is an opportunity to do so without disturbing mother and babies any soiled newspapers can be removed and replaced with clean ones.

When all the pups have been safely delivered the bitch will then settle down to recover from her exertions and the pups will find their way to the teats to suckle. If you feel the need you may wish to assist in directing the pups to the correct area and guiding them onto a teat provided this is not stressing the bitch or upsetting the pup.

Stage Three

This stage, which is the delivery of the placenta, frequently overlaps stage two. If the placenta has already been delivered with the pup all you need to do is check that there are as many placentas produced as there are pups. However, this is easier said than done, as the bitch can be very adept at removing the evidence before you get a chance to see it. If you know without a shadow of doubt that one or more placentas have been retained this could be cause for concern and you will need to seek the advice of your Vet.

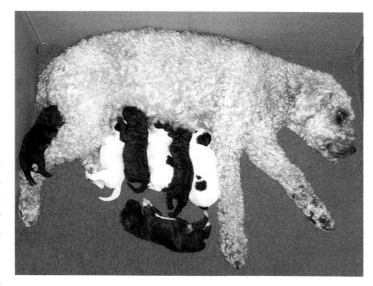

Mother and babies are doing fine!

Once all the puppies have been delivered the bitch will happily lie on her side and the pups will find their way to the teats. Ensure that all of the puppies have 'latched' on and are suckling but try to disturb mother and babies as little as possible. The action of suckling will cause contraction of the bitch's womb, which sometimes leads to some discomfort. This phase will pass and she will become more contented with time.

Once the bitch has settled down with her offspring and has regained her energy levels, it is essential that mum and babies are allowed to become acquainted with each other in a quiet and stress free environment. The minimum of outside interference is required in the early days, other than offering words of encouragement as you check frequently that all is well. Your bitch will be very reluctant to leave her family for the first few days so visits outside will be infrequent. Keep a watchful eye on any discharge. It should be dark red in colour but if it smells strongly or there is an excess of it you may need to consult your Vet.

If you are unable to spend any length of time in the same room but wish to keep an eye on the litter, a useful asset to your whelping equipment is a CCTV camera and monitor. The camera can be placed so that it is viewing the whelping box and the monitor can be in another room. Not only can you see that all is well but these instruments pick up the tiniest of sounds, which will alert you to any problems. They are not too expensive to buy and the sort that are used for human babies are ideal.

Within this chapter I have assumed that the birth has proceeded without complications so I have not covered the various problems that can arise during whelping. If you feel that you may have difficulty in coping with the ups and downs of whelping, or it is all new to you, it may be as well to have someone with you who is experienced in whelping to supervise and help with any sticky situations which may arise. It may be as well to read up on the complications of whelping prior to the birth. A useful source of information can be found in the bibliography at the end of this book.

N.B. From April 6th 2007 the Animal Welfare Bill made the docking of puppies illegal. Occasionally, Spanish Water Dogs are born with 'shortened' tails. This may result in a dilemma for anyone taking part in Kennel Club activities where 'docked' dogs will be banned. Should you be presented with puppies with short tails it might be wise to ask your Vet to check them over and issue a certificate stating that they were born like this.

BIRTH TO THREE WEEKS

For the first three weeks your priority will be to look after the bitch and leave her to look after the puppies. She will need frequent, small meals of high quality, but not necessarily high protein, food. She should have access to copious amounts of clean, fresh water. If, during the first few days, she appears to have little desire to eat she must be persuaded to drink so that her milk does not fail. If she will not drink enough plain water you could try asking her to drink it mixed with milk, but definitely **not** cow's milk. It is far better to give the bitch goat's milk or a milk substitute than it is to start bottle-feeding the puppies. The first milk, colostrum, is essential for the puppies since it carries the antibodies that the bitch has produced for their protection and is designed to kick-start the puppies into growth. However, there is a period around the third day when the normal milk takes over and at this point the supply sometimes seems insufficient. Puppies sucking, even if the supply is meagre, will prompt the bitch to produce more milk, so bottling the puppies at this stage may be counter-productive.

Make sure that the whelping box is sufficiently warm, but not too hot. Comfortable puppies, when not feeding, will lie loosely together. Cold puppies will huddle into a heap and those that are too hot will cling to the edges of the box and may even try to crawl up the corners to escape the heat.

Keep the bedding clean and dry. Although the bitch will be dealing with the puppies' waste during the early weeks, she herself will have a certain amount of discharge for some time after the birth. Although she may try to clean it herself she could bleed quite heavily, especially when she stands up, so good housekeeping is the order of the day!

During the first three weeks the bitch may not welcome the presence of other dogs. Please respect her wishes on this! She may also be wary of strangers who get too close to her babies. Again, be aware that she has the right to feel protective and don't worry. She will change her attitude as time goes by.

Appropriate handling of the puppies is required, even at this young age, and is covered in depth in Chapter 8, SOCIALISATION.

THREE TO SEVEN WEEKS

From three weeks onwards the bitch will begin to allow, or even encourage, greater contact with other people and dogs. You will now need to consider an extension to the living arrangements so that the puppies can begin to explore a larger area. Puppy panels are available that can be attached to, or placed around, the whelping box. A large crate may be incorporated, if desired, to facilitate the bitch's occasional escape from the little darlings! She will certainly want some time away from them now but she needs to be able to choose when to return so, please, don't forcibly shut her away. Including a crate will also prepare the puppies for crate training in their new homes. Plenty of toys should be made available, of differing types and textures. The puppies will now actively seek out 'toilet areas' that are away from their bedding so it will be necessary to provide this for them. A separate area of newspaper is all that is required, although 'puppy wee pads' are widely available. These absorbent pads are very effective and easy to use but can be quite expensive! Whatever you choose to use, the area will need to be changed at least after every meal, if not more often.

Now is the time to begin introducing some solid food. There are many opposing views as to the type of diet puppies should be given but the Authors feel that a suitable complete **puppy** food is all that is required. The brands that we have used successfully are 'James Wellbeloved Puppy', 'Royal Canin Puppy' and 'Nature Diet Puppy'. To begin with the food will be mixed with sufficient warm, boiled water to give it the consistency of porridge. The puppies should be offered very small quantities, four times a day, **before** the bitch is ready to feed them. This will reduce the amount of milk they wish to take from her and will begin the weaning process. Gradually, as the puppies' teeth develop, the amount of water will be reduced until the food is being offered dry, usually by about six weeks. As soon as solid food is being eaten regularly the puppies should have access to clean, fresh water at all times. As the weeks go by and the puppies eat more solid food the bitch will gradually start to restrict their access to the milk bar. She will feed them for shorter periods and will no longer lie down for them, but will sit or stand. Eventually she **may** refuse to feed them at all, although some do keep going right to the last day! This gradual change from milk to solid food will enable the bitch to dry off by the time the puppies are seven weeks of age.

Once the puppies are strong enough, and weather permitting, they should be allowed to go outside in a safe, enclosed play area. Five weeks is usually a good age to start. They need to experience the outside world and become 'hardened off' to differing temperatures. Once again, the vital aspects of the puppies' mental stimulation and development are covered in Chapter 8, SOCIALISATION.

Puppies' Progress

Newborn

One Week

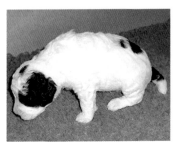

Two Weeks

Three Weeks

Four Weeks

Five Weeks

Six Weeks

Seven Weeks

SELECTING POTENTIAL OWNERS

This is one of the most important responsibilities that a breeder has towards his or her puppies. Having made certain that the puppies have received the best possible start in life it is essential to choose suitable homes and, in this breed, that is not easy! Due to the 'cute' factor and the non-shedding properties of the Spanish Water Dog a great many people become interested in owning one without any realisation of what will be involved in rearing such a 'complex' breed. Potential owners will need to be made aware of the guarding nature of the breed, the necessity for early socialisation and training as well as clear boundaries within the family. They must understand that this is not a fluffy toy that the children can sit and cuddle all day without serious consequences.

The Breeder should meet the whole family and assess their suitability objectively. Being 'very nice' is not enough – it is far better to upset them at the outset by saying "No" than it is to pick up the pieces for them **and** the puppy several months down the line. Prospective owners must have thoroughly investigated the breed, warts and all, and be prepared to put in the effort required to rear a puppy successfully. In the appendix at the back of this book there is an example of a questionnaire that could be sent out to people at the point of enquiry and returned for the Breeder to peruse at leisure. The answers would enable the Breeder to make an initial assessment before actually meeting them. Then, assuming they are potentially suitable, the family should be prepared to visit at least once **before** the puppies are ready to leave, no matter what the distance, so that a relationship can be formed between them and the Breeder.

Once it has been decided that the family are indeed suitable the Breeder should advise on choice of puppy based on his or her assessment of the family's needs and the temperament of the puppies. A strong, apparently 'dominant' puppy might not suit a family with very young children but could be perfect for an active home with older teenagers. Alternatively, a quiet, sensitive puppy might be suited to a calmer environment provided the owners are made aware that molly coddling is not required!

A puppy fitting well with his family's lifestyle and leisure pursuits

16 TWILIGHT YEARS

When we bring a dog into our homes and our lives we expect it to be with us for many years to come. So often, the new arrival has been acquired to fill an empty space that a faithful friend has left behind. I have avoided using the term 'replaced' because most of us feel that a new dog can never replace one that has been part of the family for some considerable time. However, in due course, it will have earned it's stripes and found it's way into our hearts, especially if it is a Spanish Water Dog. They have a knack for it!

All too soon it seems, your canine friend, who has lived life to the full and shared all sorts of experiences with you, slowly and imperceptibly begins to alter. You may hardly notice changes at first and you will most likely consider them of little consequence but as time passes they will become more apparent and it will be then that you realise your dog is getting old. As far as this breed is concerned it seems that they remain very active and full of life for longer than a lot of other breeds but when it does happen you need to be ready to deal with the numerous problems that may arise.

The well-known method of calculating the approximate age of your dog in human terms is to consider that one dog year is equivalent to seven human years. A more accurate method is shown in the table below:

CANINE AGE IN YEARS	0.5	1	2	3	4	5	6	7	8	9	10	11	12	13	14	15	16	17	18	19	20
HUMAN AGE IN YEARS	5	15	24	28	32	37	42	47	52	57	62	67	72	77	82	87	92	97	102	107	112

Very often, along with old age, can come ill health and I do not wish to dwell on a list of possible illnesses as each dog is different and each illness needs dealing with as it arises. However, you can expect other symptoms that will affect most dogs and are so typical of their senior years.

Your dog will begin to slow down and most probably will suffer from stiffness and arthritis. You may find that you are still fit and active but you must make allowances for your dog's painful joints and ease back on the exercise regime. He will need to spend more time sleeping and will require a quiet corner where he can enjoy a long nap without being disturbed. His bed will need to be well padded to give better support and may need to be bigger so that it is easier to get in and out of, with plenty of room to stretch out. It also needs to be draught-free and raised off the floor to ensure he is warm enough.

Less exercise means fewer calories so your dog's diet needs to be adjusted according to his needs. It is important that your dog receives the correct nutrients and a smaller amount in order to maintain condition without putting on too much weight. Excess weight will aggravate mobility problems and lead to other health problems as well. There are a number of good quality senior diets now available and quite a few veterinary practices hold obese pet clinics where sound advice on suitable diets can be obtained and your dog can be regularly weighed. As dogs age they need a lower level of protein but higher in quality and this is provided by manufacturers of good quality senior complete dog food. In most breeds seven years is considered to be the age that a senior diet becomes necessary but in a breed with the life expectancy of the Spanish Water Dog eight or nine years may be more reasonable, provided the dog is in good health.

Both sight and hearing may deteriorate so do not be surprised if your dog has difficulty in following movement or appears to be ignoring you. Many dogs suffer from cataracts in old age where the eyes appear cloudy but dogs are very good at coping with restricted eyesight and rely more on their other senses. You can help by keeping the furniture where it is and staying within reaching distance on a walk so that the dog is aware of your presence. Dogs that have lost their hearing can be taught to follow basic commands using hand signals. So often we use our hands along with our voices so he may know them already.

Be prepared for toilet accidents with an older dog. Your dog may have been clean in the house for almost all of his life so far and will not choose to be dirty but unfortunately he may not have the same control of his bladder or bowels. Take your dog outside more often than you used to and keep your eye on him for signs that he needs to go out. At night your dog may need to be confined to an area where the odd accident is of no consequence; an area that is not carpeted and the floor can be easily cleaned. Newspaper may help here.

It is not unusual for spayed bitches to lose control of the bladder in later life but this could well be a condition that responds to treatment so it is worth consulting your veterinarian. Certainly, you will need to learn tolerance and have plenty of patience.

Older dogs can often appear to be confused and begin to act strangely, like wandering from room to room for no apparent reason. Senility is just as prevalent in dogs as it is in humans. It may be that your dog has just lost interest in life and lacks motivation. Peace and quiet is all he needs with plenty of understanding of his requirements and feelings.

It is important to keep an eye on certain aspects of your dog's physical condition that can possibly be dealt with easily by yourself. Check your dog's nails for overgrowth and clip them as necessary. Less exercise will lead to them growing longer than they should be. It may be easier for you and more comfortable for your dog if the coat is kept shorter so be prepared to have him clipped more frequently. Teeth need checking regularly for deterioration and when you take your dog to the Vet's for any reason it may be worth asking him to have a look, too. An older dog often has lumps and bumps appearing under the skin. Most of these are probably harmless fatty lumps but again ask your Vet to check them if you are concerned.

In spite of being blind, Azor remained active and he continued to participate in his favourite pastimes well into old age. With the assistance of his owner, Faye, he still took part in water training, agility and flyball. What a tribute to his outstanding character and successful early training.

As your dog becomes frailer and more inactive it is time to prepare yourself for the inevitable. Ideally, it may happen suddenly and be taken out of your hands or it may be that you are faced with a decision you would prefer not to make. Each of us has it in our power to prevent the suffering that often accompanies a dog's last days and this is our final responsibility to the friend who has given us so much love without question for so long. Whilst no-one would wish to make this awful decision too soon, when quality of life is such that your companion is still enjoying some degree of comfort and happiness, it is imperative not to leave it until it is too late. Always remember this: if you delay for too long you can never take back those few days or weeks that your old friend had to endure. Is it right that he should suffer to spare you the pain? It is never easy to say goodbye but let your love allow your dog to retain his dignity to the last. You owe it to him.

Let the last two verses of Rudyard Kipling's poem '*His Apologies*' have the final word:

Master, pity Thy Servant! He is deaf and three parts blind.
He cannot catch Thy Commandments. He cannot read Thy Mind.
Oh, leave him not in his loneliness; nor make him that kitten's scorn.
He has had none other God than Thee since the year that he was born!

Lord, look down on Thy Servant! Bad things have come to pass.
There is no heat in the mid-day sun, nor health in the wayside grass.
His bones are full of an old disease – his torments run and increase.
Lord, make haste with Thy Lightnings and grant him a quick release!

Dilita continued to be successful in the show ring well into her twilight years. She was a credit to her owner, Diane, and an ambassador to the breed

17 WELFARE AND REHOMING

The Spanish Water Dog Club Welfare & Rehoming Group was formed in 2005 in the certain knowledge that it would be needed before long. Dogs of all breeds get into trouble or fall on hard times and the SWD is going to be no exception, even though there are so few in this country. Several dogs have already been taken into Welfare, rehabilitated and successfully rehomed. In such a numerically small and much sought-after breed this is a very sad state of affairs.

The nature of the problems that have presented in the dogs that have already come into welfare for rehoming confirms the importance of early socialisation and correct information being given to prospective owners **before** they purchase a puppy. If potential puppy buyers are given a true picture of the breed, its needs and its training requirements beforehand they will be better able to decide if this is a suitable breed for them and their personal circumstances. Socialisation must begin with the Breeder and continue in the new home. Early training must be motivational and non-threatening. Care must be taken not to reinforce or punish fearful, apprehensive or inappropriate guarding behaviour, as has been the case with the dogs that have needed rehoming to date. Owners need to understand the different developmental stages that these dogs go through, and learn how to approach such times positively and appropriately to prevent problems escalating.

Taking a welfare dog into the family can be a very rewarding experience and, providing the correct help and support is available, should result in a needy dog finding a permanent, loving home. However, it is important that rehoming is approached in the right way and that the emotional and physical needs of the dog are considered beforehand.

Dogs find themselves in need of rehoming for all sorts of different reasons: breakdown of the family unit; changes in financial circumstances; unacceptable behaviour; lack of socialisation and training; aggression, either actual or nervous; abuse and neglect. At the time of writing the main issues that have resulted in Spanish Water Dogs needing to be rehomed are those stated earlier: lack of knowledge and inappropriate training methods. Due to the rarity of this breed many **professionals** have little or no knowledge of the nature of these dogs or the way they respond to the treatment that they receive. Vets and dog trainers alike are inclined to assume that they are fearful, nervous or even 'aggressive' when they react badly to frightening situations or new experiences. All of the dogs that we have rehomed up to the present time were labelled in this way when, in fact, they were neither 'nervous' nor 'aggressive' in the true sense of the words. They had been handled abusively by 'dog trainers' and Vets, insufficiently socialised and completely misunderstood. Following a period of rehabilitation and training they were placed in carefully chosen homes with owners who were willing to learn how to understand them and train them so that they could live with them successfully.

REHOMING WITHOUT TEARS
For the first week or two in his new home the dog is off balance, unsure of his new family and surroundings, almost certainly being treated very differently from what he has been used to. The dog cannot possibly know he now has a good home. All he knows is that, once again, the world has turned upside down. The new owner probably feels quite confident, overjoyed to have a dog at last and ready to lavish upon him all the love and attention that they think has been lacking previously. They are very likely

to feel sorry for the dog and understandably want to compensate for the injustices they perceive that the dog has suffered. Unfortunately, the way humans do this is likely to give the dog the message that he has been given carte blanche to walk in and take over! After a couple of weeks this can result in the appearance of undesirable tendencies. On the other hand, some new owners expect that because they have taken an adult dog they can assume that the dog understands all their house rules without needing to be taught. They sometimes imagine that the dog should come with a full understanding of the English language!

In an ideal world the new owner of a rehomed dog will follow certain guidelines that will ensure the happiness of both dog and owner resulting in a strong, successful bond between them for years to come. The following 'rules and regulations' should be applied from day one until the dog is completely settled, confident and trained. The dog, of course, will still be loved and cherished, but he will be shown that life is great at the bottom of the human/canine pack. He will have no responsibilities, no worries and no misleading signals. His early mistakes will be ignored; his good behaviour will be encouraged and always rewarded.

I am now going to make two lists - one of 'Don'ts' and one of 'Do's'. I shall list the 'Don'ts' first because although it sounds very negative, what you don't do right at the beginning is usually more important than the things you need to do later as the dog gets his feet under the table!

DON'T.............
- Don't feel sorry for the dog. It will not help him feel better. You cannot alter how a dog feels retrospectively by how you treat him. Dogs live for today and spoiling a dog today to make up for abuse it suffered yesterday will have no effect other than to teach it that from today it's in charge!
- Don't expect the dog to be grateful for what you are doing now. The concept of gratitude in relation to past experiences is totally unknown to the dog.
- Don't get cross and start punishing the dog if he is not clean in the house. Stress can cause toilet problems and if not handled carefully from the outset the problem will surely escalate. Simply pretend the dog is a pup and house-train accordingly, remembering that you cannot punish a dog for something that happened while you were not there.
- Don't leave any dog, male or female, alone with children or very elderly people. Even where past history is known (and owners parting with dogs are notoriously economical with the truth!) you can never be sure how a dog is going to react in unfamiliar surroundings and circumstances.
- Don't mess about with different types of food. Decide what is a suitable diet for that particular dog and stick to it. Feed the dog after he has seen the family eat and remove the bowl after 15 minutes whether it has been eaten or not. Food is the first and most important way that a dog learns his position in the family. Only give tit-bits as a reward for something the dog has done for you, never because he just came and looked at you with big, sad eyes, saying "I'm hungry, feed me!"
- Don't expect the dog to understand immediately what you want. There may have been different rules, or no rules at all in his previous home and the dog is not a mind reader!
- Don't allow the dog to go upstairs or get on the furniture. The one who sleeps in the highest and best places is the Leader! However, furniture, and removing a dog from it, is a frequent source of confrontation so please seek advice from a behaviour counsellor if this is a problem. Place a child-gate

at the bottom of the stairs and prevent the dog having access to the living room when you are not there.

- Don't punish the dog if it starts to destroy your home. Again, stress has a big part to play and inappropriate punishment will only increase the stress. Buy (or beg, borrow or steal!) an indoor kennel (crate), accustom the dog to it gradually and leave him in that when you have to go out. Always leave something to chew and never use the crate as punishment - it must always be a nice place to be for the dog. While teaching the dog to go into the crate, remember to praise him for being inside, not for coming out.
- Don't allow visitors to make too much of the dog. Teach them (the visitors!) to ignore him when they arrive by folding their arms, turning their heads away and not looking at him, speaking to him or touching him. When the dog has gone away and settled down they can call him, make a fuss briefly, and then send him away again by adopting the same body posture as before. In this way the dog will realise that all your visitors are welcome and he has no right to try to control them.
- Don't play any fighting or tug-of-war games until the relationship between you and the dog is really solid. When that time comes only play tug games with toys that belong to **you.**
- Don't play on the floor with the dog or let the dog be in a higher position than you. This applies especially to children (and husbands!)
- Don't let the dog charge through doorways ahead of you. Get yourself in the doorway first (be quick!) and use your leg to bar his way. Wait until the dog hangs back then go through first. Don't grab the dog's collar and don't speak to him - let your body do the talking so the dog can understand.
- Don't give preference to the new dog if there is an established dog (or cat) in the house. Let the established dog see that he is still number one by doing everything first with **him** - feed first, call first, put lead on first, pet first, etc. etc.
- Don't try to contact the dog's previous owners. They may wish to visit the dog to check that all is well. This can be very unsettling for the dog, especially if the meeting is distressing for his former family. Their unhappiness may be passed to the dog so that he becomes fretful and takes a while to settle down again. A clean break is best and is always insisted upon by the SWDC Welfare & Rehoming Group.

DO.........

- Do have the dog castrated or spayed if the previous owner has not already done so. (Dogs rehomed by the SWDC Welfare & Rehoming Group will have been neutered before rehoming takes place). It is sensible from the point of view of preventing illness and unwanted puppies but, in addition it will help reduce the likely-hood of sexual dominance in males. Castration alone will never cure established problems without the support of behavioural advice, but young males that are beginning to feel their feet can benefit greatly.
- Do worm the dog as soon as possible unless you know for sure that this has been done recently. Always get your worming treatment from the Vet, not the Pet Shop.
- Do give sensitive or nervous dogs time and space to find their feet. Trying to overcome their fear or reluctance through fussing or constant attention will actually make the problem worse. Whatever a dog is doing when you fuss or verbally reassure him is the behaviour he will think you are praising him for - so he will continue to exhibit that behaviour. Prevent people from trying to reach out to nervous dogs and completely ignore a dog when he is afraid. You set an example by not showing fear yourself and eventually the dog will follow suit.

- Do teach the dog right from the word go that he can cope when you are not there. Leave him alone for very short periods from the first day, gradually lengthening the time as you see fit. If you are with a dog constantly during the early days (through understandable concern) you will eventually make him so dependant on your company that when you do have to leave him alone he will suffer from separation anxiety. Once this starts it tends to escalate from barking, through chewing the furniture and eventually to house soiling. This is especially true of rescue dogs because of their insecurity and the owner's attempts to compensate for previous experiences.

- Do start training as soon as you can. Short sessions are best, as often throughout the day as you can manage. Teach one thing at a time and remember always to praise the behaviour you want and ignore the behaviour you don't want. Never punish a dog for getting it wrong when you are training - if he understood he would have done it!

- Do use food as a reward as long as your timing is right and you are rewarding what you have asked for. Most dogs will do what you ask as long as they understand and can see that there is a pay-off so they need to be motivated, not bullied into doing something they cannot see the point in doing! Once the dog has learned, through using food as a lure, you can begin to use it less frequently as a reward for a job well done. The possibility of an occasional food reward results in a very prompt response. Dogs who are not food-orientated may respond to really enthusiastic verbal praise or a toy.

- Do go to training classes as soon as you can. Many rescue dogs need to be socialised with other people and dogs, so classes provide the perfect environment for this. If you do not know where there are good classes in your area the A.P.B.C., A.P.B.T. and the Kennel Club have a list of accredited trainers and will be pleased to help you. Your Vet should also be able to help if you ask.

- Do play with the dog when you want to and for as long as you feel like it, not when the dog demands it and until he gets fed-up! Put the toys in a cupboard - they are **your** toys and **you** decide when to get them out and play with them.

- Do ignore the dog whenever he demands attention from you. When he comes and puts his paw on your knee, leans on you, sits in front staring at you, barks at you etc. he is saying "Hey, you! I'm here, pay attention to me!" What you must say is "on yer bike!" but you must say it in dog language. Fold your arms, turn your head away and completely ignore him. When he has gone away and settled down you can call him to you, in a really nice voice, ask him to "Sit!" and praise him with some fuss. Then send him away again in dog language before he gets bored and goes of his own accord.

- Do 'hand groom' the dog regularly to reinforce your position as pack leader, but do it gently and gradually to begin with. Until the dog has got used to you don't be too forceful or too thorough, and always reward as soon as you have finished with a tit-bit. If the dog objects to being handled in this way, or fools around, seek advice. If he has been clipped recently you could massage him instead then, as his coat grows, start separating the cords.

- Do think about the future. If you are likely to go on holiday and need to put your dog in kennels do something about it straight away. See 'Boarding Kennels, Chapter 10, THE AGGRESSION MYTH.

- Please do consider learning all about 'clicker training'. Many Spanish Water Dogs that have been mis-handled are, quite understandably, wary of people that they do not know. Clicker training is a 'hands off' method of rewarding a dog so it is invaluable for building the confidence of a dog that does not trust people. It enables them to receive a reward without being touched by the person they are meeting.

- Do, please, remember that you will need to be patient! Rome was not built in a day and neither is a sound, working relationship between a dog and a new owner. If the dog's trust in people has already been damaged a **great deal** of patience may be required! Spanish Water Dogs have a phenomenal memory, which means that any bad experiences will be as strongly imprinted as the good ones. Time heals eventually, and the dog will learn to trust again.

Most dogs will settle into their new homes beautifully if given half a chance. With the combined help of the Spanish Water Dog Welfare & Rehoming Group and this book any teething problems should be fairly easily overcome.

The four dogs successfully rehomed at the time of writing

Jasper

Max

Lago

Josh

18 THE LAW AND DOGS

Choosing to own a dog is a conscious decision you yourself have taken so **you** must be prepared to accept total responsibility for your dog, its well-being, welfare and actions for the rest of its life. Through responsible dog ownership, not only are you protecting your own interests and the dog in your care but you are also safeguarding the general public. If you have regularly attended well-organised training classes with your dog or have been involved with the Kennel Club's Good Citizen Dog Scheme you will already be familiar with the correct way for your dog to behave in a public place, with people and with other dogs. Remember, Spanish Water Dogs have a strong instinct to guard and this can include barking at strangers. It is all too easy for 'Joe Public' to misunderstand what the dog is doing and to accuse it of being aggressive. This can potentially lead to all sorts of problems with the authorities, causing you much upset and heartache. Public feeling can run high, especially immediately after a particularly serious biting incident that has been sensationalised by the press. Even a well trained dog can get into trouble so you should never let your guard down for an instant when out in a public place.

As a dog owner it is important that you are familiar with the various laws pertaining to dogs, yourself and the environment. The laws are too numerous to go into in any detail here but perhaps the most important one is The Dangerous Dogs Act (1991). Others cover aspects of owning, treatment, control of dogs and of the environment.

Protection of Animals Act 1911
You are required to provide necessary care and attention for your dog and it is a criminal offence to cause or allow unnecessary suffering to an animal. This includes ill-treating, terrifying, kicking, beating torturing or causing suffering through transportation.

Dogs (Protection of Livestock) Act 1953
The owner and anyone else under whose control the dog is at the time will be guilty of an offence if it worries livestock on agricultural land. The dog must have been attacking or chasing livestock in such a way that it could cause injury or suffering. The definition of 'livestock' includes cattle, sheep, goats, pigs, horses and poultry. Game birds are not included. The Animals Act 1971 goes further to state that the keeper of the dog is liable for damage caused and includes pheasants, partridges and grouse.

The Abandonment of Animals Act 1960
This states that it is an offence to abandon any animal in circumstances likely to cause unnecessary suffering.

The Animals Act 1971
This act provides that the keeper of an animal is liable for any damage it causes through negligence on your part.

The Road Traffic Act 1988
This states that dogs must be kept on a lead on a highway. If a dog is injured as a result of a car

accident the driver is obliged to stop and give details to the person in charge of the dog or to the police within twenty-four hours if the dog was unattended. Dogs travelling in vehicles should not be a nuisance or distract the driver.

The Environmental Protection Act 1990
This act states that dog wardens are obliged to seize stray dogs; the police have discretionary powers to seize a dog. They are entitled to charge a fee for the return of your dog.

If a member of the public finds a stray dog they must return it to its owner, or take it to the local police or dog warden. If the finder wants to retain the dog, this will probably be allowed, provided they are considered to be capable of looking after a dog and they agree to keep it for at least 28 days. However, the original owner could still have a claim for the dog's return. Remember that it is illegal to take a found dog into your home without reporting it to the police first.

The Dangerous Dogs Act 1991
You may not necessarily agree with the legislation of this act and one can argue that it was rushed through Parliament, poorly drafted but we have to abide by it. It is the second part of the act that most concerns us as it is relevant to all dogs, regardless of breed. It makes it a criminal offence for a dog to be dangerously out of control in a public place. Not only does it include an instance where injury takes place but also if there is a fear that injury might occur.

If convicted of the above offence you could be fined, receive a criminal record, banned from keeping dogs or even sent to prison, depending upon the seriousness of the incident. Meanwhile, your dog would have been destroyed.

Control of Dogs Order 1992
This advises that any dog in a public place must wear a collar and tag with name and address of the owner on it.

Clean Neighbourhoods and Environment Act 2005
If your dog's barking causes a serious nuisance with neighbours the local authority can serve a noise abatement notice, which if unheeded can result in fines and legal expenses.

If your dog defecates and you fail to remove the faeces forthwith, you will be committing an offence, which could result in a fine of up to £1,000.

The Animal Welfare Act 2007
This act marks a milestone in animal welfare legislation and has been introduced in order to extend the duty of care to animals (farmed and non-farmed), so reducing suffering.

As well as increasing the penalties for those who inflict the most serious offences, the Animal Welfare Act makes it a legal requirement for pet owners to do what is reasonable to provide for their animal's needs. These are: a proper diet (food and water), somewhere suitable to live, protection from pain, suffering, injury and disease.

The majority of pet owners will not need to change the way they care for their animals to comply with the new law, most people already provide for their pet's needs but the new law will help to tackle cases of ongoing neglect.

The key elements of the act that are relevant to dog owners are:

• To reduce animal suffering by enabling preventive action before suffering occurs
• To place on owners a duty of care for their pets
• To increase from 12 to 16 the minimum age at which a child can buy an animal
• To ban mutilations of animals, with certain specified exceptions

The last clause refers partly to the docking of dogs' tails, which has been banned with the exception of working dogs.

It is hoped that your knowledge and understanding of the above laws and how they affect yourself and your dog will stand you in good stead for the time that your dog is part of your family. If, however, you encounter any problems and find yourself in breach of one of the laws it is advisable that you seek help from a solicitor who is conversant with Dog Law. Alternatively, you may wish to seek the advise of the group 'Justice for Dogs' who offer free legal advice and assistance on all matters relating to canine welfare to persons in need and can be reached at www.gsdhelpline.com .

"I feel the earth move under my feet."

"Me and my shadow."

Who can do recall races? Marron can!

*Spanish Water Dogs can enjoy terrier racing for fun – although ear flapping
is not always the winning strategy!*

19 THE FUTURE OF THE BREED

We hope that within these pages we have covered enough about this wonderful but complex breed to give you the information you require so that you understand and appreciate Spanish Water Dogs, as they should be. In order to do justice to this breed in the future, it is imperative that the history and working aspects are fully appreciated and are very much taken into account, particularly in the areas of breeding and showing.

A walk around a dog show will reveal something that we hope will never be seen in this breed. A number of other breeds, bred for a purpose in life, have been subjected to changes in looks and structure through selective breeding that would inhibit or prevent an individual dog doing the job it was originally bred for. So many breeds have become pampered and coiffured so that a walk in muddy countryside in the winter or a dip in the river would be considered most inappropriate. For instance, Poodles, so closely related to Spanish Water Dogs, can spend hours on a grooming table being combed, clipped and cut to perfection in order to be considered a good specimen by the judge when originally they were bred for working in water and sported natural coats, either curled or corded.

The appearance, physical attributes, character and temperament of the Spanish Water Dog have been developed over hundreds of years, resulting in the breed as we see it today; athletic, focused, natural and rustic. Please don't change it.

As well as emphasising the correct look of the breed we have endeavoured to give you the facts about the health issues that have already affected a small but significant number of dogs. Only by understanding these health problems in detail and, where possible, the mode of inheritance that influences them can breeders make informed and educated decisions about how to go forward with a breeding programme that addresses these problems and ultimately leads to improvement of stock. All breeders owe it to their puppy owners to do everything within their power to test their breeding stock and try to prevent passing on inherited health problems to their offspring. We should never underestimate the effects of owning an unhealthy dog. Apart from the suffering that poor creature has to endure there is also the ongoing heartache and worry that the whole of the family has to deal with. If we know that, through making careful choices before producing a litter, we can avoid distress to both dog and owner then surely this has to be the way forward.

Within these pages you will have found aspects covering temperament, behaviour, socialisation and training, in fact a wealth of knowledge gained through many years of experience by the author of these chapters. All of these subjects can never be emphasised enough where this complicated breed is concerned and we can only hope that the information provided will give you a much better understanding of Spanish Water Dogs in general and your own dog in particular. If, by reading through this information and applying it, you have a dog that is well adjusted and fun to live with we feel we will have done our job. Ultimately, we hope that the 'trickle' of dogs coming into Breed Welfare and Rehoming remains just that and never develops into a 'deluge'

We would like to think that, by taking time to look through our book, you are as enthusiastic about these wonderful but intricate dogs as we are and that our aims become your aims.

If we, in our small way by writing this book, can encourage owners and breeders of the future to consider the above points and to love this breed as it is and not what it can be changed into then we will feel humbled and honoured that you have taken the time to read what we have written.

It is not a breed you 'own', it is a breed you live with!"

Wanda Sooby   Di Williamson

AND FINALLY...

.......So, what does SWD really stand for?

'Sad Women with Dogs' of course!

*"Gracias Antonio García Pérez por tener la visión
y la determinación de sacar del anonimato
esta maravillosa raza y traerla a nuestras vidas".*

APPENDIX

Prospective Home Questionnaire

In order to assess the suitability of your home and lifestyle for a Spanish Water Dog puppy would you please answer the following questionnaire? The information that you provide will be confidential. Please answer all the questions as completely and honestly as you can. The more information that you provide the better we will be able to match you with a suitable puppy.

When buying a puppy, you need to understand that there may be some initial teething problems. We will provide you with all the help and support you need to make sure that the transition is as easy as possible for you both.

Filling in this application form does not guarantee that you will be offered a puppy. It is essential to ensure that this is the breed for you.

Applicant's name(s)……………………………………………………………………......

Address……………………………………………………………………………………

…………………………………………………………………………………………......

Tel. Number(s)………………………………e.mail……………………………….........

About your family/household

Names of adults in the family……………………………………………………………......

No. of children…………………Their ages……………………………………………......

Their
names……………………………………………………………………………………......

If you do not have children, but plan to, what would happen to the dog?……………........

…………………………………………………………………………………………......

Does every member of your household agree that a Spanish Water Dog is the right dog for you? Please ask all adults to sign below to affirm their consent:

Signature(s)……………………………………………………………………………......

Do you work outside the home?……………Yes……………No……………No. of hours

Does your spouse/partner?………………Yes……………No……………No. of hours

About your home

Is your home rented?……………………………………………………………………..

Does your tenancy agreement allow you to keep pets?…………………………………

Landlord's name………………………….……………Tel. no…………………………….…..

Do you have a garden……………………..……Is it safely fenced?………………………

What type of fence?…………..…………………How high is it?………………………….

About your experience of dogs

Have you ever met a Spanish Water Dog?……...If yes, where?……………………………

Do you already own a Spanish Water Dog?…….If yes, dog's full name…………………

………………………………………………………………………………………………..

Do you currently own any other dogs?…………..If yes, please give details of

breed/type, age, gender, whether neutered……………………………………………….....

………………………………………………………………………………………………..

Please give details of previous dogs and their cause and age of death…………………

………………………………………………………………………………………………..

About other pets

Do you have any cats?……………………………If yes, how many?………………………

Are they familiar with dogs?…………………………...…..If not, please describe what

facilities you have for making them feel safe while they get used to a new dog in their

home…………………………………………………………………………………………

………………………………………………………………………………………………..

Do you have any other pets?……………………………………………………………………

Do you have any
livestock?…………………………………………………………………………………….....

About Responsibility for Ownership of a Spanish Water Dog

Why do you want to own a Spanish Water Dog?…………………………………………..

………………………………………………………………………………………………..

Where will the dog sleep?…………………………………………………………………..

The Spanish Water Dog

Where will the dog spend most of the day?..

Do you own a crate/indoor kennel?.................Where is it?.....................

Will the dog ever be tethered?.......................Kennelled?............................

What type of exercise will the dog be given?..................................

Are you aware of the coat care required?......................................

Have you investigated the nature of the breed?....Where?..........................

Are you fully aware of the 'guarding nature' of the breed?.......................

Are you willing to train the dog?.......................Go to classes?...................

Have you ever given up a dog to a rescue organisation?..........................

If yes, please give details...

Would you agree to keep in contact with the breeder?...........................

If you purchase a Spanish Water Dog and experience problems later on, where would you turn for help and advice?...

If you could not keep the dog what would you do?................................

Would you consider joining the Spanish Water Dog Club?.......................

Would you consider taking part in some Club activities?.........................

Additional comments...

....

....

I/We declare that all of the information provided in this application form is accurate and true.

Applicant signature...Date.......................

Applicant signature...Date.......................

BIBLIOGRAPHY

25 Stupid Mistakes Dog Owners Make	Janine Adams
After You Get Your Puppy	Dr Ian Dunbar
Agility Fun – The Hobday Way	Ruth Hobday
Care Of The Older Dog	Geoff Little
Click To Calm	Emma Parsons
Clicker Training For Dogs	Karen Pryor
Dog Breeding – The Theory And Practice	Frank Jackson
Dog Tricks: Fun And Games For Your Clever Canine	Mary Rae
Dogs: A Startling New Understanding Of Canine Origin, Behavior And Evolution	Raymond Coppinger and Lorna Coppinger
Dogwise	John Fisher
El Nuevo Libro Del Perro De Agua Español	Josefina Gomez-Toldra
Fast Track Puppy Survival Kit & Fast Track Dog Survival Kit	Lyn Fleet and Helen Roberts
Fun Nose Work For Dogs	Roy Hunter
Getting In Touch With Your Dog	Linda Tellington-Jones
Give Your Dog A Bone	Dr Ian Billinghurst
Help For Your Shy Dog	Deborah Wood
High Achievers Programme	Carmen L Battaglia www.breedingbetterdogs.com
How To Say It To Your Dog	Janine Adams
On Talking Terms With Dogs: Calming Signals	Turid Rugaas
Reading The Dog's Mind	John and Mary Holmes
The Complete Idiot's Guide To Positive Dog Training	Pamela Dennison
The Power Of Positive Dog Training	Pat Miller
Understanding Your Dog	Barbara Sykes
Clicker Puppy DVD	www.doggonecrazy.ca
The Spanish Water Dog Club	www.spanishwaterdogclub.co.uk
Association of Pet Dog Trainers	www.apdt.co.uk
Association of Pet Behaviour Counsellors	www.apbc.org.uk

ACKNOWLEDGEMENTS

Antonio Garcia Perez	For his information on the history of the breed and for photographs
John Sooby	Husband of Wanda, for his support, encouragement and patience
Faye Allen	For lending us her collection of articles and references about the Spanish Water Dog
Sue Williams	For all her hard work proof reading the draft and her help with the preparation prior to publishing.
Kylee Noad	For all her help with the presentation
Angie Hodges	For her help with the draft and supportive comments and her contribution to Search Work in the chapter on Working with your Spanish Water Dog
Jenny Johnson	For her contribution to Gundog and Obedience Training in the chapter on Working with your Spanish Water Dog
Hazel Peel	Photographer, for all of the studio photographs in the chapter on Training and the front cover photo
Steve Williams	Photographer
Julian (Titch) Noad	Photographer
Robin Walker	Photographer
Margaret Mills	Photographer
Lyn Fleet and Helen Roberts	For allowing us to use their 'I have socialised my puppy with...' list, which we feel cannot be bettered
'Our Dogs'	For the references to and quotes from Harry Baxter, supporter of the breed in the early days
Miguel and Squiffy	For their patience and intelligence, their inspiration, for what they have taught us and for being different!

INDEX

Index